INTRODUCTION

By 1621, the probable date of *Women Beware Women*, the dramatic and nondramatic influences on Jacobean plays were diffuse and intermingled. Aristotle, Seneca and the followers of both, Shakespeare and other playwrights, Protestant and Catholic points of view, political attitudes, all made their contributions to the drama of the period.

Changing tastes and dramatic theories between 1621 and 1641 are well illustrated by the modification or omission of principles associated with Aristotle: kings and princes had largely disappeared as the focal points of tragedy, new definitions of heroic or tragic figures had evolved, innovations of attitudes towards the traditional tragic flaw had occurred. By the third decade of the seventeenth century the most popular form of tragedy was Italianate intrigue (with some debt to Machiavelli), centred on the private lives of the protagonists. In two of the plays in this volume the careers of women, neither of them queens or rulers, provide the principal interest. In the third play, a chronicle history with tragic overtones, the central figure is, historically, a man with a fraudulent claim to the throne of England, potentially a very unheroic hero.

A familiarity with earlier English tragedies will make a reader aware of many changes of emphasis. Although revenge is still an important element of both *Women Beware Women* and *The Cardinal*, the revenge of Jacobean and later plays is often not that of a Hieronymo or a Hamlet (heroic victims attempting to right a wrong). It is a retaliation provoked by illicit ambitions – the family aggrandizement and sexual desires of the Cardinal, the social aspirations of Bianca, the affection of Livia for her brother and her subsequent passion for Leantio. This kind of revenge implied, moreover, a perversion of values in the society of which these characters were an important or representative part; in both plays the crisis or problem has its source in the corruptibility of at least one of the highest ranking persons of church or state, with little opportunity for their victims to obtain justice. Although history plays had not been in vogue for some time, Ford's *Perkin Warbeck* is not merely a copy of a type once popular. Interest is as much in the motivations and psychology of Warbeck as in the historical events.

In both *Women Beware Women* and *The Cardinal* national affairs are incidental. Middleton was primarily concerned with Bianca's upbringing, the major episodes in her life and the development of her character. It is almost by chance that the Duke of Florence, the head of the state, became one of Bianca's victims; such an outcome had not been a part of her intended plan of revenge. In the background to *The Cardinal* was a war between Navarre and Aragon, but it is simply a convenient device for moving people on and off stage and for revealing character. Attention

centres on Rosaura, who, like Bianca, wished to marry out of her class.
Both heroines owe much, in temperament and action, to the Duchess of
Malfi, whom John Webster brought on stage about 1613. Shirley's Cardinal
is depicted as a manipulator, a sensual man devoted to self-interest.

The insights of these three seventeenth-century dramatists into the
minds of women give their plays a particular relevance in the twentieth
century. The independent, partially liberated spirit of each led to
conflicts with parental or similar authority and to the violation of
contemporary codes of behaviour. These tragedies reinforce the familiar
theme from earlier English plays that it was indisputably a man's world.
Despite this, the playwrights portrayed deeply and sympathetically the
characters of the central women, with a clear regret that in their own
times they were treated like chattels. All three develop clearly during
the course of the plays: Katherine Gordon suffered and survived, Bianca
was tempted and corrupted, and Rosaura, the most tragic, became the
victim of injustice. Each, however, contributed something to her own
suffering or downfall. As Livia cynically observed in *Women Beware
Women*, 'Nothing o'erthrows our sex but indiscretion' (II,i,164). However,
the Cardinal's grudging tribute to Rosaura is as relevant to Katherine and
Bianca, 'This woman has a spirit ...' (II,iii,167).

Shakespeare's and other English tragedies, influenced by Senecan
stoicism, had stressed the role of fate in life, but in the plays in this
collection the authors allowed their principal characters a substantial
freedom to create their own destinies. Freedom makes misjudgment
possible, and herein is a foundation for tragedy. Each of the major figures
broke 'the cake of custom', the conventional destiny that might be expected
for them, but misjudgments within a larger framework brought about
their downfall. Although illustrating realistically the individual choices or
decisions that are an accepted part of twentieth-century experience, each
play also incorporates some element of chance or fate.

Bianca impetuously eloped with Leantio, an action that had in it a
potential for happiness. By chance she was seen by the lecherous Duke of
Florence, who tempted her with his world of luxury and sensuousness, a
world she rashly accepted. Duchess Rosaura's life similarly combined fate
and freedom of will. After the accidental death of her first husband, she
rebelled against a second arranged marriage, with the Cardinal's nephew,
General Columbo, in order to wed the man she loved. Of the three
central figures in these plays, Perkin Warbeck proposed the largest
challenge to whatever obscure destiny should have been his. The stirrings
of ambition and his acceptance of persuasion and flattery led him to the
supreme effrontery – to claim the throne of England.

A realization that destiny does not drive these characters, that the
fates of nations do not directly hang on their lives, that they do not have
a pervasive flaw may diminish the tragic impact of the drama. One may
sympathize with their plights and admire their aggressive vitality, but
not deeply pity the protagonists. If the Jacobean and Caroline modifications of Aristotelian and related concepts of tragedy are accepted, then

In this volume

Thomas Middleton WOMEN BEWARE WOMEN

John Ford PERKIN WARBECK

James Shirley THE CARDINAL

Jacobean and Caroline Tragedies

Edited with an Introduction by
ROBERT G. LAWRENCE

Associate Professor of English
at the University of Victoria, British Columbia

J. M. Dent & Sons Ltd, London

© Introduction, notes and editing
J.M. Dent & Sons Ltd, 1974

This book if bound as a paperback is
subject to the condition that it may not
be issued on loan or otherwise except in
its original binding.

This book is set in 8 on 9pt Press Roman

No. 147   Hardback ISBN 0 460 10147 1

CONTENTS

the plays of Italianate intrigue are tragedies, but one may argue that
Perkin Warbeck is not a tragedy at all.

Perkin the pretender is a long way from being a traditional Aristotelian
hero; he should not be capable of attracting more than a minimum of
compassion, as the contemporary prose accounts of his career demonstrate.
John Ford, however, saw Perkin Warbeck more as a victim than a villain,
with an intensity of self-belief that some critics have labelled insanity.
Keenly interested in the psychological make-up of this man, Ford was
willing to ignore the historical fact of Warbeck's confession of imposture
to present a more sympathetic, if slanted, characterization.

With this approach to a chronicle-tragedy, Ford created a duality of
attitude towards Perkin Warbeck. The author laid stress on Warbeck's
heroic characteristics from the claimant's first appearance on stage in
Act II, with a gradual revelation that he was, in his naïveté, the tool of
several ambitious people. This positive characterization must be balanced
against an awareness that the hero is in fact a non-hero, who must in the
end be defeated, in order to maintain stability in the state. Ford used this
unresolved duality as a part of the dramatic tension of the play, and the
element of tragedy is based on the sufferings of a dedicated young man
who went to death bravely, for a cause to which he was passionately committed.
The tragic impact is intensified by Warbeck's marriage to the innocent and
loyal Katherine. She participates in the atmosphere of tragedy, but not
wholly, for she survives the dénouement, and evidently Henry VII treated
her generously. The sexual irregularities so important to plot and characterization in the two Continental plays have no part in this play set in England
and Scotland.

Women Beware Women, Perkin Warbeck, The Cardinal and other plays
of the period are comments on politics and society, dramatic mirrors for
magistrates. Although the plays in this volume were not intended primarily as social and political analysis, given conditions in England between
1621 and 1641[1], some allegory was almost inevitable between accounts
of events, real or fictitious, of years past and the contemporary scene. Both
Middleton and Shirley had written many comedies which were explicit satiric
comments on their times; they came to tragedy late in their careers.[2]

Parallels in *Women Beware Women* between sixteenth-century Italy and
seventeenth-century England are only general. The play includes the
themes of the abuse of power by rulers and nobles, the arranged marriages,
the acquisitiveness and ruthlessness, the newly rich and the predictable use
they made of their wealth, and the general breakdown of older standards
of morality. There were, of course, some dangers in writing into a play
explicit political allegory, as Middleton discovered only a few years later
in the uproar over *A Game at Chesse*. The opening scenes of both *Women
Beware Women* and *The Cardinal* immediately prepared seventeenth-century

[1] See, for example, P. Akrigg, *Jacobean Pageant* (1962) and C. Hibbert,
Charles I (1968).
[2] Biographical notes precede the plays by these authors.

audiences for social and political attitudes or commentary, Italy and Spain having been the traditional settings for tragedies of intrigue.

Perkin Warbeck, although removed from the contemporary scene, was even closer to home in the sense that it dealt with many familiar names in English legend and history, and the play reveals its author's political consciousness.[1] In the extended character sketches of King Henry VII, King James IV (both of whom are ancestors of King Charles I) and 'King Perkin' are explicit observations on royal responsibility and irresponsibility.

Implicit contemporary themes appear in *The Cardinal,* in regal, religious and military contexts. This play was written and performed in 1641, just before the outbreak of England's only civil war, when a weak, autocratic monarch brought the nation close to disaster. In a minor role in the play is an ineffectual king, in a secondary one an aggressive militarist, and in a dominant one a hated ecclesiastic.

Although religion was a major force in many plays of the period, the subject seems not to have concerned Thomas Middleton deeply.[2] In *Perkin Warbeck* religion plays a small part: Bishop Fox is depicted as sincere and dependable; the values he represents contribute to the stability of the state. *The Cardinal,* however, brings to a climax a series of plays, beginning perhaps with *The Duchess of Malfi,* that condemned the clergy for self-interest, corruption and sexual indulgence. It may be indicative of the times that *The Cardinal* (1641) ends with the destruction of all that is good or potentially good.

Each of these plays has in totality a relevance to the present century. *Perkin Warbeck* is especially meaningful, dealing as it does with a challenge to traditional authority; *Women Beware Women* concerns itself with equally familiar themes, the malignant power of ambition and the use and misuse of sex; *The Cardinal* is obliquely a study of political and religious influence and prestige.

This edition has been modernized in punctuation and spelling for the convenience of the twentieth-century reader. Square brackets enclose words and punctuation marks not in the original editions. A glossary of unfamiliar words that appear frequently in the plays is at the end of the book. The texts are based on the earliest published editions (no manuscript versions survive); they have few errors or problems.

The University of Victoria provided stenographic and research assistance and the Canada Council a leave fellowship, both of which have facilitated the work on this anthology.

1975   Robert G. Lawrence

[1] This subject is studied in the introduction to the play, pp. 92-7.
[2] A Cardinal appears in *Women Beware Women,* but only to berate conventionally his brother, the Duke, for profligate behaviour.

SELECT BIBLIOGRAPHY

GENERAL

T.S. Eliot, *Selected Essays 1917-32*, 1932.

F.T. Bowers, *Elizabethan Revenge Tragedy, 1587-1642.* Princeton, 1940.

G.E. Bentley, *The Jacobean and Caroline Stage*, 7 vols., Oxford 1941-68. An invaluable reference work.

M. Doran, *Endeavors of Art, a Study of Form in Elizabethan Drama.* Madison, 1954. Aesthetic and literary backgrounds.

B. Ford, ed., *The Age of Shakespeare* (A Guide to English Literature), 1955.

U. Ellis-Fermor, *The Jacobean Drama.* New York, 1964. A very useful critical study.

J.W. Lever, *The Tragedy of State,* 1971.

MIDDLETON

S. Schoenbaum, *Middleton's Tragedies.* New York, 1955.

T. Middleton, *Women Beware Women*, ed. R. Gill, 1968.

D.M. Holmes, *The Art of Thomas Middleton.* Oxford, 1970.

D. Dodson, 'Middleton's Livia', *Philological Quarterly, XXVII* (1948), pp. 376-81.

G.R. Hibbard, 'The Tragedies of Thomas Middleton and the Decadence of the Drama', *Renaissance and Modern Studies*, I (1957), pp. 35-64.

I. Ribner, 'Middleton's *Women Beware Women*: Poetic Imagery and the Moral Vision', *Tulane Studies in English*, IX (1959), pp. 19-33.

E. Engelberg, 'Tragic Blindness in *The Changeling* and *Women Beware Women*', *Modern Language Quarterly*, XXIII (1962), pp. 20-8.

FORD

J. Gairdner, *History of the Life and Reign of Richard the Third, to Which is Added the Story of Perkin Warbeck from Original Documents*, 1878. Useful for information about Warbeck and other contemporary figures.

H.J. Oliver, *The Problem of John Ford.* Carlton, Victoria, Aust., 1955.

C. Leech, *John Ford and the Drama of his Time*, 1957. *Perkin Warbeck* as tragedy.

E. Simons, *Henry VII, the First Tudor King,* 1968.

M. Stavig, *John Ford and the Traditional Moral Order.* Madison, 1968.

J. Ford, *The Chronicle History of Perkin Warbeck*, ed. P. Ure, 1968.

D.K. Anderson, Jr., *John Ford.* New York, 1972.

L. Babb, 'Abnormal Psychology in Ford's *Perkin Warbeck*', *Modern Language Notes,* LI (1936), pp. 234-7.

J. Barish, *'Perkin Warbeck* as anti-history', *Essays in Criticism,* XX (1970), pp. 151-71. Hypothesis that Ford may have believed in the legitimacy of Warbeck's claim to the crown of England.

SHIRLEY

R.S. Forsythe, *The Relations of Shirley's Plays to the Elizabethan Drama.* New York, 1914. Parallels between the plays of Shirley and those of other playwrights of the period.

A.H. Nason, *James Shirley, Dramatist; a Biographical and Critical Study.* New York, 1915. Uncritical and out of date.

M.C. Bradbrook, *Themes and Conventions in Elizabethan Tragedy.* Cambridge, 1935.

H.R. Trevor-Roper, *Archbishop Laud*, second edition, 1962.

J. Shirley, *The Cardinal*, ed. C. Forker. Bloomington, 1964.

F. Manly, 'The Death of Hernando in Shirley's *Cardinal*', *Notes and Queries,* CCX (1965), pp. 342-3.

R. Morton, 'Deception and Social Dislocation, an Aspect of James Shirley's Drama', *Renaissance Drama,* IX (1966), pp. 227-46.

WOMEN BEWARE WOMEN (c.1621)[1]

by THOMAS MIDDLETON
(1580-1627)

[Born London; studied at Queen's College, Oxford. Wrote pageants, masques, and pamphlets; was City Chronologer (1620-7). A varied dramatic achievement: comedies, among them *A Trick to Catch the Old One, A Chaste Maid in Cheapside*; tragedies, *Women Beware Women, The Change- ling* (with Rowley); and a political satire, *A Game at Chesse.*]

Women Beware Women exemplifies a very popular form of late Jacobean drama: Italianate intrigue growing out of ambition and sexual passion. Middleton drew from contemporary stories, such as Malespini's *Ducento Novelle* and Moryson's *Itinerary,* which modified and coloured the histori- cal relationship between Francesco de Medici, Grand Duke of Tuscany (1541-1587), and Bianca Capello (1548-1587). The playwright's ultimate source of the Isabella-Hippolito plot, no doubt chosen for its echoes of the Medici story, was a romance, *Histoire Veritable des Infortunatees et Tragiques Amours d'Hypolite et d'Isabella, Neopolitains,* Rouen, 1597.

Middleton developed themes, motivations, and actions by means of apparent inconsistencies of character. Leantio is first introduced as a smug, conscientious clerk, who can dutifully tear himself away from his bride on Monday morning. A few days later he is a flashily-dressed court hanger-on, the possessor of a sinecure, the kept man of Livia. Bianca is starry-eyed in the first scene, malevolent in the last. Isabella is a pleasant, virtuous girl who must marry the simple-minded ward at her father's command; however, she promptly accepts her aunt's fabrication which makes permissible an incestuous liason with Hippolito, even after she is married. Hippolito com- bines a superficially platonic friendship with Isabella and a hidden passion for her.

Such dualism is evident in almost everyone in the play; duality easily shades into hypocrisy, with Duke Francesco as a prominent example. Livia's ambivalence makes her both a confidante and a trickster, and her successful manipulation of chess men is a microcosm of the human situation she so confidently controls: "She that can place her man well ... can never lose her game." (II, ii, 297-8)

[1] The play parallels Middleton and Rowley's *The Changeling* (produced in 1622) in many aspects of situation, characterization, and imagery, but there are no early records of performance of *Women Beware Women,* which was first published, along with *More Dissemblers Besides Women,* in *Two New Plays* (London, Humphrey Moseley, 1657).

1

In a world of insincerities and artificialities (represented by animal figures in marzipan) status symbols are a significant reinforcement of the themes. Bianca yearns for a silver ewer, an embroidered cushion, a bigger house in the high street; Livia takes an off-hand pride in the monument and other *objets d'art* in her house; Fabricio parades his expensively reared daughter like a purebred animal offered for sale: Leantio is proud of his new treasure, Bianca, and of his costly clothes, provided later by Livia.

Status symbols are inevitably linked to materialism, greed, and corruption. The duke uses money and power to acquire what he wants, the mother unwittingly contributes to Bianca's downfall for a few sweets; Leantio is bribed with a captainship, even though his business sense tells him that he was better off as a factor. Sexual gratification and marriage are closely related to the themes of corruption and self-delusion.

These subjects are vitalized by Middleton's subtle use of images. They often echo one another, with ironies of which the speaker is unaware. There are frequent metaphors of blindness, death, and disease (especially leprosy and venereal infections), of food to illustrate self-indulgence, of destructive or distorted aspects of nature (storms, contaminating mists, fire, monsters), of business and commerce.

Middleton had a special affinity for games to portray character and develop situations. The ward is preoccupied with his achievements in childish games, Livia keeps Leantio's mother engaged at the chess board whilst the duke seduces Bianca, the masque is a game of make-believe.

Equally important is Middleton's use of dramatic irony. Many episodes illustrate the ironic juxtaposition of aristocratic society – glittering and desirable, but in fact cynical and corrupt – and lower middle class society, with its genteel poverty.

Leantio is most deeply involved in the ironic situations, partly because he straddles these two worlds. He watches Bianca leave in the duke's caroche, unaware of Lady Livia beside him trying to attract his attention, and muses, "This cannot be but of some close bawd's working." (III, ii, 267)

The final act has numerous ironies as appropriate justice turns the plotters into victims, notably Guardiano, who is literally trapped in his own trap.

The title conveys more than one irony. Ostensibly, naïve girls like Bianca and Isabella are warned to be cautious of worldly women like Livia, but Middleton also suggests that women should be wary of their own natures. He makes clear as well that men should be careful of their choice of women to trust.

Much of the humour in this tragedy is incorporated in Middleton's verbal and situational irony. The coarse interchanges between the ward and Sordido (an overlooked minor character with no illusions and much commen sense) counterbalance the sophisticated dialogue of their betters. The viciousness of Guardiano's plan to entrap Hippolito is relieved by the ward's incomprehension and his disappointment that there will be no fire-crackers.

Temptation is a major motivating force in the play, especially in self-centred adolescents like Leantio and Bianca. Significantly, she yields, not to the duke's threats or lecherous suggestions, but to his bait of luxury and security, which she has given up by marrying Leantio. One would expect the dynamic Livia to be impervious to temptation. Seemingly cool-headed and ruthless, unwilling to resign her independence to a third husband, even she is not immune to sexual demands and, with a neat irony, is overwhelmingly attracted to the handsome Leantio.

In Act IV Duke Francesco appears to resist temptation after hearing the exhortations of his brother, the Cardinal, but the reader knows that the duke has already made arrangements to have his mistress's husband murdered. The playwright was less interested in the churchman's earnest morality than in the duke's specious logic: that he can purify his relationship with Bianca by eliminating Leantio.

The integration of important dramatic elements makes the first four acts of *Women Beware Women* artistically very satisfying, deeply revealing of human nature, but to many the short final act is disappointing.

Middleton showed unusually sensitive insights into feminine psychology and motivations, but he chose to utilize a traditional dénouement. It is a morally conventional, manipulative ending of interlocking recriminations and vengeances. The concluding scene focuses on the masque, itself a mask, with its obvious echoes of *The Spanish Tragedy,* then over twenty years old. The classical catharsis of tragedy is modified by the ambivalence of the characters; they are not moving because none has an enormous potential that is extinguished.

Women Beware Women has recently been revived on stage several times, notably at Stratford-upon-Avon in 1969. Twentieth century audiences and readers respond to the modern, non-heroic qualities of the central characters, the themes of alienation and materialism, the distorted moral order. It is a play of facades – like so much in contemporary life and relationships, where few things are really what they seem – the magnificent monument hides, metaphorically at least, a licentious duke, an apparently idyllic romantic marriage lasts only a fortnight, and an intellectual companionship of a man and a woman is destroyed by passion.

Upon the Tragedy of my Familiar Acquaintance, Thomas Middleton

> *Women beware Women*; 'tis a true text
> Never to be forgot. Drabs of state vex'd
> Have plots, poisons, mischiefs that seldom miss,
> To murder virtue with a venom-kiss.
> Witness this worthy tragedy, express'd
> By him that well-deserv'd among the best
> Of poets in his time; he knew the rage,
> Madness of women cross'd, and for the stage
> Fitted their humours; hell-bred malice, strife
> Acted in state, presented to the life.
> I that have seen't can say, having just cause,
> Never came tragedy off with more applause.
>   Nath. Richards.[1]

---

[1] Nathanael Richards (*c.* 1600-*post* 1641), a London poet (*The Celestiall Publican,* 1630) and playwright (*The Tragedy of Messallina,* 1640).

WOMEN BEWARE WOMEN
by Thomas Middleton
[*c.* 1621]
[*Dramatis Personnae*]

Duke of Florence
Lord Cardinal, *brother to the Duke*
Two cardinals more
A lord
Fabricio, *father to Isabella*
Hippolito, *brother to Fabricio*
Guardiano, *uncle to the foolish ward*
The Ward, *a rich young heir*
Leantio, *a factor,*[1] *husband to Bianca* [2]
Sordido, *the ward's man*
Livia, *sister to Fabricio* [*and Hippolito*]
Isabella, *niece to Livia* [*and daughter to Fabricio*]
Bianca [Capello], *Leantio's wife*
Widow, *his mother* ·
States[3] of Florence
Citizens, an apprentice, boys, messenger, servants.

The scene: Florence.

[1] The agent of a merchant.   [2] The edition of 1657 has Brancha throughout, evidently a printing house error.   [3] Noblemen.

ACT I SCENE I

[*Outside the house of* Leantio's *mother*]
Enter Leantio *with* Bianca, *and* [*his*] *mother* [*meets them*]

Mother.   Thy sight was never yet more precious to me!
　　　　Welcome, with all the affection of a mother
　　　　That comfort can express from natural love.
　　　　Since thy birth-joy,　a mother's chiefest gladness,
　　　　After sh'as undergone her curse of sorrows,
　　　　Thou wast not more dear to me than this hour
　　　　Presents thee to my heart. Welcome again.
Leant.   [*Aside.*] 'Las, poor affectionate soul, how her joys speak to me.
　　　　I have observ'd it often, and I know it is
10　　　The fortune commonly of knavish children
　　　　To have the loving'st mothers.
Mother.　　　　　　　　　　　What's this gentlewoman?
Leant.   Oh, you have nam'd the most unvalued'st[1] purchase
　　　　That youth of man had ever knowledge of.
　　　　As often as I look upon that treasure
　　　　And know it to be mine – there lies the blessing –
　　　　It joys me that I ever was ordain'd
　　　　To have a being and to live 'mongst men;
　　　　Which is a fearful living and a poor one,
　　　　Let a man truly think on't,
20　　　To have the toil and griefs of fourscore years
　　　　Put up in a white sheet tied with two knots.
　　　　Methinks it should strike earthquakes in adulterers,
　　　　When ev'n the very sheets they commit sin in
　　　　May prove, for aught they know, all their last garments.
　　　　Oh, what a mark were there for women then!
　　　　But beauty, able to content a conqueror
　　　　Whom earth could scarce content, keeps me in compass;
　　　　I find no wish in me bent sinfully
　　　　To this man's sister or to that man's wife;
30　　　In love's name let 'em keep their honesties
　　　　And cleave to their own husbands – 'tis their duties.
　　　　Now when I go to church I can pray handsomely,
　　　　Not come, like gallants, only to see faces,
　　　　As if lust went to market still on Sundays.
　　　　I must confess I am guilty of one sin, mother,
　　　　More than I brought into the world with me,
　　　　But that I glory in. 'Tis theft, but noble,
　　　　As ever greatness yet shot up withal.
Mother.   How's that?

---

[1] Valuable.

Leant.   Never to be repented, mother,
40   Though sin be death. I had died if I had not sinn'd,
        And here's my masterpiece! Do you now behold her.
        Look on her well; she's mine. Look on her better;
        Now say if't be not the best piece of theft
        That ever was committed! And I have my pardon for't;
        'Tis seal'd from Heaven by marriage.
Mother.   Married to her!
Leant.   You must keep counsel, mother, I am undone else.
        If it be known, I have lost her. Do but think now
        What that loss is; life's but a trifle to't.
        From Venice her consent and I have brought her
50   From parents great in wealth, more now in rage,
        But let storms spend their furies; now we have got
        A shelter o'er our quiet innocent loves,
        We are contented. Little money sh'as brought me;
        View but her face, you may see all her dowry,
        Save that which lies lock'd up in hidden virtues,
        Like jewels kept in cabinets.
Mother.   Y'are to blame,
        If your obedience will give way to a check,
        To wrong such a perfection.
Leant.   How?
Mother.   Such a creature,
        To draw her from her fortune, which no doubt,
60   At the full time, might have prov'd rich and noble.
        You know not what you have done. My life can give you
        But little helps, and my death lesser hopes;
        And hitherto your own means has but made shift
        To keep you single, and that hardly[1] too.
        What ableness have you to do her right then
        In maintenance fitting her birth and virtues,
        Which ev'ry woman of necessity looks for,
        And most to go above it, not confin'd
        By their conditions, virtues, bloods, or births,
70   But flowing to affections,[2] wills, and humours?
Leant.   Speak low, sweet mother; you are able to spoil as many
        As come within the hearing; if it be not
        Your fortune to mar all, I have much marvel.
        I pray do not you teach her to rebel,
        When she's in a good way to obedience,
        To rise with other women in commotion
        Against their husbands for six gowns a year,
        And so maintain their cause, when they're once up,
        In all things else that require cost enough.

[1] With difficulty.   [2]/Affectations.

80   They are all of 'em a kind of spirits soon rais'd,
            But not so soon laid, mother. As for example,
            A woman's belly is got up in a trice,
            A simple charge ere it be laid down again;
            So ever in all their quarrels and their courses.[1]
            And I'm a proud man, I hear nothing of 'em;
            They're very still, I thank my happiness,
            And sound asleep; pray let not your tongue wake 'em.
            If you can but rest quiet, she's contented
            With all conditions that my fortunes bring her to:
90   To keep close, as a wife that loves her husband,
            To go[2] after the rate of my ability,
            Not the licentious swinge[3] of her own will,
            Like some of her old schoolfellows. She intends
            To take out other works in a new sampler,
            And frame the fashion of an honest love
            Which knows no wants, but, mocking poverty,
            Brings forth more children, to make rich men wonder
            At divine Providence, that feeds mouths of infants,
            And sends them none to feed, but stuffs their rooms
100   With fruitful bags, their beds with barren wombs.
            Good mother, make not you things worse than they are
            Out of your too much openness; pray take heed on't;
            Nor imitate the envy of old people,
            That strive to mar good sport, because they are perfect.
            I would have you more pitiful to youth,
            Especially to your own flesh and blood.
            I'll prove an excellent husband, here's my hand:
            Lay in provision, follow my business roundly,
            And make you a grandmother in forty weeks.
110   Go, pray salute her, bid her welcome cheerfully.
      Mother.   Gentlewoman, thus much is a debt of courtesy,

                                        [*Kisses her repeatedly*]

            Which fashionable strangers pay each other
            At a kind meeting; then there's more than one,
            Due to the knowledge I have of your nearness.
            I am bold to come again, and now salute you
            By th' name of daughter, which may challenge more
            Than ordinary respect.
      Leant.   [*Aside*]   Why, this is well now,
            And I think few mothers of threescore will mend it.
      Mother.   What I can bid you welcome to is mean,
120   But make it all your own; we are full of wants
            And cannot welcome worth.

      [1] Actions   [2] Proceed.   [3] Influence.

Leant.   [*Aside*]   Now this is scurvy,
       And spoke as if a woman lack'd her teeth.
       These old folks talk of nothing but defects,
       Because they grow so full of 'em themselves.
Bian.   Kind mother, there is nothing can be wanting
       To her that does enjoy all her desires.
       Heaven send a quiet peace with this man's love,
       And I am as rich as virtue can be poor,
       Which were enough, after the rate of mind,[1]
130   To erect temples for content plac'd here.
       I have forsook friends, fortunes, and my country,
       And hourly I rejoice in't. Here's my friends,
       And few is the good number. Thy successes,
       Howe'er they look, I will still name my fortunes;
       Hopeful or spiteful, they shall all be welcome.
       Who invites many guests has of all sorts,
       As he that traffics much drinks of all fortunes;
       Yet they must all be welcome and us'd well.
       I'll call this place the place of my birth now,
140   And rightly too, for here my love was born,
       And that's the birthday of a woman's joys.
       [*To* Leantio] You have not bid me welcome since I came.
Leant.   That I did questionless.
Bian.   No, sure, how was't?
       I have quite forgot it.
Leant.   Thus.

                                                    [*Kisses her*]

Bian.   Oh, sir, 'tis true;
       Now I remember well. I have done thee wrong;
       Pray take't again, sir.
Leant.   How many of these wrongs
       Could I put up in an hour, and turn up the glass[2]
       For twice as many more?
Mother.   Will't please you to walk in, daughter?
Bian.   Thanks, sweet mother;
150   The voice of her that bare me is not more pleasing.

                                     Exeunt [Mother *and* Bianca].

Leant.   Though my own care and my rich master's trust
       Lay their commands both on my factorship,
       This day and night I'll know no other business
       But her and her sweet welcome. 'Tis a bitterness
       To think upon tomorrow, that I must leave her

[1] In proportion.   [2] Hour-glass.

Still to the sweet hopes of the week's end.
That pleasure should be so restrain'd and curb'd
After the course[1] of a rich work-master,
That never pays till Saturday night! Marry,
160   It comes together in a round sum then
And does more good you'll say. O fair-ey'd Florence!
Didst thou but know what a most matchless jewel
Thou now art mistress of, a pride would take thee,
Able to shoot destruction through the bloods
Of all thy youthful sons. But 'tis great policy
To keep choice treasures in obscurest places;
Should we show thieves our wealth 'twould make 'em bolder.
Temptation is a devil will not stick
To fasten upon a saint. Take heed of that.
170   The jewel is cas'd up from all men's eyes;
Who could imagine now a gem were kept
Of that great value under this plain roof?
But how in times of absence? What assurance
Of this restraint then? Yes, yes, there's one with her;
Old mothers know the world, and such as these,
When sons lock chests, are good to look to keys.

                                                          Exit.

[ACT I] SCENE 2

[Fabricio's *house*]
Enter Guardiano, Fabricio *and* Livia

Guard.   What, has your daughter seen him yet? Know you that?
Fab.   No matter; she shall love him.
Guard.   Nay, let's have fair play,
He has been now my ward some fifteen year,
And 'tis my purpose, as time calls upon me,
By custom seconded and such moral virtues,
To tender him a wife. Now, sir, this wife
I'ld fain elect out of a daughter of yours;
You see my meaning's fair. If now this daughter
So tendered — let me come to your own phrase, sir —
Should offer to refuse him I were handsell'd.[2]
[*Aside*] Thus am I fain to calculate all my words

---

[1] Custom.   [2] Lit., to be offered a new year's gift; here used ironically: to receive something of no value; i.e. to be tricked.

For the meridian[1] of a foolish old man,
To take his understanding! – What do you answer, sir?
Fab.   I say still, she shall love him.
Guard.   Yet again?
And shall she have no reason for this love?
Fab.   Why, do you think that women love with reason?
Guard.   [*Aside*] I perceive fools are not at all hours foolish,
No more than wise men wise.
Fab.   I had a wife;
She ran mad for me; she had no reason for't,
20   For aught I could perceive. What think you,
Lady sister?
Guard.   [*Aside*]   'Twas a fit match that,
Being both out of their wits! A loving wife, it seemed,
She strove to come as near you as she could,
Fab.   And if her daughter prove not mad for love too,
She takes not after her – nor after me,
If she prefer reason before my pleasure.
You're an experienced widow, lady sister;
I pray let your opinion come amongst us.
Livia.   I must offend you then, if truth will do't,
30   And take my niece's part, and call't injustice
To force her love to one she never saw,
Maids should both see and like, all little enough;
If they love truly after that, 'tis well.
Counting the time, she takes one man till death;
That's a hard task, I tell you, but one may
Inquire at three years' end amongst young wives,
And mark how the game goes.
Fab.   Why, is not man
Tied to the same observance, lady sister,
And in one woman?
Livia.   'Tis enough for him;
40   Besides, he tastes of many sundry dishes
That we poor wretches never lay our lips to,
As obedience forsooth, subjection, duty, and such kickshaws,
All of our making, but served in to them;
And if we lick a finger then sometimes,
We are not to blame; your best cooks use it.
Fab.   Th'art a sweet lady sister, and a witty.
Livia.   A witty! Oh, the bud of commendation,
Fit for a girl of sixteen! I am blown,[2] man!
I should be wise by this time; and, for instance,
50   I have buried my two husbands in good fashion,
And never mean more to marry.
Guard.   No? Why so, lady?

[1] Capacity.   [2] Stale.

Livia.   Because the third shall never bury me.
      I think I am more than witty; how think you, sir?
Fab.   I have paid often fees to a counsellor
      Has had a weaker brain.
Livia.   Then I must tell you,
      Your money was soon parted.
Guard.   Light[1] her now, brother![2]
Livia.   Where is my niece? Let her be sent for straight.
      If you have any hope 'twill prove a wedding,
      'Tis fit i' faith, she should have one sight of him,
60   And stop upon't, and not be joined in haste,
      As if they went to stock a new-found land.[3]
Fab.   Look out her uncle, and y'are sure of her;
      Those two are nev'r asunder. They've been heard
      In argument at midnight; moonshine nights
      Are noondays with them; they walk out their sleeps,
      Or rather at those hours appear like those
      That walk in 'em, for so they did to me.
      Look you, I told you truth; they're like a chain:
      Draw but one link, all follows.

Enter Hippolito *and* Isabella, *the niece*

Guard.   [*Aside*]   O affinity,
70   What piece of excellent workmanship art thou?
      'Tis work clean wrought, for there's no lust, but love in't,
      And that abundantly; when in stranger things
      There is no love at all but what lust brings.
Fab.   [*To* Isabella] On with your mask, for 'tis your part to see now,
      And not be seen. Go to, make use of your time.
      See what you mean to like; nay, and I charge you,
      Like what you see. Do you hear me? There's no dallying;
      The gentleman's almost twenty, and 'tis time
      He were getting lawful heirs, and you a-breeding on 'em.
Isab.   Good father, –
80 *Fab.*   Tell not me of tongues and rumours.
      You'll say the gentleman is somewhat simple;
      The better for a husband, were you wise,
      For those that marry fools live ladies' lives.
      On with the mask! I'll hear no more. He's rich;
      The fool's hid under bushels.
Livia.   Not so hid neither,
      But here's a foul great piece of him methinks.
      What will he be when he comes altogether?

_____
[1] Settle. [2] Addressed to Fabricio, brother to Livia. [3] Efforts to colonize
Newfoundland in the seventeenth century were largely unsuccessful.

Enter the Ward *with a trap-stick,*[1] *and* Sordido, *his man*

Ward.   Beat him?
     I beat him out o' th' field with his own cat-stick,
     Yet gave him the first hand.
Sord.   Oh, strange!
90 *Ward.*   I did it,
     Then he set jacks[2] on me.
Sord.   What, my lady's tailor?
Ward.   Ay, and I beat him too.
Sord.   Nay, that's no wonder,
     He's us'd to beating.
Ward.   Nay, I tickl'd him
     When I came once to my tippings.[3]
Sord.   Now you talk on 'em,
     There was a poulterer's wife made a great complaint
     Of you last night to your guardianer, that you struck
     A bump in her child's head, as big as an egg.
Ward.   An egg may prove a chicken; then in time
     The poulterer's wife will get[4] by't. When I am
100 In game I am furious; came my mother's eyes
     In my way, I would not lose a fair end.[5] No,
     Were she alive, but with one tooth in her head,
     I should venture the striking out of that.
     I think of nobody when I am in play,
     I am so earnest. Coads me,[6] my guardianer!
     Prithee lay up my cat and cat-stick safe.
Sord.   Where, sir, i' th' chimney-corner?
Ward.   Chimney-corner?
Sord.   Yes, sir, your cats are always safe i' th' chimney-corner,
110 unless they burn their coats.[7]
Ward.   Marry, that I am afraid on.
Sord.   Why, then, I will bestow your cat i' th' gutter,
     And there she's safe, I am sure.
Ward.   If I but live
     To keep a house, I'll make thee a great man,
     If meat and drink can do't. I can stoop[8] gallantly
     And pitch out[9] when I list; I'm dog at a hole.[10]
     I mar'l my guardianer does not seek a wife for me;
     I protest I'll have a bout with the maids else,
     Or contract myself at midnight to the larder-woman,

---

[1] In the game of trap, a trap-stick or cat-stick is used to knock a tapered
piece of wood, the cat, into the air and to strike it away.
[2] Knaves. [3] Strokes. [4] Profit. [5] A win. [6] God save me. [7] Here and
elsewhere in this exchange are allusions to prostitution and venereal
disease. [8] Condescend. [9] Settle upon a matter. [10] Stubborn.

120   In presence of a fool[1] or a sack-posset.[2]
        Guard.   Ward!
        Ward.   I feel myself after any exercise
              Horribly prone. Let me but ride, I'm lusty,
              A cock-horse straight, i' faith.
        Guard.   Why, ward, I say —
        Ward.   I'll forswear eating eggs in moonshine nights;[3]
              There's nev'r a one I eat but turns into a cock
              In four-and-twenty hours. If my hot blood
              Be not took down in time, sure 'twill crow shortly.
        Guard.   Do you hear, sir? Follow me; I must new-school you.
130   *Ward.*   School me? I scorn that; I am past schooling.
              I am not so base to learn to write and read;
              I was born to better fortunes in my cradle.

                                    Exit [*with* Guardiano *and* Sordido].

        Fab.   How do you like him, girl? This is your husband.
              Like him or like him not, wench, you shall have him
              And you shall love him.
        Livia.   Oh, soft there, brother. Though you be a justice,
              Your warrant cannot be serv'd out of your liberty.[4]
              You may compel, out of the power of father,
              Things merely harsh to a maid's flesh and blood;
140   But when you come to love, there the soil alters.
              Y'are in another country, where your laws
              Are no more set by than the cacklings
              Of geese in Rome's great Capitol.[5]
        Fab.   Marry him she shall then;
              Let her agree upon love afterwards.

                                                            Exit.

        Livia.   You speak now, brother, like an honest mortal
              That walks upon th' earth with a staff;[6]
              You were up i' th' clouds before. You'ld command love,
              And so do most old folks that go without it.
              My best and dearest brother, I could dwell here;

                                            [*Kisses* Hippolito]

150   There is not such another seat on earth
              Where all good parts better express themselves.

        [1] Trifle, custard.   [2] A drink made with sack, eggs, and sugar.   [3] Eggs were
        reputed to be aphrodisiac in effect.   [4] Jurisdiction.   [5] The geese, sacred
        to Juno, warned of an invasion by the Gauls.   [6] i.e. a pilgrim.

Hipp. You'll make me blush anon.
Livia. 'Tis but like saying grace before a feast then,
 And that's most comely; thou art all a feast,
 And she that has thee a most happy guest.
 Prithee cheer up that niece with special counsel.

                                                    [*Exit.*]

Hipp. [*Aside*] I would 'twere fit to speak to her what I would, but
 'Twas not a thing ordain'd; Heaven has forbid it,
 And 'tis most meet that I should rather perish
60 Than the decree divine receive least blemish.
 Feed inward, you my sorrows, make no noise,
 Consume me silent, let me be stark dead
 Ere the world know I'm sick. You see my honesty,
 If you befriend me, so.
Isab. [*Aside*]   Marry a fool!
 Can there be greater misery to a woman
 That means to keep her days true to her husband
 And know no other man, so virtue wills it?
 Why, how can I obey and honour him,
 But I must needs commit idolatry?
70 A fool is but the image of a man,
 And that but ill-made neither. O the heartbreakings
 Of miserable maids, where love's enforc'd!
 The best condition is but bad enough;
 When women have their choices, commonly
 They do but buy their thraldoms, and bring great portions
 To men to keep 'em in subjection,
 As if a fearful prisoner should bribe
 The keeper to be good to him, yet lies in still,
 And glad of a good usage, a good look
80 Sometimes. By 'r Lady, no misery surmounts a woman's.
 Men buy their slaves, but women buy their masters.
 Yet honesty and love makes all this happy
 And, next to angels', the most bless'd estate.
 That Providence, that has made ev'ry poison
 Good for some use, and sets four warring elements
 At peace in man, can make a harmony
 In things that are most strange to human reason!
 Oh, but this marriage! – What, are you sad too, uncle?
 Faith, then there's a whole household down together.
90 Where shall I go to seek my comfort now,
 When my best friend's distressed? What is't afflicts you, sir?
Hipp. Faith, nothing but one grief that will not leave me,
 And now 'tis welcome; ev'ry man has something
 To bring him to his end, and this will serve,

     Join'd with your father's cruelty to you,
     That helps it forward.
Isab.   Oh, be cheer'd, sweet uncle!
     How long has't been upon you? I nev'r spied it.
     What a dull sight have I! How long, I pray, sir?
Hipp.   Since I first saw you, niece, and left Bologna.
200 *Isab.*   And could you deal so unkindly with my heart,
     To keep it up so long hid from my pity?
     Alas, how shall I trust your love hereafter?
     Have we pass'd through so many arguments,
     And miss'd of that still, the most needful one?
     Walk'd out whole nights together in discourses,
     And the main point forgot? We are to blame both.
     This is an obstinate, wilful forgetfulness,
     And faulty on both parts. Let's lose no time now,
     Begin, good uncle, you that feel't; what is it?
210 *Hipp.*   You of all creatures, niece, must never hear on't;
     'Tis not a thing ordain'd for you to know.
Isab.   Not I, sir? All my joys that word cuts off.
     You made profession once you lov'd me best;
     'Twas but profession!
Hipp.   Yes, I do't too truly,
     And fear I shall be chid for't. Know the worst then:
     I love thee dearlier than an uncle can.
Isab.   Why, so you ever said, and I believ'd it.
Hipp.   [*Aside*] So simple is the goodness of her thoughts
     They understand not yet th'unhallowed language
220   Of a near sinner; I must yet be forced,
     Though blushes be my venture,[1] to come nearer. –
     As a man loves his wife, so love I thee.
Isab.   What's that?
     Methought I heard ill news come toward me,
     Which commonly we understand too soon,
     Then over-quick at hearing. I'll prevent[2] it,
     Though my joys fare the harder; welcome it;
     It shall nev'r come so near mine ear again.
     Farewell all friendly solaces and discourses;
     I'll learn to live without ye, for your dangers
230   Are greater than your comforts. What's become
     Of truth in love if such we cannot trust,
     When blood that should be love is mix'd with lust?

                                           Exit.

Hipp.   The worst can be but death, and let it come.

[1] Hazard.   [2] Anticipate.

He that lives joyless, ev'ry day's his doom.

Exit.

[ACT I] SCENE 3

[Outside house of Leantio's *mother]*
Enter Leantio *alone*

Leant.   Methinks I'm ev'n as dull now at departure
As men observe great gallants the next day
After a revels; you shall see 'em look
Much of my fashion if you mark 'em well.
'Tis ev'n a second Hell to part from pleasure
When [a] man has got a smack on't; as many holidays
Coming together makes your poor heads idle
A great while after, and are said to stick
Fast in their finger's ends, ev'n so does game
10   In a new-married couple for the time;
It spoils all thrift, and indeed lies abed
To invent all the new ways for great expenses.

[Enter] Bianca *and* Mother *above*

See, and she be not got on purpose now
Into the window to look after me.
I have no power to go now and I should be hang'd.
Farewell all business! I desire no more
Than I see yonder; let the goods at quay
Look to themselves. Why should I toil my youth out?
It is but begging two or three year sooner,
20   And stay with her continually. Is't a match?
Oh, fie, what a religion have I leap'd into!
Get out again, for shame. The man loves best
When his care's most; that shows his zeal to love.
Fondness is but the idiot to affection,[1]
That plays at hot-cockles[2] with rich merchants' wives,
Good to make sport withal when the chest's full
And the long warehouse cracks. 'Tis time of day
For us to be more wise; 'tis early with us;

[1] 'Love is merely the idiot when contrasted to affection.'   [2] A game in which a kneeling blindfolded person guesses who has struck him from behind.

And if they lose the morning of their affairs
30   They commonly lose the best part of the day.
Those that are wealthy and have got enough,
'Tis after sunset with 'em; they may rest,
Grow fat with ease, banquet, and toy and play,
When such as I enter the heat o' th' day,
And I'll do't cheerfully.
Bian.   I perceive, sir,
Y'are not gone yet; I have good hope you'll stay now.
Leant.   Farewell, I must not.
Bian.   Come, come; pray return.
Tomorrow, adding but a little care more,
Will dispatch all as well; believe me 'twill, sir.
40 *Leant.*   I could well wish myself where you would have me,
But love that's wanton must be rul'd awhile
By that that's careful, or all goes to ruin.
As fitting is a government in love
As in a kingdom. Where 'tis all mere lust
'Tis like an insurrection in the people
That rais'd, in self-will, wars against all reason.
But love that is respective for increase
Is like a good king that keeps all in peace.
Once more, farewell.
Bian.   But this one night, I prithee.
50 *Leant.*   Alas, I'm in for twenty if I stay,
And then for forty more, I have such luck to flesh;
I never bought a horse but he bore double.
If I stay any longer I shall turn
An everlasting spendthrift. As you love
To be maintain'd well, do not call me again,
For then I shall not care which end goes forward.
Again, farewell to thee.

                                                                    Exit.

Bian.   Since it must, farewell too.
Mother.   Faith, daughter, y'are to blame; you take the course
To make him an ill husband, troth you do,
60   And that disease is catching, I can tell you;
Ay, and soon taken by a young man's blood,
And that with little urging. Nay, fie, see now,
What cause have you to weep? Would I had no more,
That have liv'd threescore years; there were a cause,
And 'twere well thought on. Trust me, y'are to blame;
His absence cannot last five days at utmost.
Why should those tears be fetch'd forth? Cannot love
Be ev'n as well express'd in a good look,

But it must see her face still in a fountain?
70   It shows like a country maid dressing her head
By a dish of water. Come, 'tis an old[1] custom
To weep for love.

Enter two or three boys, *and a* citizen *or two, with an* apprentice

Boys.   Now they come, now they come!
2 Boy.   The duke!
3 Boy.   The state![2]
Cit.   How near, boy?
1 Boy.   I' th' next street, sir, hard at hand.
Cit.   You, sirrah, get a standing for your mistress,
    The best in all the city.
Apprent.   I have't for her, sir;
    'Twas a thing I provided for her overnight.
    'Tis ready at her pleasure.
Cit.   Fetch her to't then. Away, sir!

[*Exeunt* boys, citizens, *and* apprentice.]

Bian.   What's the meaning of this hurry,
    Can you tell, mother?
80 *Mother.*   What a memory
Have I! I see by that years come upon me.
Why, 'tis a yearly custom and solemnity,
Religiously observ'd by th' duke and state,
To Saint Mark's temple,[3] the fifteenth of April.
See if my dull brains had not quite forgot it.
'Twas happily question'd of thee; I had gone down else,
Sat like a drone below, and never thought on't.
I would not, to be ten years younger again,
That you had lost the sight. Now you shall see
90   Our duke, a goodly gentleman of his years.
Bian.   Is he old then?
Mother.   About some fifty-five.[4]
Bian.   That's no great age in man; he's then at best
    For wisdom and for judgment.
Mother.   The Lord Cardinal,
    His noble brother – there's a comely gentleman,
    And greater in devotion than in blood.[5]
Bian.   He's worthy to be mark'd.
Mother.   You shall behold

---

[1] i.e. old-fashioned. [2] Noblemen. [3] A notable thirteenth-century church in Florence. Saint Mark's feast day was, in fact, the twenty-fifth of April. [4] Historically he would have been approximately twenty-two. [5] Passion.

    All our chief states of Florence. You came fortunately
    Against this solemn day.
Bian.   I hope so always.

Music

Mother.   I hear 'em near us now. Do you stand easily?
Bian.   Exceeding well, good mother.
100 *Mother.*   Take this stool.
Bian.   I need it not, I thank you.
Mother.   Use your will then.

        *Enter in great solemnity six knights bare-headed, then two cardinals,
        and then the* Lord Cardinal, *then the* duke; *after him the* states *of
        Florence by two and two, with variety of music and song*

                                                        Exeunt.

Mother.   How like you, daughter?
Bian.   'Tis a noble state.
    Methinks my soul could dwell upon the reverence
    Of such a solemn and most worthy custom.
    Did not the duke look up? Methought he saw us.
Mother.   That's ev'ryone's conceit that sees a duke;
    If he look steadfastly, he looks straight at them;
    When he perhaps, good careful gentleman,
    Never minds any, but the look he casts
110 Is at his own intentions, and his object
    Only the public good.
Bian.   Most likely so.
Mother.   Come, come, we'll end this argument below.

                                                        Exeunt.

[ACT II] SCENE 1

[Livia's *house*]
Enter Hippolito *and* Lady Livia, *the widow*

Livia.   A strange affection, brother, when I think on't.
    I wonder how thou cam'st by't.
Hipp.   Ev'n as easily
    As man comes by destruction, which oft-times
    He wears in his own bosom.

Livia.   Is the world
So populous in women, and Creation
So prodigal in beauty and so various,
Yet does love turn thy point to thine own blood?
'Tis somewhat too unkindly. Must thy eye
Dwell evilly on the fairness of thy kindred
10 And seek not where it should? It is confin'd
Now in a narrower prison than was made for't.
It is allow'd a stranger; and where bounty
Is made the great man's honour, 'tis ill husbandry
To spare, and servants shall have small thanks for't.
So he Heaven's bounty seems to scorn and mock
That spares free means, and spends of his own stock.
Hipp.   Never was man's misery so soon sew'd up,
Counting how truly.
Livia.   Nay, I love you so
That I shall venture much to keep a change from you
20 So fearful as this grief will bring upon you.
Faith, it even kills me when I see you faint
Under a reprehension,[1] and I'll leave it,
Though I know nothing can be better for you.
Prithee, sweet brother, let not passion waste
The goodness of thy time and of thy fortune;
Thou keep'st the treasure of that life I love
As dearly as mine own, and if you think
My former words too bitter, which were minist'red
By truth and zeal, 'tis but a hazarding
30 Of grace and virtue, and I can bring forth
As pleasant fruits as sensuality wishes
In all her teeming longings. This I can do.
Hipp.   Oh, nothing that can make my wishes perfect!
Livia.   I would that love of yours were pawn'd to't, brother,
And as soon lost that way as I could win.
Sir, I could give as shrewd a lift[2] to chastity
As any she that wears a tongue in Florence;
Sh'ad need be a good horsewoman and sit fast,
Whom my strong argument could not fling at last.
40 Prithee take courage, man; though I should counsel
Another to despair, yet I am pitiful
To thy afflictions, and will venture hard —
I will not name for what, 'tis not handsome;
Find you the proof and praise me.
Hipp.   Then I fear me
I shall not praise you in haste.
Livia.   This is the comfort;

[1] Rebuke.   [2] Theft.

You are not the first, brother, has attempted
Things more forbidden than this seems to be.
I'll minister all cordials now to you,
Because I'll cheer you up, sir.

Hipp.   I am past hope.
50 *Livia.*   Love, thou shalt see me do a strange cure then,
As e'er was wrought on a disease so mortal
And near akin to shame. When shall you see her?

Hipp.   Never in comfort more.

Livia.   Y'are so impatient too.

Hipp.   Will you believe? Death, sh'as forsworn my company
And seal'd it with a blush.

Livia.   So, I perceive
All lies upon my hands then. Well, the more glory
When the work's finish'd.

Enter Servant

                              How now, sir? The news?

Serv.   Madam, your niece, the virtuous Isabella,
Is lighted now to see you.

Livia.   That's great fortune.
60   Sir, your stars bless. You, simple,[1] lead her in.

                                        Exit Servant.

Hipp.   What's this to me?

Livia.   Your absence, gentle brother;
I must bestir my wits for you.

Hipp.   Ay, to great purpose.

                                        Exit Hippolito.

Livia.   Beshrew you! Would I lov'd you not so well.
I'll go to bed and leave this deed undone.
I am the fondest where I once affect,
The carefull'st of their healths and of their ease, forsooth,
That I look still but slenderly[2] to mine own.
I take a course to pity him so much now
That I have none left for modesty and myself.
70   This 'tis to grow so liberal; y'have few sisters
That love their brothers' ease 'bove their own honesties.
But if you question my affections,
That will be found my fault.

[1] Fool.   [2] Scantily.

Enter Isabella, *the niece*

                            Niece, your love's welcome.
Alas, what draws that paleness to thy cheeks?
This enforc'd marriage towards?[1]

Isab.   It helps, good aunt,
Amongst some other griefs; but those I'll keep
Lock'd up in modest silence, for they're sorrows
Would shame the tongue more than they grieve the thought.

Livia.   Indeed, the ward is simple.

Isab.   Simple! That were well;
80   Why, one might make good shift with such a husband
But he's a fool entail'd;[2] he halts downright in't.

Livia.   And, knowing this, I hope 'tis at your choice
To take or refuse, niece.

Isab.   You see it is not.
I loathe him more than beauty can hate death
Or age, her spiteful neighbour.

Livia.   Let't appear then.

Isab.   How can I, being born with that obedience
That must submit unto a father's will?
If he command, I must of force consent.

Livia.   Alas, poor soul! Be not offended, prithee,
90   If I set by the name of niece awhile,
And bring in pity in a stranger fashion.
It lies here in this breast, would cross this match.

Isab.   How! Cross it, aunt?

Livia.   Ay, and give thee more liberty
Than thou hast reason yet to apprehend.

Isab.   Sweet aunt, in goodness keep not hid from me
What may befriend my life.

Livia.   Yes, yes, I must.
When I return to reputation,
And think upon the solemn vow I made
To your dead mother, my most loving sister[3] –
100 As long as I have her memory 'twixt mine eyelids,
Look for no pity now.

Isab.   Kind, sweet, dear aunt, –

Livia.   No, 'twas a secret I have took special care of,
Delivered by your mother on her deathbed
(That's nine years now), and I'll not part from't yet,
Though nev'r was fitter time nor greater cause for't.

Isab.   As you desire the praises of a virgin –

Livia.   Good sorrow! I would do thee any kindness
Not wronging secrecy or reputation.

[1] Approaching.   [2] Absolutely.   [3] In fact, sister-in-law.

Isab.   Neither of which, as I have hope of fruit[ful] ness,
          Shall receive wrong from me.
110 *Livia.*   Nay, 'twould be your own wrong,
          As much as any's, should it come to that once.
Isab.   I need no better means to work persuasion then.
Livia.   Let it suffice, you may refuse this fool,
          Or you may take him, as you see occasion
          For your advantage. The best wits will do't.
          Y'have liberty enough in your own will;
          You cannot be enforc'd. There grows the flower,
          If you could pick it out, makes whole life sweet to you.
          That which you call your father's command's nothing;
120   Then your obedience must needs be as little.
          If you can make shift here to taste your happiness,
          Or pick out aught that likes you, much good do you.
          You see your cheer, I'll make you no set dinner.
Isab.   And trust me, I may starve for all the good
          I can find yet in this. Sweet aunt, deal plainlier.
Livia.   Say I should trust you now upon an oath,
          And give you, in a secret, that would start you,
          How am I sure of you, in faith and silence?
Isab.   Equal assurance may I find in mercy
          As you for that in me.
130 *Livia.*   It shall suffice.
          Then know, however custom has made good,
          For reputation's sake, the names of niece
          And aunt 'twixt you and I, w'are nothing less.
Isab.   How's that?
Livia.   I told you I should start your blood.
          You are no more alli'd to any of us,
          Save what the courtesy of opinion casts
          Upon your mother's memory and your name,
          Than the mer'st stranger is, or one begot
          At Naples when the husband lies at Rome;
140   There's so much odds betwixt us. Since your knowledge
          Wish'd more instruction, and I have your oath
          In pledge for silence, it makes me talk the freelier.
          Did never the report of that fam'd Spaniard,
          Marquess of Coria,[1] since your time was ripe
          For understanding, fill your ear with wonder?
Isab.   Yes; what of him? I have heard his deeds of honour
          Often related when we liv'd in Naples.
Livia.   You heard the praises of your father then.
Isab.   My father!

[1] One of the titles of the Duke of Alba, a Spanish general who was at war
with Pope Paul IV during the 1550's, and was Viceroy of Naples in 1556.

Livia. | That was he; but all the business
150   So carefully and so discreetly carried
         That fame receiv'd no spot by't, not a blemish.
         Your mother was so wary to her end,
         None knew it but her conscience and her friend,
         Till penitent confession made it mine,
         And now my pity, yours; it had been long else.
         And I hope care and love alike in you,
         Made good by oath, will see it take no wrong now.
         How weak his commands now, whom you call father!
         How vain all his enforcements, your obedience!
160   And what a largeness in your will and liberty
         To take or to reject, or to do both!
         For fools will serve to father wise men's children.
         All this y'have time to think on. Oh, my wench,
         Nothing o'erthrows our sex but indiscretion;
         We might do well else of a brittle[1] people
         As any under the great canopy.
         I pray forget not but to call me aunt still;
         Take heed of that – it may be mark'd in time else –
         But keep your thoughts to yourself, from all the world,
170   Kindred, or dearest friend; nay, I entreat you,
         From him that all this while you have call'd uncle,
         And though you love him dearly, as I know
         His deserts claim as much ev'n from a stranger,
         Yet let not him know this, I prithee, do not;
         As ever thou hast hope of second pity,[2]
         If thou shouldst stand in need on't, do not do't.
Isab.   Believe my oath, I will not.
Livia.   Why, well said.
         [Aside] Who shows more craft t'undo a maidenhead,
         I'll resign my part to her. –

         Enter Hippolito

                        She's thine own; go.

                                                           Exit.

180 Hipp.   [Aside] Alas, fair flattery cannot cure my sorrows.
     Isab.   [Aside] Have I pass'd so much time in ignorance,
         And never had the means to know myself
         Till this bless'd hour? Thanks to her virtuous pity
         That brought it now to light. Would I had known it

[1] Vulnerable.   [2] The first pity is Livia's (line 155), the second is that of
Heaven.

But one day sooner. He had then receiv'd
In favours what, poor gentleman, he took
In bitter words, a slight and harsh reward
For one of his deserts.
Hipp.   [*Aside*]   There seems to me now
More anger and distraction in her looks.
190   I'm gone; I'll not endure a second storm;
The memory of the first is not past yet.
Isab.   [*Aside*]   Are you return'd, you comforts of my life,
In this man's presence? I will keep you fast now,
And sooner part eternally from the world
Than my good joys in you. — Prithee forgive me;
I did but chide in jest. The best loves use it
Sometimes; it sets an edge upon affection.
When we invite our best friends to a feast
'Tis not all sweetmeats that we set before them;
200   There's somewhat sharp and salt, both to whet appetite
And make 'em taste their wine well. So methinks,
After a friendly, sharp and savoury chiding,
A kiss tastes wondrous well and full o' th' grape.
How think'st thou, does't not?
Hipp.   'Tis so excellent
I know not how to praise it, what to say to't.
Isab.   This marriage shall go forward.
Hipp.   With the ward?
Are you in earnest?
Isab.   'Twould be ill for us else.
Hipp.   [*Aside*]   For us? How means she that?
Isab.   Troth, I begin
To be so well methinks within this hour,
210   For all this match able to kill one's heart,
Nothing can pull me down now. Should my father
Provide a worse fool yet, which I should think
Were a hard thing to compass, I'd have him either.
The worse the better; none can come amiss now,
If he want wit enough. So discretion love me,
Desert and judgment, I have content sufficient.
She that comes once to be a housekeeper
Must not look every day to fare well, sir,
Like a young waiting-gentlewoman in service,
220   For she feeds commonly as her lady does;
No good bit passes her but she gets a taste on't,
But when she comes to keep house for herself
She's glad of some choice cates[1] then once a week,
Or twice at most, and glad if she can get 'em;

---

[1] Delicacies.

So must affection learn to fare with thankfulness.
Pray make your love no stranger, sir, that's all.
[*Aside*] Though you be one yourself and know not on't,
And I have sworn you must not.

Exit.

Hipp.   This is beyond me!
  Never came joys so unexpectedly
230   To meet desires in man. How came she thus?
  What has she[1] done to her, can any tell?
  'Tis beyond sorcery this, drugs or love-powders,
  Some art that has no name sure; strange to me
  Of all the wonders I e'er met withal
  Throughout my ten years' travels, but I'm thankful for't.
  This marriage now must of necessity forward;
  It is the only veil wit can devise
  To keep our acts hid from sin-piercing eyes.

Exit.

[ACT II] SCENE 2

[Livia's *house*]
Enter Guardiano *and* Livia

Livia.   How, sir? A gentlewoman, so young, so fair,
  As you set forth, spied from the widow's window?
Guard.   She!
Livia.   Our Sunday-dinner woman?
Guard.   And Thursday-supper woman, the same still.
  I know not how she came by her, but I'll swear
  She's the prime gallant for a face in Florence,
  And no doubt other parts follow their leader.
  The duke himself first spied her at the window;
10   Then in a rapture, as if admiration
  Were poor when it were single, beck'ned me
  And pointed to the wonder warily,
  As one that fear'd she would draw in her splendour
  Too soon if too much gaz'd at. I nev'r knew him
  So infinitely taken with a woman,
  Nor can I blame his appetite or tax

[1] i.e. Livia.

His raptures of slight folly; she's a creature
Able to draw a state from serious business,
And make it their best piece[1] to do her service.
20   What course shall we devise? H'as spoke twice now.
Livia.   Twice?
Guard.   'Tis beyond your apprehension
How strangely that one look has catch'd his heart.
'Twould prove but too much worth in wealth and favour
To those should work his peace.
Livia.   And if I do't not,
Or at least come as near it (if your art
Will take a little pains and second me)
As any wench in Florence of my standing,
I'll quite give o'er, and shut up shop in cunning.
Guard.   'Tis for the duke, and if I fail your purpose,
30   All means to come, by riches or advancement,
Miss me and skip me over!
Livia.   Let the old woman then
Be sent for with all speed; then I'll begin.
Guard.   A good conclusion follow, and a sweet one,
After this stale beginning with old ware.
Within there!

Enter Servant

Serv.   Sir, do you call?
Guard.   Come near, list hither.

                              [*Speaks aside to* Servant]

Livia.   I long myself to see this absolute creature
That wins the heart of love and praise so much.
Guard.   Go, sir, make haste.
Livia.   Say I entreat her company.
Do you hear, sir?
Serv.   Yes, madam.

                                        Exit.

Livia.   That brings her quickly.
40 *Guard.*   I would 'twere done; the duke waits the good hour,
And I wait the good fortune that may spring from't.
I have had a lucky hand these fifteen year
At such court-passage[2] with three dice in a dish.

---

[1] Task.   [2] A game played with three dice.

Enter Fabricio

Signor Fabricio!

Fab.   Oh, sir, I bring an alteration in my mouth now.

Guard.   [*Aside*] An alteration? No wise speech, I hope.
He means not to talk wisely, does he, trow? –
Good! What's the change I pray, sir?

Fab.   A new change.

Guard.   Another yet! Faith, there's enough already.

Fab.   My daughter loves him now.

50 *Guard.*   What! Does she, sir?

Fab.   Affects him beyond thought. Who but the ward, forsooth?
No talk but of the ward; she would have him
To choose 'bove all the men she ever saw.
My will goes not so fast as her consent now;
Her duty gets before my command still.

Guard.   Why then, sir, if you'll have me speak my thoughts,
I smell 'twill be a match.

Fab.   Ay, and a sweet young couple,
If I have any judgment.

Guard.   [*Aside*]   Faith, that's little. –
Let her be sent tomorrow before noon,
60   And handsomely trick'd up, for 'bout that time
I mean to bring her in and tender her to him.

Fab.   I warrant you for handsome. I will see
Her things laid ready, every one in order,
And have some part of her trick'd up tonight.

Guard.   Why, well said.

Fab.   'Twas a use her mother had
When she was invited to an early wedding;
She'ld dress her head o'ernight, sponge up herself,
And give her neck three lathers.

Guard.   [*Aside*]   Ne'er a halter?[1]

Fab.   On with her chain of pearl, her ruby bracelets;
70   Lay ready all her tricks and jiggumbobs.

Guard.   So must your daughter.

Fab.   I'll about it straight, sir.

Exit Fabricio.

Livia.   How he sweats in the foolish zeal of fatherhood
After six ounces an hour, and seems
To toil as much as if his cares were wise ones.

Guard.   Y'have let his folly[2] blood in the right vein, lady.

Livia.   And here comes his sweet son-in-law that shall be.

[1] Guardiano develops a lather-leather pun. [2] Foolish.

They're both alli'd in wit before the marriage;
What will they be hereafter, when they are nearer?
Yet they can go no further than the fool;
There's the world's end in both of 'em.

Enter Ward *and* Sordido, *one with a shuttlecock, the other a battledore.*

80 *Guard.*   Now, young heir!
Ward.   What's the next business after shuttlecock now?
Guard.   Tomorrow you shall see the gentlewoman
Must be your wife.
Ward.   There's ev'n another thing too
Must be kept up with a pair of battledores.
My wife! What can she do?
Guard.   Nay, that's a question you should ask yourself, ward,
When y'are alone together.
Ward.   That's as I list.
A wife's to be ask['d] anywhere, I hope;
I'll ask her in a congregation,[1] if I have a mind to't, and so save a
90   licence. – [*To* Sordido] My guardianer has no more wit than an
herb-woman, that sells away all her sweet herbs and nosegays, and
keeps a stinking breath for her own pottage.
Sord.   Let me be at the choosing of your beloved,
If you desire a woman of good parts.
Ward.   Thou shalt, sweet Sordido.
Sord.   I have a plaguy guess. Let me alone to see what she is.
If I but look upon her – 'way, I know all the faults to a hair that you
may refuse her for.
Ward.   Dost thou? I prithee let me hear 'em, Sordido.
100 *Sord.*   Well, mark 'em then; I have 'em all in rhyme:
The wife your guardianer ought to tender
Should be pretty, straight, and slender;
Her hair not short, her foot not long,
Her hand not huge, nor too too loud her tongue;
No pearl[2] in eye, nor ruby[3] in her nose,
No burn or cut but what the catalogue shows.
She must have teeth, and that no black ones,
And kiss most sweet when she does smack once;
Her skin must be both white and plump,
110   Her body straight, not hopper-rump'd,[4]
Or wriggle sideways like a crab.
She must be neither slut nor drab,
Nor go too splay-foot with her shoes,
To make her smock lick up the dews.

---

[1] Publishing the banns of marriage would save the cost of a special licence.
[2] Cataract.   [3] Carbuncle.   [4] Deformed, with projecting buttocks.

     And two things more which I forgot to tell ye:
     She neither must have bump in back nor belly.
     These are the faults that will not make her pass.
Ward.   And if I spy not these I am a rank ass.
Sord.   Nay, more: By right, sir, you should see her naked,
     For that's the ancient order.
120 *Ward.*   See her naked?
     That were good sport, i' faith. I'll have the books turn'd over,
     And if I find her naked on record,
     She shall not have a rag on. But stay, stay:
     How if she should desire to see me so too?
     I were in a sweet case then; such a foul skin!
Sord.   But y'have a clean shirt, and that makes amends, sir.
Ward.   I will not see her naked for that trick though.

                                       Exit.

Sord.   Then take her with all faults, with her clothes on,
     And they may hide a number with a bum-roll.[1]
130   Faith, choosing of a wench in a huge farthingale
     Is like the buying of ware under a great penthouse;[2]
     What with the deceit of one
     And the false light of th'other, mark my speeches,
     He may have a diseas'd wench in's bed
     And rotten stuff in's breeches.

                                       Exit.

Guard.   It may take handsomely.
Livia.   I see small hind'rance.

   Enter Mother

     How now, so soon return'd?
Guard.   She's come.
Livia.   That's well.
     Widow, come, come; I have a great quarrel to you.
     Faith, I must chide you that you must be sent for!
140   You make yourself so strange, never come at us,
     And yet so near a neighbour, and so unkind.
     Troth, y'are to blame. You cannot be more welcome
     To any house in Florence, that I'll tell you.
Mother.   My thanks must needs acknowledge so much, madam.
Livia.   How can you be so strange then? I sit here

---

[1] A large roll of cloth worn about the hips to hold out from the body a straight skirt or farthingale.   [2] Canopy.

Sometimes whole days together without company
When business draws this gentleman from home,
And should be happy in society,
Which I so well affect, as that of yours.
150   I know y'are alone too; why should not we,
Like two kind neighbours, then supply the wants
Of one another, having tongue discourse,
Experience in the world, and such kind helps
To laugh down time and meet age merrily?[1]

Mother.   Age, madam? You speak mirth. 'Tis at my door,
But a long journey from your ladyship yet.

Livia.   My faith, I'm nine-and-thirty, ev'ry stroke, wench,
And 'tis a general observation
'Mongst knights' wives or widows, we accompt
160   Ourselves then old when young men's eyes leave looking at's.
'Tis a true rule amongst us, and ne'er fail'd yet
In any but in one that I remember;
Indeed, she had a friend at nine-and-forty.
Marry, she paid well for him, and in th'end
He kept a quean or two with her own money,
That robb'd her of her plate and cut her throat.

Mother.   She had her punishment in this world, madam,
And a fair warning to all other women,
That they live chaste at fifty.

Livia.   Ay, or never, wench.
170   Come, now I have thy company I'll not part with't
Till after supper.

Mother.   Yes, I must crave pardon, madam.

Livia.   I swear you shall stay supper. We have no strangers, woman,
None but my sojourners[2] and I, this gentleman,
And the young heir, his ward. You know our company.

Mother.   Some other time I will make bold with you, madam.

Guard.   Nay, pray stay, widow.

Livia.   Faith, she shall not go.
Do you think I'll be forsworn?

                              [Servants *bring in*] *table and chess* [*game*]

Mother.   'Tis a great while
Till supper-time; I'll take my leave then now, madam,
And come again i' th'evening, since your ladyship
Will have it so.

180 *Livia.*   I' th'evening? By my troth, wench,
I'll keep you while I have you. You have great business sure
To sit alone at home; I wonder strangely

---

[1] 1657 edition has 'meerly.'   [2] Visitors.

What pleasure you take in't. Were't to me now,
I should be ever at one neighbour's house
Or other all day long, having no charge,
Or none to chide you if you go or stay.
Who may live merrier, ay, or more at heart's ease?
Come, we'll to chess or draughts; there are an hundred tricks
To drive out time till supper, never fear't, wench.

190 *Mother.*   I'll but make one step home and return straight, madam.

    Livia.   Come, I'll not trust you; you use more excuses
To your kind friends than ever I knew any.
What business can you have, if you be sure
Y'have lock'd the doors? And that being all you have,
I know y'are careful on't. One afternoon
So much to spend here? Say I should entreat you now
To lie a night or two, or a week with me,
Or leave your own house for a month together,
It were a kindness that long neighbourhood[1]

200 And friendship might well hope to prevail in.
Would you deny such a request? I' faith,
Speak truth, and freely.

    Mother.   I were then uncivil, madam.

    Livia.   Go to then, set your men; we'll have whole nights
Of mirth together ere we be much older, wench.

    Mother.   [*Aside*] As good now tell her then, for she will know't;
I have always found her a most friendly lady.

    Livia.   Why, widow, where's your mind?

    Mother. |Troth, ev'n at home, madam.
To tell you truth, I left a gentlewoman
Ev'n sitting all alone, which is uncomfortable,
Especially to young bloods.

210 *Livia.*   Another excuse!

    Mother.   No, as I hope for health, madam, that's a truth.
Please you to send and see.

    Livia.   What gentlewoman? Pish!

    Mother.   Wife to my son indeed, but not known, madam,
To any but yourself.

    Livia.   Now I beshrew you.
Could you be so unkind to her and me
To come and not bring her? Faith, 'tis not friendly.

    Mother.   I fear'd to be too bold.

    Livia.   Too bold? Oh what's become
Of the true hearty love was wont to be
'Mongst neighbours in old time?

    Mother.   And she's a stranger, madam.

220 *Livia.*   The more should be her welcome. When is courtesy

---

[1] Association.

In better practice than when 'tis employ'd
In entertaining strangers? I could chide, i' faith.
Leave her behind, poor gentlewoman, alone too?
Make some amends and send for her betimes; go.
Mother.   Please you command one of your servants, madam.
Livia.   Within there!

    Enter Servant

Serv.   Madam?
Livia.   Attend the gentlewoman.
Mother.   It must be carried wondrous privately
From my son's knowledge; he'll break out in storms else.
Hark you, sir.

                       [*Speaks to* Servant, *who exits*]

Livia.   [*To* Guardiano] Now comes in the heat of your part.
230 *Guard.*   [*To* Livia] True, I know it, lady, and if I be out,
May the duke banish me from all employments
Wanton or serious.
Livia.   So, have you sent, widow?
Mother.   Yes, madam, he's almost at home by this.
Livia.   And, faith, let me entreat you that henceforward
All such unkind faults may be swept from friendship,
Which does but dim the lustre. And think thus much:
It is a wrong to me, that have ability
To bid friends welcome, when you keep 'em from me;
You cannot set greater dishonour near me,
240 For bounty is the credit and the glory
Of those that have enough. I see y'are sorry,
And the good mends is made by't.
Mother.   Here she's, madam.

    Enter Bianca *and* Servant [, *who leaves*]

Bian.   [*Aside*] I wonder how she comes to send for me now?
Livia.   Gentlewoman, y'are most welcome, trust me y'are,
As courtesy can make one, or respect
Due to the presence of you.
Bian.   I give you thanks, lady.
Livia.   I heard you were alone, and 't had appear'd
An ill condition in me, though I knew you not,
Nor ever saw you (yet humanity
250 Thinks ev'ry case her own), to have kept your company[1]

---

[1] i.e. Leantio's mother.

Here from you and left you all solitary.
I rather ventur'd upon boldness then
As the least fault, and wish'd your presence here,
A thing most happily motion'd[1] of that gentleman,
Whom I request you, for his care and pity,
To honour and reward with your acquaintance,
A gentleman that ladies' rights stands for —
That's his profession.

Bian.   'Tis a noble one,
And honours my acquaintance.

Guard.   All my intentions
Are servants to such mistresses.

260 *Bian.*   'Tis your modesty,
It seems, that makes your deserts speak so low, sir.

Livia.   Come, widow. Look you, lady, here's our business.
Are we not well employ'd, think you? An old quarrel
Between us that will never be at an end.

Bian.   No, and methinks there's men enough to part you, lady.

Livia.   Ho! But they set us on; let us come off
As well as we can, poor souls, men care no farther.
I pray sit down forsooth, if you have the patience
To look upon two weak and tedious gamesters.

270 *Guard.*   Faith, madam, set these by till evening;
You'll have enough on't then. The gentlewoman,
Being a stranger, would take more delight
To see your rooms and pictures.

Livia.   Marry, good sir,
And well rememb'red. I beseech you show 'em her;
That will beguile time well. Pray heartily, do, sir;
I'll do as much for you. Here, take these keys;
Show her the monument too, and that's a thing
Everyone sees not. You can witness that, widow.

Mother.   And that's worth sight indeed, madam.

Bian.   Kind lady,
280 I fear I came to be a trouble to you.

Livia.   Oh, nothing less forsooth!

Bian.   And to this courteous gentleman,
That wears a kindness in his breast so noble
And bounteous to the welcome of a stranger.

Guard.   If you but give acceptance to my service,
You do the greatest grace and honour to me
That courtesy can merit.

Bian.   I were to blame else,
And out of fashion much. I pray you lead, sir.

Livia.   After a game or two w'are for you, gentlefolks.

[1] Instigated.

Guard.   We wish no better seconds[1] in society
290   Than your discourses, madam, and your partner's there.
Mother.   I thank your praise. I listen'd to you, sir,
Though when you spoke there came a paltry rook
Full in my way, and chokes up all my game.

Exeunt Guardiano *and* Bianca

Livia.   Alas, poor widow, I shall be too hard for thee.
Mother.   Y'are cunning at the game, I'll be sworn, madam.
Livia.   It will be found so ere I give you over.
She that can place her man well —
Mother.   As you do, madam.
Livia.   As I shall, wench — can never lose her game.
Nay, nay, the black king's mine.
Mother.   Cry you mercy, madam.
Livia.   And this my queen.
Mother.   I see't now.
300 *Livia.*   Here's a duke[2]
Will strike a sure stroke for the game anon;
Your pawn cannot come back to relieve itself.
Mother.   I know that, madam.
Livia.   You play well the whilst.
[*Aside*] How she belies her skill. — I hold two ducats[3]
I give you check and mate to your white king,
Simplicity itself, your saintish king there.
Mother.   Well, ere now, lady,
I have seen the fall of subtlety. Jest on.
Livia.   Ay, but simplicity receives two for one.
Mother.   What remedy but patience!

Enter above Guardiano *and* Bianca

310 *Bian.*   Trust me, sir,
Mine eye nev'r met with fairer ornaments.
Guard.   Nay, livelier, I'm persuaded, neither Florence
Nor Venice can produce.
Bian.   Sir, my opinion
Takes your part highly.
Guard.   There's a better piece
Yet than all these.

Duke [*is revealed*] *above*[4]

[1] Supporters.   [2] i.e. rook. Middleton used the same equivalence in his
political allegory *A Game at Chesse* (1625).   [3] A ducat was worth about
50p.   [4] i.e. on the same level as Bianca and Guardiano.

Bian.   Not possible, sir!
Guard.   Believe it;
　　You'll say so when you see't. Turn but your eye now,
　　Y'are upon't presently.

Exit.

Bian.   Oh, sir!
Duke.   He's gone, beauty.
　　Pish, look not after him; he's but a vapour
　　That when the sun appears is seen no more.
Bian.   Oh, treachery to honour!
320 *Duke.*   Prithee tremble not.
　　I feel thy breast shake like a turtle[1] panting
　　Under a loving hand that makes much on't.
　　Why art so fearful? As I'm friend to brightness,
　　There's nothing but respect and honour near thee.
　　You know me, you have seen me; here's a heart
　　Can witness I have seen thee.
Bian.   The more's my danger.
Duke.   The more's thy happiness. Pish, strive not, sweet!
　　This strength were excellent employ'd in love now,
　　But here 'tis spent amiss.[2] Strive not to seek
330　Thy liberty and keep me still in prison.
　　I' faith, you shall not out till I'm releas'd now;
　　We'll be both freed together or stay still by't;
　　So is captivity pleasant.
Bian.   Oh, my Lord!
Duke.   I am not here in vain; have but the leisure
　　To think on that, and thou'lt be soon resolv'd.
　　The lifting of thy voice is but like one
　　That does exalt his enemy, who, proving high,
　　Lays all the plots to confound him that rais'd him.
　　Take warning, I beseech thee; thou seem'st to me
340　A creature so compos'd of gentleness
　　And delicate meekness, such as bless the faces
　　Of figures that are drawn for goddesses,
　　And make art proud to look upon her work,
　　I should be sorry the least force should lay
　　An unkind touch upon thee.
Bian.   Oh, my extremity!
　　My Lord, what seek you?
Duke.   Love.
Bian.   'Tis gone already;

---

[1] Turtle dove.　[2] This sentence, like others spoken by the duke, has a
sexual *double entendre*.

        I have a husband.
Duke.   That's a single comfort;
     Take a friend to him.
Bian.   That's a double mischief,
     Or else there's no religion.
Duke.   Do not tremble
     At fears of thine own making.
350 *Bian.*   Nor, great Lord,
     Make me not bold with death and deeds of ruin
     Because they fear not you. Me they must fright;
     Then am I best in health. Should thunder speak
     And none regard it, it had lost the name
     And were as good be still. I'm not like those
     That take their soundest sleeps in greatest tempests;
     Then wake I most, the weather fearfullest,
     And call for strength to virtue.
Duke.   Sure I think
     Thou know'st the way to please me; I affect[1]
360   A passionate pleading 'bove an easy yielding,
     But never pitied any. They deserve none
     That will not pity me. I can command;
     Think upon that. Yet if thou truly knewest
     The infinite pleasure my affection takes
     In gentle, fair entreatings, when love's businesses
     Are carried courteously 'twixt heart and heart,
     You'ld make more haste to please me.
Bian.   Why should you seek, sir,
     To take away that you can never give?
Duke.   But I give better in exchange: wealth, honour.
370   She that is fortunate in a duke's favour
     Lights on a tree that bears all women's wishes.
     If your own mother saw you pluck fruit there,
     She would commend your wit, and praise the time
     Of your nativity. Take hold of glory.
     Do not I know y'have cast away your life
     Upon necessities, means merely doubtful
     To keep you in indifferent health and fashion,
     A thing I heard too lately and soon pitied.
     And can you be so much your beauty's enemy,
380   To kiss away a month or two in wedlock,
     And weep whole years in wants forever after?
     Come, play the wise wench, and provide forever;
     Let storms come when they list, they find thee shelter'd.
     Should any doubt arise, let nothing trouble thee;
     Put trust in our love for the managing

[1] Like.

Of all to thy heart's peace. We'll walk together,
And show a thankful joy for both our fortunes.

Exeunt above.

Livia.	Did not I say my duke would fetch you over,[1] widow?
Mother.	I think you spoke in earnest when you said it, madam.

390 *Livia.*   And my black king makes all the haste he can too.
    Mother.   Well, madam, we may meet with him in time yet.
    Livia.   I have given thee blind mate twice.
    Mother.   You may see, madam,
My eyes begin to fail.
    Livia.   I'll swear they do, wench.

Enter Guardiano

Guard.   [*Aside*] I can but smile as often as I think on't,
How prettily the poor fool was beguil'd,
How unexpectedly. It's a witty age;
Never were finer snares for women's honesties
Than are devis'd in these days; no spider's web
Made of a daintier thread than are now practis'd
400   To catch love's flesh-fly by the silver wing.
Yet to prepare her stomach by degrees
To Cupid's feast, because I saw 'twas queasy,
I show'd her naked pictures by the way,
A bit to stay[2] the appetite. Well, advancement,
I venture hard to find thee; if thou com'st
With a greater title set upon thy crest,
I'll take that first cross patiently, and wait
Until some other comes greater than that.
I'll endure all.
    Livia.   The game's ev'n at the best now; you may see, widow,
How all things draw to an end.
410 *Mother.*   Ev'n so do I, madam.
    Livia.   I pray take some of your neighbours along with you.[3]
    Mother.   They must be those are almost twice your years then,
If they be chose fit matches for my time, madam.
    Livia.   Has not my duke bestirr'd himself?
    Mother.   Yes, faith, madam.
H'as done me all the mischief in this game.
    Livia.   H'as show'd himself in's kind.[4]
    Mother.   In's kind, call you it?
I may swear that.

---

[1] Trick you.   [2] Appease.   [3] i.e. towards death, echoing Mother's pious interpretation of 'all things draw to an end.'   [4] In his true form.

Livia.   Yes, faith, and keep your oath.
Guard.   Hark, list! There's somebody coming down; 'tis she.

Enter Bianca

Bian.   [*To* Guardiano.] Now bless me from a blasting. I saw that now
420   Fearful for any woman's eye to look on.
          Infectious mists and mildews hang at's eyes;
          The weather of a doomsday dwells upon him.
          Yet since mine honour's leprous, why should I
          Preserve that fair that caus'd the leprosy?
          Come, poison all at once. Thou in whose baseness
          The bane of virtue broods, I'm bound in soul
          Eternally to curse thy smooth-brow'd treachery
          That wore the fair veil of a friendly welcome,
          And I a stranger. Think upon't, 'tis worth it;
430   Murders pil'd up upon a guilty spirit
          At his last breath will not lie heavier
          Than this betraying act upon thy conscience.
          Beware of off'ring the first-fruits to sin;
          His weight is deadly who commits[1] with strumpets
          After they have been abas'd and made for use;
          If they offend to th' death, as wise men know,
          How much more they then that first make 'em so?
          I give thee that to feed on. I'm made bold now,
          I thank thy treachery; sin and I'm acquainted,
440   No couple greater; and I'm like that great one[2]
          Who, making politic use of a base villain:
          'He likes the treason well, but hates the traitor;'
          So I hate thee, slave.
Guard.   [*Aside*]   Well, so the duke love me
          I fare not much amiss then; two great feasts
          Do seldom come together in one day;
          We must not look for 'em.
Bian.   What, at it still, mother?
Mother.   You see we sit by't. Are you so soon return'd?
Livia.   So lively and so cheerful, a good sign that.
Mother.   You have not seen all since, sure?
Bian.   That have I, mother,
450   The monument and all. I'm so beholding
          To this kind, honest, courteous gentleman —
          You'ld little think it, mother — show'd me all,
          Had me from place to place so fashionably;
          The kindness of some people, how't exceeds!
          Faith, I have seen that I little thought to see

[1] i.e. commits adultery.   [2] i.e. Machiavelli.

I' th' morning when I rose.
Mother.   Nay, so I told you
   Before you saw't, it would prove worth your sight.
   I give you great thanks for my daughter, sir,
   And all your kindness towards her.
Guard.   O good widow!
60   [*Aside*] Much good may['t] do her, forty weeks hence, i' faith!

Enter Servant

Livia.   Now, sir?
Serv.   May't please you, madam, to walk in,
   Supper's upon the table.
Livia.   Yes, we come.
   Will't please you, gentlewoman?
Bian.   Thanks, virtuous lady, –
   [*To* Livia] Y'are a damn'd bawd – I'll follow you, forsooth.
   Pray take my mother in; [*To* Livia] an old ass go with you –
   This gentleman and I vow not to part.
Livia.   Then get you both before.
Bian.   There lies his art.

Exeunt [Bianca *and* Guardiano].

Livia.   Widow, I'll follow you.

[*Exit* Mother.]

                          Is't so, 'Damn'd bawd'?
   Are you so bitter? 'Tis but want of use.
70   Her tender modesty is seasick a little,
   Being not accustom'd to the breaking billow
   Of woman's wavering faith, blown with temptations.
   'Tis but a qualm of honour, 'twill away;
   A little bitter for the time, but lasts not.
   Sin tastes at the first draught like wormwood water,
   But drunk again, 'tis nectar ever after.

Exit.

ACT III SCENE 1

[*House of* Leantio's *mother*]
Enter Mother

Mother.   I would my son would either keep at home
          Or I were in my grave.
          She was but one day abroad, but ever since
          She's grown so cutted,[1] there's no speaking to her.
          Whether the sight of great cheer at my lady's,
          And such mean fare at home, work discontent in her,
          I know not, but I'm sure she's strangely alter'd.
          I'll nev'r keep daughter-in-law i' th' house with me
          Again, if I had an hundred. When read I of any
10   That agreed long together, but she and her mother
          Fell out in the first quarter? Nay, sometime
          A grudging of a scolding the first week, by 'r Lady.
          So takes the new disease methinks in my house.
          I'm weary of my part; there's nothing likes her.
          I know not how to please her here alate,
          And here she comes.

Enter Bianca

Bian.   This is the strangest house
          For all defects as ever gentlewoman
          Made shift withal to pass away her love in.
          Why is there not a cushion-cloth of drawn work,[2]
20   Or some fair cut-work[3] pinn'd up in my bed-chamber,
          A silver-and-gilt casting-bottle[4] hung by't?
          Nay, since I am content to be so kind to you,
          To spare you for a silver basin and ewer,[5]
          Which one of my fashion looks for of duty;
          She's never offered under,[6] where she sleeps.
Mother.   [*Aside*] She talks of things here my whole state's not worth.
Bian.   Never a green silk quilt is there i' th' house, mother,
          To cast upon my bed?
Mother.   No, by troth, is there,
          Nor orange-tawny neither.
Bian.   Here's a house
30   For a young gentlewoman to be got with child in!
Mother.   Yes, simple though you make it, there has been three
          Got in a year in't, since you move me to't,

---

[1] Curt. [2] With pulled or withdrawn threads forming a design.
[3] Embroidery. [4] A bottle for sprinkling perfume. [5] Pitcher. [6] Less.

And all as sweet-fac'd children and as lovely
As you'll be mother of. I will not spare you.
What, cannot children be begot, think you,
Without gilt casting-bottles? Yes, and as sweet ones.
The miller's daughter brings forth as white boys[1]
As she that bathes herself with milk and bean-flour.
'Tis an old saying, 'One may keep good cheer
40   In a mean house'; so may true love affect[2]
After the rate of princes in a cottage.

Bian.   Troth, you speak wondrous well for your old house here;
'Twill shortly fall down at your feet to thank you,
Or stoop when you go to bed, like a good child,
To ask you blessing. Must I live in want
Because my fortune match'd me with your son?
Wives do not give away themselves to husbands
To the end to be quite cast away; they look
To be the better us'd and tender'd rather,
50   Highlier respected, and maintain'd the richer;
They're well rewarded else for the free gift
Of their whole life to a husband. I ask less now
Than what I had at home when I was a maid
And at my father's house, kept short of that
Which a wife knows she must have, nay, and will —
Will, mother, if she be not a fool born.
And report went of me that I could wrangle
For what I wanted when I was two hours old;
And by that copy,[3] this land still I hold.
You hear me, mother.

                                                                Exit.

60 *Mother.*   Ay, too plain methinks,
And were I somewhat deafer when you spake,
'Twere nev'r a whit the worse for my quietness.
'Tis the most sudden'st, strangest alteration,
And the most subtlest that ev'r wit at threescore
Was puzzled to find out. I know no cause for't, but
She's no more like the gentlewoman at first
Than I am like her that nev'r lay with man yet,
And she's a very young thing where'er she be.
When she first lighted here I told her then
70   How mean she should find all things; she was pleas'd forsooth,
None better. I laid open all defects to her;
She was contented still, but the devil's in her;
Nothing contents her now. Tonight my son

[1] Darlings.   [2] Aspire.   [3] Right.

     Promis'd to be at home; would he were come once[1]
     For I'm weary of my charge, and life too.
     She'ld be serv'd all in silver by her good will
     By night and day. She hates the name of pewterer[2]
     More than sick men the noise, or diseas'd bones
     That quake at fall o' th' hammer, seeming to have
80   A fellow feeling with't at every blow.[3]
     What course shall I think on? She frets me so.

                         [Stands apart]

   Enter Leantio

Leant.   How near am I now to a happiness
     That earth exceeds not! Not another like it.
     The treasures of the deep are not so precious
     As are the conceal'd comforts of a man
     Lock'd up in woman's love. I scent the air
     Of blessings when I come but near the house.
     What a delicious breath marriage sends forth!
     The violet bed's not sweeter. Honest wedlock
90   Is like a banqueting house built in a garden,
     On which the spring's chaste flowers take delight
     To cast their modest odours; when base lust
     With all her powders, paintings, and best pride
     Is but a fair house built by a ditch side.
     When I behold a glorious, dangerous strumpet,
     Sparkling in beauty and destruction too,
     Both at a twinkling, I do liken straight
     Her beautified body to a goodly temple
     That's built on vaults where carcasses lie rotting,
100   And so by little and little I shrink back again,
     And quench desire with a cool meditation,
     And I'm as well methinks. Nor for a welcome
     Able to draw men's envies upon man,
     A kiss now that will hang upon my lip
     As sweet as morning dew upon a rose,
     And full as long. After five days' fast
     She'll be so greedy now and cling about me,
     I take care how I shall be rid of her;
     And here't begins.

   [Enter Bianca, *and* Mother *steps forward]*

[1] i.e. once for all.   [2] The maker of inexpensive housewares.   [3] Perhaps an allusion to the construction of coffins.

Bian.   Oh, sir, y'are welcome home.
Mother.   Oh, is he come? I am glad on't.
10 *Leant.*   [*Aside*]   Is that all?
     Why this? As dreadful now as sudden death
     To some rich man that flatters all his sins
     With promise of repentance when he's old,
     And dies in the mid way before he comes to't. –
     Sure y'are not well, Bianca? How dost, prithee?
Bian.   I have been better than I am at this time.
Leant.   Alas, I thought so.
Bian.   Nay, I have been worse too
     Than now you see me, sir.
Leant.   I'm glad thou mend'st yet;
     I feel my heart mend too. How came it to thee?
20 Has any thing dislik'd[1] thee in my absence?
Bian.   No, certain; I have had the best content
     That Florence[2] can afford.
Leant.   Thou makest the best on't.
     Speak, mother, what's the cause? You must needs know.
Mother.   Troth, I know none, son; let her speak herself.
     Unless it be the same gave Lucifer
     A tumbling cast: that's pride.
Bian.   Methinks this house stands nothing to my mind;
     I'ld have some pleasant lodging i' th' high street, sir,
     Or if 'twere near the court, sir, that were much better.
30 'Tis a sweet recreation for a gentlewoman
     To stand in a bay window and see gallants.
Leant.   Now I have another temper, a mere stranger
     To that of yours it seems; I should delight
     To see none but yourself.
Bian.   I praise not that;
     Too fond is as unseemly as too churlish;
     I would not have a husband of that proneness
     To kiss me before company for a world.
     Beside, 'tis tedious to see one thing still, sir,
     Be it the best that ever heart affected.
40 Nay, were't yourself, whose love had power, you know,
     To bring me from my friends, I would not stand thus
     And gaze upon you always; troth, I could not, sir.
     As good be blind and have no use of sight
     As look on one thing still. What's the eye's treasure
     But change of objects? You are learned, sir,
     And know I speak not ill. 'Tis full as virtuous
     For woman's eye to look on several men
     As for her heart, sir, to be fixed on one.

[1] Displeased.   [2] *Double entendre:* the city or the Duke of Florence.

Leant.   Now thou com'st home to me; a kiss for that word.
150 *Bian.*   No matter for a kiss, sir; let it pass.
        'Tis but a toy; we'll not so much as mind it.
        Let's talk of other business and forget it.
        What news now of the pirates?[1] Any stirring?
        Prithee discourse a little.
Mother.   [*Aside*]   I am glad he's here yet
        To see her tricks himself; I had lied monstrously
        If I had told 'em first.
Leant.   Speak, what's the humour, sweet,
        You make your lip so strange? This was not wont.
Bian.   Is there no kindness betwixt man and wife
        Unless they make a pigeon-house of friendship
160   And be still billing? 'Tis the idlest fondness
        That ever was invented, and 'tis pity
        It's grown a fashion for poor gentlewomen.
        There's many a disease kiss'd in a year by't,
        And a French curtsy[2] made to't. Alas, sir,
        Think of the world, how we shall live, grow serious;
        We have been married a whole fortnight now.
Leant.   How? A whole fortnight? Why, is that so long?
Bian.   'Tis time to leave off dalliance; 'tis a doctrine
        Of your own teaching, if you be rememb'red,
        And I was bound to obey it.
170 *Mother.*   [*Aside*]   Here's one fits him! –
        This was well catch'd, i' faith, son, like a fellow
        That rids another country of a plague
        And brings it home with him to his own house.

                                                        Knock within

        Who knocks?
Leant.   Who's there now? Withdraw you, Bianca;
        Thou art a gem no stranger's eye must see,
        Howev'r thou pleas'd now to look dull on me.

                                                        Exit [Bianca].

        Enter Messenger

        Y'are welcome, sir; to whom your business, pray?
Mess.   To one I see not here now.
Leant.   Who should that be, sir?
Mess.   A young gentlewoman I was sent to.

[1] In the sixteenth century the coasts of Italy were plagued with Italian and Turkish pirates.   [2] An allusion to the 'French disease,' syphilis.

Leant.   A young gentlewoman?
80 *Mess.*   Ay, sir, about sixteen.
    Why look you wildly, sir?
Leant.   At your strange error;
    Y'have mistook the house, sir. There's none such here
    I assure you.
Mess.   I assure you too,
    The man that sent me cannot be mistook.
Leant.   Why, who is't sent you, sir?
Mess.   The duke.
Leant.   The duke?
Mess.   Yes, he entreats her company at a banquet
    At Lady Livia's house.
Leant.   Troth, shall I tell you, sir,
    It is the most erroneous business
    That ere your honest pains was abus'd with?
90 I pray forgive me if I smile a little;
    I cannot choose, i' faith, sir, at an error
    So comical as this − I mean no harm though.
    His grace has been most wondrous ill-inform'd.
    Pray so return it, sir. What should her name be?
Mess.   That I shall tell you straight too: Bianca Capello.
Leant.   How, sir, 'Bianca'? What do you call th'other?
Mess.   Capello. Sir, it seems you know no such then?
Leant.   Who should this be? I never heard o' th' name.
Mess.   Then 'tis a sure mistake.
Leant.   What if you enquir'd
00 In the next street, sir? I saw gallants there
    In the new houses that are built of late.
    Ten to one, there you find her.
Mess.   Nay, no matter;
    I will return the mistake and seek no further.
Leant.   Use your own will and pleasure, sir; y'are welcome.

                                        Exit Messenger.

    What shall I think of first? Come forth, Bianca.
    Thou art betray'd, I fear me.

    Enter Bianca

Bian.   Betray'd? How, sir?
Leant.   The duke knows thee.
Bian.   Knows me? How know you that, sir?
Leant.   Has got thy name.
Bian.   [*Aside*]   Ay, and my good name too,

That's worse o' th' twain!

Lean.   How comes this work about?

210 *Bian.*   How should the duke know me? Can you guess, mother?

Mother.   Not I, with all my wits. Sure, we kept house close.

Leant.   Kept close? Not all the locks in Italy
   Can keep you women so! You have been gadding,
   And ventur'd out at twilight to th' court-green yonder,
   And met the gallant bowlers coming home,
   Without your masks too, both of you; I'll be hang'd else!
   Thou has been seen, Bianca, by some stranger;
   Never excuse it.

Bian.   I'll not seek the way, sir.
   Do you think y'have married me to mew me up

220 Not to be seen? What would you make of me?

Leant.   A good wife, nothing else.

Bian.   Why, so are some
   That are seen ev'ry day, else the devil take 'em.

Leant.   No more then. I believe all virtuous in thee
   Without an argument. 'Twas but thy hard chance
   To be seen somewhere; there lies all the mischief,
   But I have devis'd a riddance.

Mother.   Now I can tell you, son,
   The time and place.

Leant.   When? Where?

Mother.   What wits have I!
   When you last took your leave, if you remember,
   You left us both at window.

Leant.   Right, I know that.

230 *Mother.*   And not the third part of an hour after
   The duke pass'd by in a great solemnity
   To Saint Mark's temple, and to my apprehension
   He look'd up twice to th' window.

Leant.   Oh, there quick'ned
   The mischief of this hour.

Bian.   [*Aside*]   If you call't mischief,
   It is a thing I fear I am conceiv'd with.

Leant.   Look'd he up twice, and could you take no warning?

Mother.   Why once may do as much harm, son, as a thousand.
   Do not you know one spark has fir'd an house
   As well as a whole furnace?

Leant.   My heart flames for't.

240 Yet let's be wise and keep all smother'd closely.
   I have bethought a means. Is the door fast?

Mother.   I lock'd it myself after him.

Leant.   You know, mother,
   At the end of the dark parlour there's a place

So artificially contriv'd for a conveyance[1]
No search could ever find it – when my father
Kept in for manslaughter, it was his sanctuary –
There will I lock my life's best treasure up.
Bianca?
Bian.   Would you keep me closer yet?
Have you the conscience? Y'are best ev'n choke me up, sir.
50   You make me fearful of your health and wits,
You cleave to such wild courses. What's the matter?
Leant.   Why, are you so insensible of your danger
To ask that now? The duke himself has sent for you
To Lady Livia's, to a banquet forsooth!
Bian.   Now I beshrew you heartily! Has he so?
And you the man would never yet vouchsafe
To tell me on't till now! You show your loyalty
And honesty at once, and so farewell, sir.
Leant.   Bianca, whither now?
Bian.   Why, to the duke, sir;
You say he sent for me.
60 Leant.   But thou dost not mean
To go, I hope!
Bian.   No? I shall prove unmannerly,
Rude and uncivil, mad, and imitate you.
Come, mother, come; follow his humour no longer.
We shall be all executed for treason shortly.
Mother.   Not I, i' faith; I'll first obey the duke
And taste of a good banquet. I'm of thy mind.
I'll step but up, and fetch two handkerchiefs
To pocket up some sweetmeats, and o'ertake thee.

                                            Exit.

Bian.   [*Aside*] Why, here's an old wench would trot into a bawd now
For some dry sucket[2] or a colt in marchpane.[3]

                                            Exit.

Leant.   Oh, thou the ripe time of man's misery, wedlock,
When all his thoughts, like over-laden trees,
Crack with the fruits they bear, in cares, in jealousies;
Oh, that's a fruit that ripens hastily
After 'tis knit to marriage; it begins
As soon as the sun shines upon the bride
A little to show colour. Blessed powers,

[1] Passage.   [2] Candied fruit.   [3] Marzipan, a confectionery made up in
ornamental forms.

Whence comes this alteration? The distractions,
The fears and doubts it brings are numberless,
280 And yet the cause I know not. What a peace
Has he that never marries! If he knew
The benefit he enjoy'd, or had the fortune
To come and speak with me, he should know then
The infinite wealth he had, and discern rightly
The greatness of his treasure by my loss.
Nay, what a quietness has he 'bove mine
That wears his youth out in a strumpet's arms,
And never spends more care upon a woman
Than at the time of lust; but walks away,
290 And if he find her dead at his return,
His pity is soon done; he breaks a sigh
In many parts and gives her but a piece on't.
But all the fears, shames, jealousies, costs and troubles,
And still renew'd cares of a marriage bed
Live in the issue[1] when the wife is dead.

Enter Messenger

Mess.   A good perfection[2] to your thoughts.
Leant.   The news, sir?
Mess.   Though you were pleas'd of late to pin an error on me,
    You must not shift another in your stead too:
    The duke has sent me for you.
Leant.   How for me, sir?
300 [*Aside*] I see then 'tis my theft; w'are both betray'd.
    Well, I'm not the first has stol'n away a maid;
    My countrymen have us'd it. – I'll along with you, sir.

                                                        Exeunt.

[ACT III] SCENE 2

[Livia's *house*]
A banquet prepared. Enter Guardiano *and* Ward

Guard.   Take you especial note of such a gentlewoman;
    She's here on purpose. I have invited her,
    Her father, and her uncle to this banquet.
    Mark her behaviour well, it does concern you;

[1] Offspring.   [2] Completion.

And what her good parts are, as far as time
And place can modestly require a knowledge of,
Shall be laid open to your understanding.
You know I'm both your guardian and your uncle;
My care of you is double, ward and nephew,
And I'll express it here.
10 *Ward.*   Faith, I should know her
Now by her mark among a thousand women.
A little, pretty, deft, and tidy thing, you say?
Guard.   Right.
Ward.   With a lusty sprouting sprig in her hair?
Guard.   Thou goest the right way still. Take one mark more:
Thou shalt nev'r find her hand out of her uncle's,
Or else his out of hers if she be near him.
The love of kindred never yet stuck closer
Than theirs to one another; he that weds her
Marries her uncle's heart too.

Cornets

Ward.   Say you so, sir?
20 Then I'll be ask'd i' th' church to both of them.
Guard.   Fall back, here comes the duke.
Ward.   He brings a gentlewoman,
I should fall forward rather.

Enter Duke, Bianca, Fabricio, Hippolito, Livia, Mother, Isabella,
     and Attendants

Duke.   Come, Bianca,
Of purpose sent into the world to show
Perfection once in woman; I'll believe
Henceforward they have ev'ry one a soul too,[1]
'Gainst all the uncourteous opinions
That man's uncivil rudeness ever held of 'em.
Glory of Florence, light into my arms!

Enter Leantio

Bian.   Yon comes a grudging man will chide you, sir.
30 The storm is now in's heart and would get nearer
And fall here if it durst; it pours down yonder.
Duke.   If that be he, the weather shall soon clear.
List and I'll tell thee how.
Leant.   [*Aside*]   A-kissing too?

[1] An allusion to the belief that God gave a soul only to man (Genesis 2:7).

     I see 'tis plain lust now, adultery bold'ned.
     What will it prove anon, when 'tis stuff'd full
     Of wine and sweetmeats, being so impudent fasting?
Duke.   We have heard of your good parts, sir, which we honour
     With our embrace and love. Is not the captainship
     Of Rouens'[1] citadel, since the late deceas'd,
     Suppli'd by any yet?
40 *Gent.*   By none, my Lord.
   Duke.   Take it; the place is yours then, and as faithfulness
     And desert grows, our favour shall grow with't.

                                        [*Leantio kneels*]

     Rise now the captain of our fort at Rouens.
Leant.   The service of whole life give Your Grace thanks.
Duke.   Come sit, Bianca.
Leant.   [*Aside*]   This is some good yet,
     And more than ev'r I look'd for, a fine bit
     To stay a cuckold's stomach! All preferment
     That springs from sin and lust, it shoots up quickly,
     As gardeners' crops do in the rotten'st grounds;
50   So is all means rais'd from base prostitution,
     Ev'n like a sallet growing upon a dunghill.
     I'm like a thing that never was yet heard of,
     Half merry and half mad, much like a fellow
     That eats his meat with a good appetite,
     And wears a plague-sore that would fright a country;
     Or rather like the barren,[2] hard'ned ass,
     That feeds on thistles till he bleeds again;
     And such is the condition of my misery.
Livia.   Is that your son, widow?
Mother.   Yes; did your ladyship
     Never know that till now?
60 *Livia.*   No, trust me, did I.
     [*Aside*] Nor ever truly felt the power of love
     And pity to a man till now I knew him.
     I have enough to buy me my desires
     And yet to spare; that's one good comfort. – Hark you,
     Pray let me speak with you, sir, before you go.
Leant.   With me, lady? You shall; I am at your service.
     [*Aside*] What will she say now, trow? More goodness yet?
Ward.   I see her now, I'm sure; the ape's so little
     I shall scarce feel her; I have seen almost

---

[1] Presumably Rouen, France. This city has no clear connection with
sixteenth-century Florence, but one of Middleton's possible sources (see
Intro., p. 1) was published in Rouen in 1597. [2] Stupid.

70   As tall[1] as she sold in the fair for ten pence.
      See how she simpers it, as if marmalade
      Would not melt in her mouth. She might have the kindness, i' faith,
      To send me a gilded bull from her own trencher,[2]
      A ram, a goat, or somewhat to be nibbling.
      These women, when they come to sweet things once,
      They forget all their friends they grow so greedy,
      Nay, oftentimes their husbands.
   Duke.   Here's a health now, gallants,
      To the best beauty at this day in Florence.
   Bian.   Whoe'er she be, she shall not go unpledg'd, sir.
   Duke.   Nay, you're excus'd for this.
80 *Bian.*   Who, I, my Lord?
   Duke.   Yes, by the law of Bacchus. Plead your benefit;[3]
      You are not bound to pledge your own health, lady.
   Bian.   That's a good way, my Lord, to keep me dry.
   Duke.   Nay, then I will not offend Venus so much;
      Let Bacchus seek his 'mends in another court.
      Here's to thyself, Bianca.
   Bian.   Nothing comes
      More welcome to that name than Your Grace.
   Leant.   [*Aside*]   So, so.
      Here stands the poor thief now that stole the treasure,
      And he's not thought on. Ours is near kin now
90   To a twin misery born into the world:
      First, the hard-conscienc'd worldling; he hoards wealth up;
      Then comes the next, and he feasts all upon't.
      One's damn'd for getting, th'other for spending on't.
      O equal justice, thou hast met my sin
      With a full weight. I'm rightly now oppress'd;
      All her friends' heavy hearts lie in my breast.
   Duke.   Methinks there is no spirit amongst us, gallants,
      But what divinely sparkles from the eyes
      Of bright Bianca. We sat all in darkness
100   But for that splendour. Who was't told us lately
      Of a match-making rite, a marriage tender?
   Guard.   'Twas I, my Lord.
   Duke.   'Twas you indeed. Where is she?
   Guard.   This is the gentlewoman.
   Fab.   My Lord, my daughter.
   Duke.   Why, here's some stirring yet.
   Fab.   She's a dear child to me.
   Duke.   That must needs be: you say she is your daughter!
   Fab.   Nay, my good Lord, dear to my purse I mean,
      Beside my person; I nev'r reckon'd that.

---

[1] Handsome.   [2] Platter.   [3] Claim your advantage.

She has the full qualities of a gentlewoman;
I have brought her up to music, dancing, what not,
110   That may commend her sex and stir her husband.
Duke.   And which is he now?
Guard.   This young heir, my Lord.
Duke.   What is he brought up to?
Hipp.   [*Aside*]   To cat and trap.
Guard.   My Lord, he's a great ward, wealthy but simple;
His parts consist in acres.
Duke.   Oh, wiseacres!
Guard.   Y'have spoke him in a word, sir.
Bian.   'Las, poor gentlewoman,
She's ill bested, unless sh'as dealt the wiselier
And laid in more provision for her youth.
Fools[1] will not keep in summer.
Leant.   [*Aside*]   No, nor such wives
From whores in winter.
Duke.   Yea, the voice too, sir?
120 *Fab.*   Ay, and a sweet breast too, my Lord, I hope,
Or I have cast away my money wisely;
She took her pricksong[2] earlier, my Lord,
Than any of her kindred ever did.
A rare child, though I say't, but I'ld not have
The baggage hear so much; 'twould make her swell straight,
And maids of all things must not be puff'd up.
Duke.   Let's turn us to a better banquet then,
For music bids the soul of a man to a feast,
And that's indeed a noble entertainment
130   Worthy Bianca's self. You shall perceive, beauty,
Our Florentine damsels are not brought up idlely.
Bian.   They're wiser of themselves it seems, my Lord,
And can take gifts when goodness offers 'em.

                                                            Music

Leant.   [*Aside*] True, and damnation has taught you that wisdom;
You can take gifts too. Oh, that music mocks me!
Livia.   [*Aside*] I am as dumb to any language now
But love's as one that never learn'd to speak.
I am not yet so old but he may think of me.
My own fault, I have been idle a long time,
140   But I'll begin the week and paint tomorrow,
So follow my true labour day by day;
I never thriv'd so well as when I us'd it.

---

[1] Punning on 'custards.'   [2] Studied written vocal music, with innuendo.

Song

[*Isab.*]   What harder chance can
    fall to woman,
    Who was born to cleave to some
      man,
    Than to bestow her time, youth,
      beauty,
    Life's observance, honour, duty
150   On a thing for no use good,
    But to make physic work or blood
    Force fresh in an old lady's cheek?
    She that would be
    Mother of fools, let her compound[1]
      with me.

Ward.   Here's a tune indeed! Pish, I had rather hear one ballad sung i' th' nose now, of the lamentable drowning of fat sheep and oxen, than all these simpering tunes played upon cats'-guts and sung by little kitlings.

Fab.   How like you her breast now, my Lord?

Bian.   [*Aside*]   Her breast?
    He talks as if his daughter had given suck
    Before she were married, as her betters have.
    The next he praises sure will be her nipples.

Duke.   Methinks now such a voice to such a husband
160   Is like a jewel of unvalued worth
    Hung at a fool's ear.

Fab.   May it please Your Grace
    To give her leave to show another quality?

Duke.   Marry, as many good ones as you will, sir;
    The more the better welcome.

Leant.   [*Aside*]   But the less
    The better practis'd. That soul's black indeed
    That cannot commend virtue; but who keeps it?
    The extortioner will say to a sick beggar,
    'Heaven comfort thee,' though he give none himself.
    This good is common.

Fab.   Will it please you now, sir,
170   To entreat your ward to take her by the hand
    And lead her in a dance before the duke?

Guard.   That will I, sir; 'tis needful. Hark you, nephew.

Fab.   Nay, you shall see, young heir, what y'have for your money,
    Without fraud or imposture.

Ward.   Dance with her?
    Not I, sweet guardianer; do not urge my heart to't.
    'Tis clean against my blood. Dance with a stranger?
    Let whos' will do't, I'll not begin first with her.

Hipp.   [*Aside*]   No, fear't not, fool; sh'as took a better order.

Guard.   Why, who shall take her then?

Ward.   Some other gentleman.

---

[1] Bargain.

180   Look, there's her uncle, a fine-timber'd reveller;
        Perhaps he knows the manner of her dancing.
        I'll have him do't before me; I have sworn, guardianer;
        Then may I learn the better.
Guard.   Thou'lt be an ass still.
Ward.   Ay, all that uncle shall not fool me out.
        Pish, I stick closer to myself than so.
.*Guard.*   I must entreat you, sir, to take your niece
        And dance with her. My ward's a little wilful;
        He would have you show him the way.
Hipp.   Me, sir?
        He shall command it at all hours; pray tell him so.
190 *Guard.*   I thank you for him; he has not wit himself, sir.
    Hipp.   Come, my life's peace, I have a strange office on't here.
        'Tis some man's luck to keep the joys he likes
        Conceal'd for his own bosom, but my fortune
        To set 'em out now for another's liking,
        Like the mad misery of necessitous man,
        That parts from his good horse with many praises,
        And goes on foot himself. Need must be obey'd
        In ev'ry action; it mars man and maid.

                                                           Music
    Duke.   Signor Fabricio, y'are a happy   *A dance, making honours*
                            father;   *to the* duke *and curtsy*
            Your cares and pains are fortunate;   *to themselves, both*
200   you see   *before and after*
            Your cost bears noble fruits. Hippolito,
                thanks.
    Fab.   Here's some amends for all my charges yet;
        She wins both prick[1] and praise where'er she comes.
    Duke.   How lik'st, Bianca?
    Bian.   All things well, my Lord;
        But this poor gentlewoman's fortune, that's the worst.
    Duke.   There is no doubt, Bianca, she'll find leisure
        To make that good enough; he's rich and simple.
    Bian.   She has the better hope o' th'upper hand indeed,
        Which women strive for most.
    Guard.   Do't when I bid you, sir!
210 *Ward.*   I'll venture but a hornpipe with her, guardianer,
        Or some such married man's dance.
    Guard.   Well, venture something, sir.
    Ward.   I have rhyme for what I do.
    Guard.   But little reason I think.
    Ward.   Plain men dance the measures,[2] the cinquepace[3] the gay,

---

[1] The bullseye (of an archery butt).   [2] A formal dance.   [3] Galliard.

Cuckolds dance the hornpipe, and farmers dance the hay;[1]
Your soldiers dance the round, and maidens that grow big,
You[r] drunkards the canaries,[2] you[r] whore and bawd the jig.
Here's your eight kind of dancers; he that finds the ninth,
Let him pay the minstrels.
Duke.   Oh, here he appears once in his own person.
220   I thought he would have married her by attorney,
And lain with her so too.
Bian.   Nay, my kind Lord,
There's very seldom any found so foolish
To give away his part there.
Leant.   [*Aside*]   Bitter scoff!
Yet I must do't. With what a cruel pride

                                                Music

The glory of her sin strikes by my afflictions.

Ward and Isabella *dance; he ridiculously imitates* Hippolito

Duke.   This thing will make shift, sirs, to make a husband,
For aught I see in him. How think'st, Bianca?
Bian.   Faith, an ill-favour'd shift, my Lord, methinks.
230   If he would take some voyage when he's married,
Dangerous or long enough, and scarce be seen
Once in nine year together, a wife then
Might make indifferent shift to be content with him.
Duke.   A kiss! That wit deserves to be made much on.
Come, our caroche.[3]
Guard.   Stands ready for Your Grace.
Duke.   My thanks to all your loves. Come, fair Bianca;
We have took special care of you and provided
Your lodging near us now.
Bian.   Your love is great, my Lord.
Duke.   Once more, our thanks to all.
Omnes.   All bless'd honours guard you.

Exeunt all but Leantio *and* Livia.   *Cornets flourish.*

240 *Leant.*   [*Aside*] Oh, hast thou left me then, Bianca, utterly?
Bianca! Now I miss thee. Oh, return
And save the faith of woman! I nev'r felt
The loss of thee till now; 'tis an affliction
Of greater weight than youth was made to bear,

[1] A country dance.   [2] A lively dance, said to have been brought from the
Canary Islands, noted for Canary wine.   [3] A luxurious carriage.

As if a punishment of after-life
Were fall'n upon man here, so new it is
To flesh and blood, so strange, so insupportable
A torment, ev'n mistook, as if a body
Whose death were drowning must needs therefore suffer it
In scalding oil.

Livia.   Sweet sir, –

250 *Leant.*   [*Aside*]   As long as mine eye saw thee
I half enjoy'd thee.

Livia.   Sir, –

Leant.   [*Aside*]   Canst thou forget
The dear pains my love took, how it has watch'd
Whole nights together in all weathers for thee,
Yet stood in heart more merry than the tempests
That sung about mine ears, like dangerous flatterers
That can set all their mischief to sweet tunes;
And then receiv'd thee from thy father's window
Into these arms at midnight, when we embrac'd
As if we had been statues only made for't,

260 To show art's life, so silent were our comforts,
And kiss'd as if our lips had grown together.

Livia.   [*Aside*] This makes me madder to enjoy him now.

Leant.   [*Aside*] Canst thou forget all this, and better joys
That we met after this, which then new kisses
Took pride to praise?

Livia.   [*Aside*] I shall grow madder yet. – Sir.

Leant.   [*Aside*] This cannot be but of some close bawd's working. –
Cry mercy, lady. What would you say to me?
My sorrow makes me so unmannerly,
So comfort bless me, I had quite forgot you.

270 *Livia.*   Nothing, but ev'n in pity to that passion
Would give your grief good counsel.

Leant.   Marry, and welcome, lady;
It never could come better.

Livia.   Then first, sir,
To make away all your good thoughts at once of her,
Know most assuredly she is a strumpet!

Leant.   Ha! 'Most assuredly.' Speak not a thing
So vilde[1] so certainly. Leave it more doubtful.

Livia.   Then I must leave all truth and spare my knowledge
A sin which I too lately found and wept for.

Leant.   Found you it?

Livia.   Ay, with wet eyes.

Leant.   O perjurious friendship!

280 *Livia.*   You miss'd your fortunes when you met with her, sir.

-----

[1] i.e. vile.

Young gentlemen that only love for beauty,
They love not wisely; such a marriage rather
Proves the destruction of affection.
It brings on want, and want's the key of whoredom.
I think y'had small means with her?

Leant.   Oh, not any, lady.

Livia.   Alas, poor gentleman! What mean'st thou, sir,
Quite to undo thyself with thine own kind heart?
Thou art too good and pitiful to woman.
Marry, sir, thank thy stars for this bless'd fortune
290 That rids the summer of thy youth so well
From many beggars that had lain a-sunning
In thy beams only else, till thou hadst wasted
The whole days of thy life in heat and labour.
What would you say now to a creature found
As pitiful to you, and as it were
Ev'n sent on purpose from the whole sex general
To requite all that kindness you have shown to't?

Leant.   What's that, madam?

Livia.   Nay, a gentlewoman,
And one able to reward good things; ay,
300 And bears a conscience to't. Couldst thou love such a one
That, blow all fortunes, would never see thee want?
Nay, more, maintain thee to thine enemy's envy,
And shalt not spend a care for't, stir a thought,
Nor break a sleep; unless love's music waked thee
No storm of fortune should. Look upon me
And know that woman.

Leant.   O my life's wealth, Bianca!

Livia.   Still with her name? Will nothing wear it out?
That deep sigh went but for a strumpet, sir.

Leant.   It can go for no other that loves me.

310 *Livia.*   [*Aside*] He's vex'd in mind; I came too soon to him.
Where's my discretion now, my skill, my judgment?
I'm cunning in all arts but my own love.
'Tis as unseasonable to tempt him now
So soon, as a widow to be courted
Following her husband's corse, or to make bargain
By the grave-side, and take a young man there.
Her strange departure stands like a hearse[1] yet
Before his eyes, which time will take down shortly.

Exit.

Leant.   Is she my wife till death, yet no more mine?

[1] A framework erected over a coffin, to hold candles and tributes.

320   That's a hard measure. Then what's marriage good for?
       Methinks by right I should not now be living,
       And then 'twere all well. What a happiness
       Had I been made of had I never seen her!
       For nothing makes man's loss grievous to him
       But knowledge of the worth of what he loses;
       For what he never had he never misses.
       She's gone for ever, utterly. There is
       As much redemption of a soul from Hell
       As a fair woman's body from his palace.
330   Why should my love last longer than her truth?
       What is there good in woman to be lov'd,
       When only that which makes her so has left her?
       I cannot love her now, but I must like
       Her sin and my own shame too, and be guilty
       Of law's breach with her, and mine own abusing,
       All which were monstrous. Then my safest course
       For health of mind and body is to turn
       My heart and hate her, most extremely hate her.
       I have no other way. Those virtuous powers
340   Which were chaste witnesses of both our troths
       Can witness she breaks first, and I'm rewarded
       With captainship o' th' fort! A place of credit,
       I must confess, but poor. My factorship
       Shall not exchange means with't; he that died last in't,
       He was no drunkard, yet he died a beggar
       For all his thrift. Besides, the place not fits me;
       It suits my resolution, not my breeding.

       Enter Livia

       Livia.   [*Aside*] I have tri'd all ways I can, and have not power
               To keep from sight of him. – How are you now, sir?
       Leant.   I feel a better ease, madam.
350 *Livia.*   Thanks to blessedness.
       You will do well, I warrant you, fear it not, sir.
       Join but your own good will to't. He's not wise
       That loves his pain or sickness, or grows fond
       Of a disease whose property is to vex him
       And spitefully drink his blood up. Out upon't, sir!
       Youth knows no greater loss. I pray let's walk, sir;
       You never saw the beauty of my house yet,
       Nor how abundantly fortune has bless'd me
       In worldly treasure. Trust me, I have enough, sir,
360   To make my friend a rich man in my life,
       A great man at my death. Yourself will say so.
       If you want anything, and spare to speak,

Troth I'll condemn you for a wilful man, sir.
Leant.   Why sure, this can be but the flattery of some dream.
Livia.   Now by this kiss, my love, my soul and riches,
'Tis all true substance.
Come, you shall see my wealth. Take what you list;
The gallanter you go, the more you please me.
I will allow you too your page and footman,
`370`   Your race horses, or any various pleasure
Exercis'd youth delights in. But to me
Only, sir, wear your heart of constant stuff;
Do but you love enough, I'll give enough.
Leant.   Troth then, I'll love enough and take enough.
Livia.   Then we are both pleas'd enough.

                                                 Exeunt.

[ACT III] SCENE 3

[Fabricio's *house*]
Enter Guardiano *and* Isabella *at one door,
and the* Ward *and* Sordido *at another*

Guard.   Now, nephew, here's the gentlewoman again.
Ward.   Mass, here she's come again. Mark her now, Sordido.
Guard.   This is the maid my love and care has chose
Out for your wife, and so I tender her to you.
Yourself has been eyewitness of some qualities
That speak a courtly breeding and are costly.
I bring you both to talk together now;
'Tis time you grew familiar in your tongues.
Tomorrow you join hands, and one ring ties you,
`10`   And one bed holds you, if you like the choice.
Her father and her friends are i' th' next room
And stay to see the contract ere they part;
Therefore dispatch, good ward; be sweet and short.
Like her or like her not, there's but two ways,
And one your body, th'other your purse pays.[1]
Ward.   I warrant you, guardianer, I'll not stand all day thrumming,[2]
But quickly shoot my bolt at your next coming.
Guard.   Well said. Good fortune to your birding then.

---

[1] If the Ward rejects Isabella, he apparently must pay some financial
penalty.   [2] Wasting time; from 'thrum,' the loose ends of woven material.

[*Exit.*]

    Ward.   I never miss'd mark yet.
20 *Sord.*   Troth I think, master, if the truth were known,
        You never shot at any but the kitchen-wench,
        And that was a she-woodcock,[1] a mere innocent,
        That was oft lost and cri'd[2] at eight-and-twenty.
    Ward.   No more of that meat, Sordido; here's eggs o' th' spit[3]
        now. We must turn gingerly, draw out the catalogue of all
        the faults of women.
    Sord.   How, all the faults? Have you so little reason to think so much
        paper will lie in my breeches? Why, ten carts will not carry it,
        if you set down but the bawds. All the faults? Pray let's be
30   content with a few of 'em; and if they were less, you would find
        'em enough I warrant you. Look you, sir.
    Isab.   [*Aside*] But that I have th'advantage of the fool,
        As much as woman's heart can wish and joy at,
        What an infernal torment 'twere to be
        Thus bought and sold and turn'd and pri'd into; when, alas,
        The worst bit is too good for him? And the comfort is
        H'as but a cater's[4] place on't, and provides
        All for another's table. Yet how curious[5]
        The ass is, like some nice professor[6] on't,
40   That buys up all the daintiest food i' th' markets,
        And seldom licks his lips after a taste on't.
    Sord.   Now to her, now y'have scann'd all her parts over.
    Ward.   But at [what] end shall I begin now, Sordido?
    Sord.   Oh, ever at a woman's lip, while you live, sir. Do you
        ask that question?
    Ward.   Methinks, Sordido, sh'as but a crabbed face to begin with.
    Sord.   A crabbed face? That will save money.
    Ward.   How, save money, Sordido?
    Sord.   Ay, sir; for having a crabbed face of her own, she'll
50   eat the less verjuice[7] with her mutton. 'Twill save verjuice
        at year's end, sir.
    Ward.   Nay, and your jests begin to be saucy once, I'll make you
        eat your meat without mustard.
    Sord.   And that in some kind is a punishment.
    Ward.   Gentlewoman, they say 'tis your pleasure to be my wife,
        and you shall know shortly whether it be mine or no to be your
        husband; and thereupon thus I first enter upon you. [*Kisses
        her*] Oh, most delicious scent! Methinks it tasted as if a

---

[1] Proverbially simple or foolish. [2] The town crier called the name of
anyone missing. [3] Matters of immediate importance. [4] i.e. caterer's.
[5] Fastidious. [6] The professor of a religious faith, an ascetic. [7] Acidic
sauce made from crab-apples, etc.

man had stepped into a comfit[1]-maker's shop to let a cart go by,
60   all the while I kiss'd her. It is reported, gentlewoman, you'll
run mad for me if you have me not.

Isab.   I should be in great danger of my wits, sir,
For being so forward. [*Aside*] Should this ass kick backward now!

Ward.   Alas, poor soul! And is that hair your own?

Isab.   Mine own? Yes, sure, sir; I owe nothing for't.

Ward.   'Tis a good hearing. I shall have the less to pay when I
have married you. – Look, does her eyes stand well?[2]

Sord.   They cannot stand better than in her head I think; where
would you have them? And for her nose, 'tis of a very good last.[3]

70 *Ward.*   I have known as good as that has not lasted a year though.

Sord.   That's in the using of a thing. Will not any strong bridge
fall down in time, if we do nothing but beat at the bottom?
A nose of buff[4] would not last always, sir, especially if it came
into th' camp once.[5]

Ward.   But, Sordido, how shall we do to make her laugh that I may
see what teeth she has? For I'll not bate her a tooth, nor take a black
one into th' bargain.

Sord.   Why, do but you fall in talk with her, you cannot choose
but one time or other make her laugh, sir.

80 *Ward.*   It shall go hard, but I will. Pray what qualities have
you beside singing and dancing? Can you play at shuttlecock
forsooth?

Isab.   Ay, and at stool-ball[6] too, sir; I have great luck at it.

Ward.   Why, can you catch a ball well?

Isab.   I have catch'd two in my lap at one game.

Ward.   What, have you, woman? I must have you learn
To play at trap too; then y'are full and whole.

Isab.   Anything that you please to bring me up to,
I shall take pains to practise.

90 *Ward.*   'Twill not do, Sordido; we shall never get her mouth open'd
wide enough.

Sord.   No, sir? That's strange. Then here's a trick for your
learning. *He yawns;* [Isabella *yawns also, but conceals her mouth*]
Look now, look now, quick, quick there!

Ward.   Pox of that scurvy mannerly trick with handkerchief! It
hind'red me a little, but I am satisfied. When a fair woman gapes
and stops her mouth so, it shows like a cloth stopple in a
cream-pot. I have fair hope of her teeth now, Sordido.

Sord.   Why, then y'have all well, sir; for aught I see, she's
100 right and straight enough now, as she stands. They'll

[1] Sweetmeat. [2] Remain steady. [3] i.e. it is durable. [4] Strong leather.
[5] Sordido alludes to the ravages of syphilis, endemic amongst camp-
followers. [6] A game in which a player throws a ball towards a stool, and
another tries to prevent the ball from hitting the stool.

commonly lie crooked; that's no matter. Wise gamesters never
find fault with that, let 'em lie still so.

Ward.   I'ld fain mark how she goes, and then I have all; for of
all creatures, I cannot abide a splay-footed woman. She's an
unlucky thing to meet in a morning; her heels keep together so,
as if she were beginning an Irish dance still, and the
wriggling of her bum playing the tune to't. But I have
bethought a cleanly shift to find it. Dab down as you
see me, and peep of one side when her back's toward you;

110   I'll show you the way.

Sord.   And you shall find me apt enough to peeping;
I have been one of them has seen mad sights
Under your scaffolds.

Ward.   Will it please you walk, forsooth,
A turn or two by yourself? You are so pleasing to me,
I take delight to view you on both sides.

Isab.   I shall be glad to fetch a walk to your love, sir;
'Twill get affection a good stomach, sir.
[*Aside*] Which I had need have, to fall to such coarse victuals.

[*Walks*]

Ward.   Now go thy ways for a clean-treading wench,
120   As ever man in modesty peep'd under.

Sord.   I see the sweetest sight to please my master.
Never went Frenchman righter upon ropes[1]
Than she on Florentine rushes.

Ward.   'Tis enough forsooth.

Isab.   And how do you like me now, sir?

Ward.   Faith, so well
I never mean to part with thee, sweetheart,
Under some sixteen children, and all boys.

Isab.   You'll be at simple pains, if you prove kind,
And breed 'em all in your teeth.[2]

Ward.   Nay, by my faith,
What serves your belly for? 'Twould make my cheeks
Look like blown bagpipes.

Enter Guardiano

130   *Guard.*   How now, ward and nephew,
Gentlewoman and niece? Speak, is it so or not?

Ward.   'Tis so; we are both agreed, sir.

---

[1] Tightrope performers were popular in the seventeenth century.   [2] 'If you
continue in character (with your apparent stupidity), you will suffer
sympathetic pains in your teeth whilst I am pregnant.' (Folk tradition)

Guard.   In to your kindred then;
   There's friends and wine and music waits to welcome you.
Ward.   Then I'll be drunk for joy.
Sord.   And I for company.
   I cannot break my nose in a better action.

                                           Exeunt.

ACT IV SCENE 1

[Bianca's *apartment*]
Enter Bianca, *attended by two* ladies

Bian.   How goes your watches, ladies? What's a-clock now?
1 Lady.   By mine, full nine.
2 Lady.   By mine, a quarter past.
1 Lady.   I set mine by Saint Mark's.
2 Lady.   Saint Anthony's[1]
   They say goes truer.
1 Lady.   That's but your opinion, madam,
   Because you love a gentleman o' th' name.
2 Lady.   He's a true gentleman then.
1 Lady.   So may he be
   That comes to me tonight, for aught you know.
Bian.   I'll end this strife straight. I set mine by the sun;
   I love to set by th' best; one shall not then
   Be troubled to set often.
10 *2 Lady.*   You do wisely in't.
Bian.   If I should set my watch as some girls do,
   By ev'ry clock i' th' town, 'twould nev'r go true,
   And too much turning of the dial's point,
   Or tamp'ring with the spring, might in small time
   Spoil the whole work too.[2] Here it wants of nine now.
1 Lady.   It does indeed, forsooth; mine's nearest truth yet.
2 Lady.   Yet I have found her lying with an advocate, which show'd
   Like two false clocks together in one parish.
Bian.   So now I thank you, ladies; I desire
   Awhile to be alone.
20 *1 Lady.*   And I am nobody
   Methinks, unless I have one or other with me.
   Faith, my desire and hers will nev'r be sisters.

---

[1] This church is shown, near Saint Mark's, on a sixteenth-century map of
Florence.   [2] This speech includes several *double entendre.*

Exeunt ladies.

Bian.   How strangely woman's fortune comes about!
           This was the farthest way to come to me
           All would have judg'd that knew me born in Venice,
           And there with many jealous eyes brought up,
           That never thought they had me sure enough
           But when they were upon me; yet my hap
           To meet it here, so far off from my birthplace,
30   My friends or kindred. 'Tis not good, in sadness,
           To keep a maid so strict in her young days.
           Restraint breeds wand'ring thoughts, as many fasting days
           A great desire to see flesh stirring again.
           I'll nev'r use any girl of mine so strictly.
           Howev'r they're kept, their fortunes find 'em out;
           I see't in me. If they be got in court
           I'll never forbid 'em the country, nor the court
           Though they be born i' th' country. They will come to't,
           And fetch their falls a thousand mile about,
40   Where one would little think on't.

           Enter Leantio

Leant.   [*Aside*] I long to see how my despiser looks
           Now she's come here to court. These are her lodgings;
           She's simply[1] now advanc'd. I took her out
           Of no such window, I remember, first;
           That was a great deal lower, and less carv'd.
Bian.   How now? What silkworm's this, i' th' name of pride?
           What, is it he?
Leant.   A bow i' th' ham to your greatness.
           You must have now three legs,[2] I take it, must you not?
Bian.   Then I must take another; I shall want else
50   The service I should have. You have but two there.
Leant.   Y'are richly plac'd.
Bian.   Methinks y'are wondrous brave,[3] sir.
Leant.   A sumptuous lodging.
Bian.   Y'have an excellent suit there.
Leant.   A chair of velvet.
Bian.   Is your cloak lin'd through, sir?
Leant.   Y'are very stately here.
Bian.   Faith, something proud, sir.
Leant.   Stay, stay; let's see your cloth-of-silver slippers.
Bian.   Who's your shoemaker? H'as made you a neat boot.
Leant.   Will you have a pair? The duke will lend you spurs.

[1] Absolutely.   [2] Bows.   [3] Finely dressed.

Bian.   Yes, when I ride.

Leant.   'Tis a brave life you lead.

Bian.   I could nev'r see you in such good clothes
     In my time.

Leant.   In your time?

60 *Bian.*   Sure I think, sir,
     We both thrive best asunder.

Leant.   Y'are a whore!

Bian.   Fear nothing, sir.

Leant.   An impudent, spiteful strumpet!

Bian.   Oh, sir, you give me thanks for your captainship;
     I thought you had forgot all your good manners.

Leant.   And to spite thee as much, look there, there read,
     Vex, gnaw; thou shalt find there I am not love-starv'd.

                               [Hands her a letter]

     The world was never yet so cold or pitiless
     But there was ever still more charity found out
     Than at one proud fool's door, and 'twere hard, faith,

70   If I could not pass that. Read to thy shame there.
     A cheerful and a beauteous benefactor too,
     As ev'r erected the good works of love.

Bian.   *[Aside]*   Lady Livia!
     Is't possible? Her worship was my pandress!
     She dote and send and give, and all to him?
     Why, here's a bawd plagu'd home! – Y'are simply happy, sir,
     Yet I'll not envy you.

Leant.   No, court-saint, not thou!
     You keep some friend of a new fashion.
     There's no harm in your devil; he's a suckling,
     But he will breed teeth shortly, will he not?

80 *Bian.*   Take heed you play not then too long with him.

Leant.   Yes, and the great one too. I shall find time
     To play a hot religious bout with some of you,
     And perhaps drive you and your course of sins
     To their eternal kennels. I speak softly now;
     'Tis manners in a noblewoman's lodgings,
     And I well know all my degrees of duty.
     But come I to your everlasting parting once,
     Thunder shall seem soft music to that tempest.

Bian.   Twas said last week there would be change of weather

90   When the moon hung so, and belike you heard it.

Leant.   Why, here's sin made, and nev'r a conscience put to't,
     A monster with all forehead[1] and no eyes.

[1] Audacity.

Why do I talk to thee of sense or virtue,
That art as dark as death? And as much madness
To set light before thee as to lead blind folks
To see the monuments, which they may smell as soon
As they behold; marry, oft-times their heads,
For want of light, may feel the hardness of 'em.
So shall thy blind pride my revenge and anger,
100   That canst not see it now, and it may fall
At such an hour when thou least see'st of all.
So to an ignorance darker than thy womb
I leave thy perjur'd soul. A plague will come.

Exit.

Bian.   Get you gone first, and then I fear no greater;
Nor thee will I fear long. I'll have this sauciness
Soon banish'd from these lodgings, and the rooms
Perfum'd well after the corrupt air it leaves.
His breath has made me almost sick, in troth.
A poor base start-up! 'Life! Because h'as got
110   Fair clothes by foul means, comes to rail and show 'em.

Enter the Duke

Duke.   Who's that?
Bian.   Cry you mercy, sir.
Duke.   Prithee, who's that?
Bian.   The former thing, my Lord, to whom you gave
The captainship; he eats his meat with grudging still.
Duke.   Still?
Bian.   He comes vaunting here of his new love
And the new clothes she gave him. Lady Livia!
Who but she now his mistress?
Duke.   Lady Livia?
Be sure of what you say.
Bian.   He show'd me her name, sir,
In perfum'd paper, her vows, her letter,
With an intent to spite me. So his heart said,
120   And his threats made it good; they were as spiteful
As ever malice utter'd and as dangerous,
Should his hand follow the copy.[1]
Duke.   But that must not.
Do not you vex your mind. Prithee, to bed, go.
All shall be well and quiet.
Bian.   I love peace, sir.

[1] Example.

Duke.   And so do all that love. Take you no care for't,
It shall be still provided to your hand.

Exit [Bianca].

Who's near us there?

Enter Messenger

Mess.   My Lord?
Duke.   Seek out Hippolito,
    Brother to Lady Livia, with all speed.
Mess.   He was the last man I saw, my Lord.

Exit.

Duke.   Make haste.
130   He is a blood soon stirr'd, and as he's quick
        To apprehend a wrong, he's bold and sudden
        In bringing forth a ruin. I know likewise
        The reputation of his sister's honour's
        As dear to him as life-blood to his heart.
        Beside, I'll flatter him with a goodness to her
        Which I now thought on, but nev'r meant to practise,
        Because I know her base, and that wind drives him.
        The ulcerous reputation feels the poise[1]
        Of lightest wrongs, as sores are vex'd with flies.
        He comes.

Enter Hippolito

                    Hippolito, welcome.
140 *Hipp.*   My lov'd Lord.
        Duke.   How does that lusty widow, thy kind sister?
        Is she not sped yet of[2] a second[3] husband?
        A bed-fellow she has, I ask not that;
        I know she's sped of him.
        Hipp.   Of him, my Lord?
        Duke.   Yes, of a bed-fellow. Is the news so strange to you?
        Hipp.   I hope 'tis so to all.
        Duke.   I wish it were, sir,
        But 'tis confess'd too fast. Her ignorant pleasures,
        Only by lust instructed, have receiv'd
        Into their services an impudent boaster,
150   One that does raise his glory from her shame,

---

[1] Burden.   [2] Provided with.   [3] Actually third; see I, ii, 50.

And tells the midday sun what's done in darkness.
Yet blinded with her appetite wastes her wealth,
Buys her disgraces at a dearer rate
Than bounteous housekeepers[1] purchase their honour.
Nothing sads me so much, as that in love
To thee and to thy blood, I had pick'd out
A worthy match for her, the great Vincentio,
High in our favour and in all men's thoughts.

Hipp.   O thou destruction of all happy fortunes,
160   Unsated blood! Know you the name, my Lord,
Of her abuser?
Duke.   One Leantio.
Hipp. He's a factor!
Duke.   He nev'r made so brave a voyage
By his own talk.
Hipp.   The poor old widow's son.
I humbly take my leave.
Duke.   [Aside]   I see 'tis done. —
Give her good counsel, make her see her error;
I know she'll hearken to you.
Hipp.   Yes, my Lord,
I make no doubt; as I shall take the course
Which she shall never know till it be acted,
And when she wakes to honour, then she'll thank me for't.
170   I'll imitate the pities of old surgeons
To this lost limb, who, ere they show their art,
Cast one asleep, then cut the diseas'd part.
So out of love to her I pity most,
She shall not feel him going till he's lost;
Then she'll commend the cure.

                                                            Exit.

Duke.   The great cure's past.
I count this done already; his wrath's sure
And speaks an injury deep. Farewell, Leantio;
This place will never hear thee murmur more.

Enter Lord Cardinal, *attended*

Our noble brother, welcome!
Card.   Set those lights down;
Depart till you be called.

                                                [*Exeunt* servants.]

[1] i.e. generous keepers (owners) of great houses.

180 *Duke.*   [*Aside*]   There's serious business
            Fixed in his look; nay, it inclines a little
            To the dark colour of a discontentment. –
            Brother, what is't commands your eye so powerfully?
            Speak. You seem lost.
    Card.   The thing I look on seems so,
            To my eyes lost for ever.
    Duke.   You look on me.
    Card.   What a grief 'tis to a religious feeling
            To think a man should have a friend so goodly,
            So wise, so noble, nay, a duke, a brother,
            And all this certainly damn'd!
    Duke   How!
    Card.   'Tis no wonder,
190   If your great sin can do't. Dare you look up,
            For thinking of a veng'ance? Dare you sleep,
            For fear of never waking but to death?
            And dedicate unto a strumpet's love
            The strength of your affections, zeal, and health?
            Here you stand now; can you assure your pleasures
            You shall once more enjoy her, but once more?
            Alas, you cannot. What a misery 'tis then
            To be more certain of eternal death
            Than of a next embrace? Nay, shall I show you
200   How more unfortunate you stand in sin
            Than the low, private man? All his offenses,
            Like enclos'd grounds, keep but about himself,
            And seldom stretch beyond his own soul's bounds;
            And when a man grows miserable 'tis some comfort
            When he's no further charg'd than with himself.
            'Tis a sweet ease to wretchedness. But, great man,
            Ev'ry sin thou commit'st shows like a flame
            Upon a mountain; 'tis seen far about,
            And with a big wind made of popular breath
210   The sparkles fly through cities. Here one takes,
            Another catches there, and in short time
            Waste all to cinders. But remember still
            What burnt the valleys first came from the hill;
            Ev'ry offence draws his particular pain,
            But 'tis example proves the great man's bane.
            The sins of mean men lie like scatter'd parcels[1]
            Of an unperfect bill, but when such fall
            Then comes example, and that sums up all.
            And this your reason grants: if men of good lives,
220   Who by their virtuous actions stir up others

[1] Details.

          To noble and religious imitation,
          Receive the greater glory after death,
          As sin must needs confess, what may they feel
          In height of torments and in weight of veng'ance;
          Not only they themselves not doing well,
          But set a light up to show men to Hell?
Duke.   If you have done, I have. No more, sweet brother.
Card.   I know time spent in goodness is too tedious;
          This had not been a moment's space in lust now.
230   How dare you venture on eternal pain,
          That cannot bear a minute's reprehension?
          Methinks you should endure to hear that talk'd of
          Which you so strive to suffer. O my brother,
          What were you, if you were taken now?
          My heart weeps blood to think on't. 'Tis a work
          Of infinite mercy you can never merit,
          That yet you are not death-struck, no, not yet.
          I dare not stay you long for fear you should not
          Have time enough allow'd you to repent in.
240   There's but this wall[1] betwixt you and destruction
          When y'are at strongest, and but poor thin clay.
          Think upon't, brother. Can you come so near it
          For a fair strumpet's love, and fall into
          A torment that knows neither end nor bottom?
          For beauty but the deepness of a skin,
          And that[2] not of their own neither. Is she a thing
          Whom sickness dare not visit or age look on
          Or death resist? Does the worm shun her grave?
          If not, as your soul knows it, why should lust
250   Bring man to lasting pain, for rotten dust?
Duke.   Brother of spotless honour, let me weep
          The first of my repentance in thy bosom,
          And show the bless'd fruits of a thankful spirit;
          And if I ere keep woman more unlawfully,
          May I want[3] penitence at my greatest need;
          And wise men know there is no barren place
          Threatens more famine than a dearth in grace.
Card.   Why, here's a conversion is at this time, brother,
          Sung for a hymn in Heaven, and at this instant
260   The powers of darkness groan, makes all Hell sorry.
          First I praise Heaven, then in my work I glory!
          Who's there attends without?

          Enter servants

_____

[1] The body, in the sense of a barrier. [2] i.e. that beauty (created with cosmetics). [3] Lack.

Serv.   My Lord?
Card.   Take up those lights; there was a thicker darkness
       When they came first. The peace of a fair soul
       Keep with my noble brother!

Exit Cardinal, *etc.*

Duke.   Joys be with you, sir.
       She lies alone tonight for't, and must still,
       Though it be hard to conquer; but I have vow'd
       Never to know her as a strumpet more,
       And I must save my oath. If fury fail not,
70   Her husband dies tonight, or at the most
       Lives not to see the morning spent tomorrow.
       Then will I make her lawfully mine own,
       Without this sin and horror. Now I'm chidden
       For what I shall enjoy then unforbidden,
       And I'll not freeze in stoves.[1] 'Tis but a while;
       Live like a hopeful bridegroom chaste from flesh,
       And pleasure then will seem new, fair, and fresh.

Exit.

[ACT IV] SCENE 2

[Livia's *house*]
Enter Hippolito

Hipp.   The morning so far wasted, yet his baseness
       So impudent? See if the very sun do not blush at him!
       Dare he do thus much and know me alive?
       Put case one must be vicious, as I know myself
       Monstrously guilty, there's a blind time made for't;
       He might use only that, 'twere conscionable;
       Art, silence, closeness, subtlety, and darkness
       Are fit for such a business; but there's no pity
       To be bestow'd on an apparent[2] sinner,
0   An impudent daylight lecher. The great zeal
       I bear to her advancement in this match
       With Lord Vincentio, as the duke has wrought it,
       To the perpetual honour of our house,
       Puts fire into my blood to purge the air

[1] A heated room.   [2] Conspicuous.

Of this corruption, fear it spread too far
And poison the whole hopes of this fair fortune.
I love her good so dearly that no brother
Shall venture farther for a sister's glory
Than I for her preferment.

Enter Leantio *and* a page

Leant.   [*Aside*]   Once again
20   I'll see that glist'ring whore shines like a serpent
Now the court sun's upon her. — Page!
Page.   Anon, sir.
Leant.   [*Aside*] I'll go in state too. — See the coach be ready.
I'll hurry away presently.

[*Exit* Page.]

Hipp.   Yes, you shall hurry,
And the devil after you. Take that at setting forth!

[*Strikes him*]

Now, and you'll draw, we are upon equal terms, sir.
Thou took'st advantage of my name in honour
Upon my sister; I nev'r saw the stroke
Come till I found my reputation bleeding,
And therefore count it I no sin to valour
30   To serve thy lust so. Now we are of even hand,
Take your best course against me. You must die!
Leant.   [*Aside*] How close sticks envy to man's happiness!
When I was poor and little car'd for life
I had no such means offer'd me to die;
No man's wrath minded[1] me. — Slave, I turn this to thee,
To call thee to account for a wound lately
Of a base stamp upon me.
Hipp.   'Twas most fit
For a base metal. Come and fetch one now
More noble then, for I will use thee fairer
40   Than thou hast done thine [own] soul or our honour,
And there I think 'tis for thee.

[*They fight, and* Hippolito *wounds* Leantio]

Within.   Help, help! Oh, part 'em!
Leant.   False wife, I feel now th'hast pray'd heartily for me.

[1] Concerned.

Rise, strumpet, by my fall; thy lust may reign now.
My heart-string and the marriage-knot that tied thee
Breaks both together.

[*Dies*]

Hipp.   There I heard the sound on't,
And never lik'd string better.

Enter Guardiano, Livia, Isabella, Ward, *and* Sordido

Livia.   'Tis my brother!
Are you hurt, sir?
Hipp.   Not anything.
Livia.   Blessed fortune!
Shift for thyself. What is he thou hast kill'd?
Hipp.   Our honour's enemy.
Guard.   Know you this man, lady?
50 *Livia.*   Leantio! My love's joy! Wounds stick upon thee
As deadly as thy[1] sins. Art thou not hurt?
The devil take that fortune. And he dead?
Drop plagues into thy bowels without voice,
Secret and fearful! Run for officers!
Let him be apprehended with all speed
For fear he 'scape away. Lay hands on him.
We cannot be too sure. 'Tis wilful murder!
You do Heaven's veng'ance and the law just service.
You know him not as I do: he's a villain,
60 As monstrous as a prodigy[2] and as dreadful.
Hipp.   Will you but entertain a noble patience
Till you but hear the reason, worthy sister?
Livia.   The reason? That's a jest Hell falls a-laughing at!
Is there a reason found for the destruction
Of our more lawful loves? And was there none
To kill the black lust 'twixt thy niece and thee
That has kept close so long?
Guard.   How's that, good madam?
Livia.   Too true, sir. There she stands, let her deny't.
The deed cries shortly in the midwife's arms
70 Unless the parents' sins strike it still-born;
And if you be not deaf and ignorant
You'll hear strange notes ere long. Look upon me, wench.
'Twas I betray'd thy honour subtly to him

[1] i.e. Hippolito's. The following words are spoken in an accusing tone,
with an implication of injustice, since the killer of Leantio is uninjured.
[2] Unnatural creature.

Under a false tale. It lights upon now.
His arm has paid me home upon thy breast,
My sweet, belov'd Leantio!
Guard.   Was my judgment
And care in choice so dev'lishly abus'd,
So beyond shamefully? All the world will grin at me.
Ward.   O Sordido, Sordido, I'm damn'd, I'm damn'd!
Sord.   Damn'd? Why, sir?
80 *Ward.*   One of the wicked. Dost not see't?
A cuckold, a plain reprobate cuckold!
Sord.   Nay, and you be damn'd for that, be of good cheer, sir;
y'have gallant company of all professions. I'll have a wife
next Sunday too, because I'll along with you myself.
Ward.   That will be some comfort yet.
Livia.   You, sir, that bear your load of injuries
As I of sorrows, lend me your griev'd strength
To this sad burden, who, in life, wore actions
Flames were not nimbler.[1] We will talk of things
90   May have the luck to break our hearts together.
Guard.   I'll list to nothing but revenge and anger,
Whose counsels I will follow.

> *Exeunt* Livia *and* Guardiano
> [*with the body of* Leantio].

Sord.   A wife, quoth 'a!
Here's a sweet plum tree of your guardianer's grafting!
Ward.   Nay, there's a worse name belongs to this fruit yet, and
you could hit on't, a more open one; for he that marries a
whore looks like a fellow bound all his lifetime to a medlar-
tree,[2] and that's good stuff: 'tis no sooner ripe but it
looks rotten, and so do some queans at nineteen. A pox on't,
I thought there was some knavery abroach, for something
100   stirr'd in her belly the first night I lay with her.
Sord.   What, what, sir?
Ward.   This is she brought up so courtly, can sing and dance, and
tumble too, methinks! I'll never marry wife again that has
so many qualities.
Sord.   Indeed, they are seldom good, master, for likely when they
are taught so many, they will have one trick more of their own
finding out. Well, give me a wench but with one good quality,
to lie with none but her husband, and that's bringing up
enough for any woman breathing.

---

[1] i.e. flames were not nimbler than his actions.   [2] Produces an apple-like
fruit, normally eaten when over-ripe. In the seventeenth century it had
overtones of sexuality.

10   *Ward.*   This was the fault when she was tend'red to me; you never
          look'd to this.
    Sord.   Alas, how would you have me see through a great farthingale,
          sir? I cannot peep through a millstone, or in the going,[1] to
          see what's done i' th' bottom.
    Ward.   Her father prais'd her breast; sh'ad the voice forsooth.
          I marvell'd she sung so small indeed, being no maid. Now I
          perceive there's a young chorister in her belly. This breeds
          a singing in my head, I'm sure!
    Sord.   'Tis but the tune of your wives' cinquepace danc'd in a
20   feather bed. Faith, go lie down, master; but take heed your
          horns do not makes holes in the pillowberes.[2] [*Aside*] I would
          not batter brows with him for a hogshead of angels.[3] He would
          prick my skull as full of holes as a scrivener's sand-box.

                                           Exeunt Ward *and* Sordido.

    Isab.   [*Aside*] Was ever maid so cruelly beguil'd
          To the confusion of life, soul, and honour,
          All of one woman's murd'ring? I'ld fain bring
          Her name no nearer to my blood than 'woman,'
          And 'tis too much of that. Oh, shame and horror!
          In that small distance from yon man[4] to me
30   Lies sin enough to make a whole world perish –
          'Tis time we parted, sir, and left the sight
          Of one another; nothing can be worse
          To hurt repentance, for our very eyes
          Are far more poisonous to religion
          Than basilisks[5] to them. If any goodness
          Rest in you, hope of comforts, fear of judgments,
          My request is, I nev'r may see you more,
          And so I turn me from you everlastingly,
          So is my hope to miss you. But for her
40   That durst so dally with a sin so dangerous
          And lay a snare so spitefully for my youth,
          If the least means but favour my revenge,
          That I may practise the like cruel cunning
          Upon her life, as she has on mine honour,
          I'll act it without pity.
    Hipp.   [*Aside*]   Here's a care
          Of reputation and a sister's fortune
          Sweetly rewarded by her! Would a silence
          As great as that which keeps among the graves
          Had everlastingly chain'd up her tongue!

[1] Action.   [2] Pillowcases.   [3] An angel had a value of approximately 50p.
[4] Hippolito.   [5] A mythical serpent capable of killing with its glance.

150   My love to her has made mine miserable.

    Enter Guardiano *and* Livia. [*They speak apart*]

Guard.   If you can but dissemble your heart's griefs now,
    Be but a woman so far.
Livia.   Peace! I'll strive, sir.
Guard.   As I can wear my injuries in a smile,
    Here's an occasion offer'd that gives anger
    Both liberty and safety to perform
    Things worth the fire it holds, without the fear
    Of danger or of law; for mischiefs acted
    Under the privilege of a marriage-triumph
    At the duke's hasty nuptials will be thought
    Things merely accidental. All's[1] by chance,
    Not got of their own natures.
Livia.   I conceive you, sir,
    Even to a longing for performance on't,
    And here behold some fruits.

            [*Kneels, speaking to* Isabella *and* Hippolito]

                Forgive me both.
    What I am now, return'd to sense and judgment,
    Is not the same[2] rage and distraction
    Presented lately to you. That rude form
    Is gone for ever. I am now myself,
    That speaks all peace and friendship, and these tears
    Are the true springs of hearty, penitent sorrow
170   For those foul wrongs which my forgetful fury
    Sland'red your virtues with. This gentleman
    Is well resolv'd now.
Guard.   I was never otherways.
    I knew, alas, 'twas but your anger spake it,
    And I nev'r thought on't more.
Hipp.   Pray rise, good sister.
Isab.   Here's ev'n as sweet amends made for a wrong now
    As one that gives a wound and pays the surgeon.
    All the smart's nothing, the great loss of blood,
    Or time of hind'rance. [*Aside*] Well, I had a mother,
    I can dissemble too. – What wrongs have slipp'd
180   Through anger's ignorance, aunt, my heart forgives.
Guard.   Why, thus tuneful now!
Hipp.   And what I did, sister,
    Was all for honour's cause, which time to come

    [1] i.e. all as.   [2] i.e. is not the same person as . . . .

Will approve[1] to you.
Livia.   Being awak'd to goodness,
I understand so much, sir, and praise now
The fortune of your arm and of your safety;
For by his death y'have rid me of a sin
As costly as ev'r woman doted on.
'T has pleas'd the duke so well too that, behold, sir,
H'as sent you here your pardon, which I kiss'd
'0   With most affectionate comfort. When 'twas brought
Then was my fit just past; it came so well methought
To glad my heart.
Hipp.   I see his grace thinks on me.
Livia.   There's no talk now but of the preparation
For the great marriage.
Hipp.   Does he marry her then?
Livia.   With all speed, suddenly, as fast as cost
Can be laid on with many thousand hands.
This gentleman and I had once a purpose
To have honoured the first marriage of the duke[2]
With an invention of his own; 'twas ready,
'0   The pains well past, most of the charge bestow'd on't;
Then came the death of your good mother, niece,
And turn'd the glory of it all to black.
'Tis a device would fit these times so well too,
Art's treasury not better. If you'll join,
It shall be done; the cost shall all be mine.
Hipp.   Y'have my voice first; 'twill well approve my thankfulness
For the duke's love and favour.
Livia.   What say you, niece?
Isab.   I am content to make one.
Guard.   The plot's[3] full then;
Your pages, madam, will make shift for cupids.
Livia.   That will they, sir.
0 *Guard.*   You'll play your old part still?
Livia.   What is't? Good troth, I have ev'n forgot it!
Guard.   Why, Juno Pronuba, the marriage goddess.
Livia.   'Tis right indeed.
Guard.   [*To* Isabella] And you shall play the nymph
That offers sacrifice to appease her wrath.
Isab.   Sacrifice, good sir?

---

[1] Demonstrate (perhaps by means of the marriage for Livia of which the duke had spoken; see IV, i, 156-7, and IV, ii, 10-16).   [2] It took place in 1564 after Bianca was already the mistress of the duke. He married Bianca in 1579 soon after his first wife's death. The second marriage lasted until the duke and Bianca died in 1587.   [3] A summary of the action of a play, including the names of the performers.

Livia.   Must I be appeased then?
Guard.   That's as you list yourself, as you see cause.
Livia.   Methinks 'twould show the more state[1] in her deity
    To be incens'd.
Isab.   [*Aside*] 'Twould, but my sacrifice
    Shall take a course to appease you, or I'll fail in't,
220   And teach a sinful bawd to play a goddess.
Guard.   [*To* Hippolito] For our parts we'll not be ambitious, sir.
    Please you walk in and see the project drawn,
    Then take your choice.
Hipp.   I weigh not, so I have one.

                Exeunt [Hippolito, Guardiano, *and* Isabella].

Livia.   How much ado have I to restrain fury
    From breaking into curses! Oh, how painful 'tis
    To keep great sorrow smother'd! Sure I think
    'Tis harder to dissemble grief than love.
    Leantio, here the weight of thy loss lies,
    Which nothing but destruction can suffice.

                                            Exit.

[ACT IV] SCENE 3

[*The palace of the* duke]
Hoboys.[2] *Enter in great state the* Duke *and* Bianca, *richly attired,
with lords, cardinals, ladies, and other attendants. They pass
solemnly over. Enter* Lord Cardinal *in a rage, seeming to break off
the ceremony*

Card.   Cease, cease! Religious honours done to sin
    Disparage virtue's reverence, and will pull
    Heaven's thunder upon Florence. Holy ceremonies
    Were made for sacred uses, not for sinful.
    Are these the fruits of your repentance, brother?
    Better it had been you had never sorrow'd
    Than to abuse the benefit and return
    To worse than where sin left you.
    Vow'd you then never to keep strumpet more,
10   And are you now so swift in your desires
    To knit your honours and your life fast to her?

[1] Dignity.   [2] Oboes.

Is not sin sure enough to wretched man
But he must bind himself in chains to't? Worse,
Must marriage, that immaculate robe of honour
That renders virtue glorious, fair, and fruitful
To her great Master, be now made the garment
Of leprosy and foulness? Is this penitence,
To sanctify hot lust? What is it otherways
Than worship done to devils? Is this the best
20   Amends that sin can make after her riots?
As if a drunkard, to appease Heaven's wrath,
Should offer up his surfeit for a sacrifice!
If that be comely, then lust's offerings are,
On wedlock's sacred altar!
Duke.   Here y'are bitter
Without cause, brother. What I vow'd I keep
As safe as you your conscience, and this needs not.
I taste more wrath in't than I do religion,
And envy more than goodness. The path now
I tread is honest, leads to lawful love,
30   Which virtue in her strictness would not check.
I vow'd no more to keep a sensual woman;
'Tis done. I mean to make a lawful wife of her.
Card.   He that taught you that craft
Call him not master long, he will undo you.
Grow not too cunning for your soul, good brother.
Is it enough to use adulterous thefts,
And then take sanctuary in marriage?
I grant, so long as an offender keeps
Close in a privileged temple, his life's safe,
40   But if he ever venture to come out
And so be taken, then he surely dies for't.
So now y'are safe, but when you leave this body,
Man's only privileg'd temple upon earth,
In which the guilty soul takes sanctuary,
Then you'll perceive what wrongs chaste vows endure
When lust usurps the bed that should be pure.
Bian.   Sir, I have read you over all this while
In silence, and I find great knowledge in you
And severe learning; yet 'mongst all your virtues
50   I see not charity written, which some call
The first-born of religion, and I wonder
I cannot see't in yours. Believe it, sir,
There is no virtue can be sooner miss'd
Or later welcom'd; it begins the rest
And sets 'em all in order. Heaven and angels
Take great delight in a converted sinner;
Why should you then, a servant and professor,

Differ so much from them? If ev'ry woman
That commits evil should be therefore kept
60   Back in desires of goodness, how should virtue
Be known and honour'd? From a man that's blind
To take a burning taper, 'tis no wrong,
He never misses it, but to take light
From one that sees, that's injury and spite.
Pray, whether is religion better serv'd,
When lives that are licentious are made honest,
Than when they still run through a sinful blood?
'Tis nothing virtue's temple to deface,
But build the ruins, there's a work of grace!
70 *Duke.*   I kiss thee for that spirit; thou hast prais'd thy wit
A modest way. On, on there!

Hoboys

Card.   Lust is bold,
And will have veng'ance speak ere't be controll'd.

Exeunt.

ACT V SCENE 1

[*The palace of the duke*]
Enter Guardiano *and* Ward

Guard.   Speak. Hast thou any sense of thy abuse? Dost thou
know what wrong's done thee?
Ward.   I were an ass else! I cannot wash my face but I am feeling
on't.[1]
Guard.   Here, take this caltrop;[2] then convey it secretly into the
place I show'd you. Look you, sir, this is the trap door to't.
Ward.   I know't of old, uncle, since the last triumph.[3] Here rose
up a devil with one eye, I remember, with a company of
fireworks at's tail.
10 *Guard.*   Prithee leave squibbing now; mark me and fail not, but
when thou hear'st me give a stamp, down with't. The villain's[4]
caught then.
Ward.   If I miss you, hang me! I love to catch a villain, and

---

[1]i.e. feeling the horns of a cuckold.   [2]A metal ball with spikes protruding
from it, a weapon of war intended to maim horses.   [3]Pageant.   [4]i.e. Hippolito.

your stamp[1] shall go current, I warrant you. But how shall I
rise up and let him down too, all at one hole? That will be a
horrible puzzle. You know I have a part in't; I play
Guard.   True, but never make you ready for't.
Ward.   No? My clothes are bought and all, and a foul fiend's head
with a long contumelious tongue i' th' chaps on't, a very fit
20   shape for Slander i' th' out-parishes.[2]
Guard.   It shall not come so far; thou understand'st it not.
Ward.   Oh, oh?
Guard.   He shall lie deep enough ere that time, and stick first
upon those.[3]
Ward.   Now I conceive you, guardianer.
Guard.   Away! List to the privy stamp, that's all thy part.
Ward.   Stamp my horns in a mortar if I miss you and give the
powder in white wine to sick cuckolds: a very present remedy
for the headache.

Exit Ward.

30 *Guard.*   If this should any way miscarry now,
As, if the fool be nimble enough, 'tis certain,[4]
The pages that present the swift-wing'd cupids
Are taught to hit him with their shafts of love,
Fitting his part, which I have cunningly poison'd.
He cannot 'scape my fury; and those ills
Will be laid all on fortune, not our wills –
That's all the sport on't, for who will imagine
That at the celebration of this night
Any mischance that haps can flow from spite?

Exit.

[ACT V]   SCENE 2

[*The palace of the* duke]
Flourish. Enter above Duke, Bianca, Lord Cardinal, Fabricio,
and other cardinals, lords and ladies in state

Duke.   Now, our fair Duchess, your delight shall witness

[1] A pun on 'stamp' meaning a mark or design which gives validity to a coin,
token, etc.   [2] i.e. outside the city boundaries, where such old-fashioned
entertainments might still be popular.   [3] Those spikes.   [4] i.e. certain to
carry.

How y'are belov'd and honour'd. All the glories
Bestow'd upon the gladness of this night
Are done for your bright sake.
Bian.   I am the more
In debt, my Lord, to loves and courtesies
That offer up themselves so bounteously
To do me honour'd grace, without my merit.
Duke.   A goodness set in greatness! How it sparkles
Afar off, like pure diamonds set in gold!
10   How perfect my desires were, might I witness
But a fair noble peace 'twixt your two spirits.
The reconcilement would be more sweet to me
Than longer life to him that fears to die.
Good sir!
Card.   I profess peace and am content.
Duke.   I'll see the seal upon't, and then 'tis firm.
Card.   You shall have all you wish.

                                        [*Kisses* Bianca]

Duke.   I have all indeed now.
Bian.   [*Aside*] But I have made surer work; this shall not blind me.

He that begins so early to reprove,
Quickly rid him, or look for little love.
20   Beware a brother's envy – he's the next heir too.
Cardinal, you die tonight; the plot's laid surely.
In time of sports death may steal in securely;
Then 'tis least thought on.
For he that's most religious, holy friend,
Does not at all hours think upon his end;
He has his times of frailty, and his thoughts
Their transportations too, through flesh and blood,
For all his zeal, his learning, and his light,
As well as we poor soul[s] that sin by night.
Duke.   What's this, Fabricio?
30 *Fab.*   Marry, my Lord, the model
Of what's presented.
Duke.   Oh, we thank their loves.
Sweet Duchess, take your seat; list to the argument.[1]

Reads.

There is a nymph that haunts the woods and springs,

---

[1] Summary; Livia indicated (IV, ii, 198-9) that the duke had devised this
masque several years before.

In love with two at once, and they with her.
Equal it runs, but to decide these things
The cause to mighty Juno they refer,
She being the marriage-goddess. The two lovers,
They offer sighs, the nymph a sacrifice,
All to please Juno, who by signs discovers
40   How the event[1] shall be; so that strife dies.
Then springs a second; for the man refus'd
Grows discontent, and out of love abus'd
He raises Slander up, like a black fiend,
To disgrace th'other, which pays him i' th'end.
Bian.   In troth, my Lord, a pretty, pleasing argument,
And fits th'occasion well. Envy and Slander
Are things soon rais'd against two faithful lovers,
But comfort is, they are not long unrewarded.

                                                                                        Music

Duke.   This music shows they're upon entrance now.
50 *Bian.*   Then enter all my wishes.

        Enter Hymen[2] *in yellow*, Ganymede[3] *in a blue robe powdered with
        stars, and* Hebe[4] *in a white robe with golden stars, with covered cups
        in their hands. They dance a short dance, then, bowing to the* duke,
        etc., Hymen *speaks.*

Hym.   To thee, fair bride, Hymen offers up
        Of nuptial joys this the celestial cup.
        Taste it, and thou shalt ever find
        Love in thy bed, peace in thy mind.
Bian.   We'll taste you sure; 'twere pity to disgrace
        So pretty a beginning.
Duke.   'Twas spoken nobly.
Gan.   Two cups of nectar have we begg'd from Jove;
        Hebe, give that to Innocence, I this to Love.

        [Hebe *proffers cup to* Cardinal, Ganymede *to* Duke; *the brothers
        drink*]

        Take heed of stumbling more; look to your way.

[1] Outcome.   [2] The god of marriage.   [3] Cup bearer to Zeus, who transformed him into the constellation Aquarius.   [4] Goddess of youth and
spring, daughter of Zeus and Hera, cup bearer to her father until she
tripped over a star, spilling a container of milk, creating the Milky Way,
the Via Lactea. (See lines 59-62 below.) Ganymede succeeded her as
cup bearer.

60   Remember still the Via Lactea.
   Hebe.   Well, Ganymede, you have more faults, though not so known;
       I spill'd one cup, but you have filch'd many a one.
   Hym.   No more; forbear for Hymen's sake.
       In love we met, and so let's part.

                                                                              Exeunt.

   Duke.   But soft, here's no such persons in the argument
       As these three, Hymen, Hebe, Ganymede.
       The actors that this model here discovers
       Are only four, Juno, a nymph, two lovers.
   Bian.   This is some antimasque[1] belike, my Lord,
70   To entertain[2] time. [*Aside*] Now my peace is perfect. –
       Let sports come on apace; now is their time, my Lord.

                                                                              Music

       Hark you, you hear from 'em.
   Duke.   The nymph indeed!

   *Enter two dressed like nymphs,[3] bearing two tapers lighted; then
       Isabella dressed with flowers and garlands, bearing a censer[4] with
       fire in it. They set the censer and tapers on Juno's altar with
       much reverence, this ditty being sung in parts*

       Ditty.
       Juno, nuptial goddess, thou that rul'st o'er coupled bodies,
       Ti'st man to woman never to forsake her,
       Thou only powerful marriage-maker,
       Pity this amaz'd affection:
       I love both, and both love me;
       Nor know I where to give rejection,
       My heart likes so equally,
       Till thou set'st right my peace of life,
80   And with thy power conclude this strife.
   Isab.   Now with my thanks depart,[5] you to the springs,
       I to these wells of love. Thou sacred goddess
       And queen of nuptials, daughter to great Saturn,
       Sister and wife to Jove, imperial Juno,
       Pity this passionate conflict in my breast,
       This tedious war 'twixt two affections;
       Crown me with victory, and my heart's at peace.

[1] An interlude before or between the acts of a masque.   [2] While away.
[3] i.e. the cupids, V, i, 31-33.   [4] A container for incense.   [5] Evidently a
metaphorical command, since the cupids are at hand at line 133.

Enter Hippolito *and* Guardiano, *like shepherds*

Hipp.   Make me that happy man, thou mighty goddess.
Guard.   But I live most in hope if truest love
    Merit the greatest comfort.
90 *Isab.*   I love both
    With such an even and fair affection,
    I know not which to speak for, which to wish for,
    Till thou, great arbitress 'twixt lovers' hearts,
    By thy auspicious grace, design[1] the man;
    Which pity I implore.
Both [*Shepherds*].   We all implore it.
Isab.   And after sighs, contrition's truest odours,

                            Livia *descends like Juno*

    I offer to thy powerful deity
    This precious incense; may it ascend peacefully.

                      [*Hands the censer to* Livia]

    [*Aside*] And if it keep true touch, my good aunt Juno,
100   'Twill try your immortality ere't be long.
    I fear you'll never get so nigh Heaven again
    When you're once down.
Livia.   Though you and your affections
    Seem all as dark to our illustrious brightness
    As night's inheritance, Hell, we pity you,
    And your requests are granted. You ask signs;
    They shall be given you; we'll be gracious to you.
    He of those twain which we determine for you
    Love's arrows shall wound twice; the later wound
    Betokens love in age, for so are all
110   Whose love continues firmly all their lifetime
    Twice wounded at their marriage, else affection
    Dies when youth ends. [*Aside*] This savour overcomes me. –
    Now for a sign of wealth and golden days,
    Bright-ey'd Prosperity, which all couples love,
    Ay, and makes love – take that!

    [*Throws the burning incense in the face of* Isabella, *who
       collapses*]

                   Our brother Jove
    Never denies us of his burning treasure

[1] Designate.

> T'express bounty.
Duke.   She falls down upon't;
  What's the conceit[1] of that?
Fab.   As overjoy'd, belike;
  Too much prosperity overjoys us all,
120 And she has her lapful it seems, my Lord.
Duke.   This swerves a little from the argument though.
  Look you, my lords.
Guard.   [*Aside*] All's fast. Now comes my part to toll[2] him[3]
  hither;
  Then with a stamp given, he's dispatch'd as cunningly.

[*Stamps, and himself falls through the trap-door.* Hippolito
kneels beside Isabella]

Hipp.   Stark dead! Oh, treachery! Cruelly made away! How's that?
Fab.   Look, there's one of the lovers dropp'd away too!
Duke.   Why sure this plot's drawn false! Here's no such thing.
Livia.   Oh, I am sick to th' death. Let me down quickly!
  This fume is deadly. Oh, 't has poison'd me!
130 My subtlety is sped; her art has quitted me;
  My own ambition pulls me down to ruin.

[*Dies*]

Hipp.   Nay, then I kiss thy cold lips and applaud
  This thy revenge in death.

Cupids shoot [*at* Hippolito]

Fab.   Look, Juno's down too.
  What makes she there? Her pride should keep aloft;
  She was wont to scorn the earth in other shows.
  Methinks her peacocks' feathers[4] are much pull'd.
Hipp.   Oh, death runs through my blood in a wild flame too!
  Plague of those cupids; some lay hold on 'em,
  Let 'em not 'scape. They have spoil'd me, the shaft's deadly!
140 *Duke.*   I have lost myself in this quite.
Hipp.   My great lords, we are all confounded.
Duke.   How!
Hipp.   Dead, and ay, worse!
Fab.   Dead? My girl dead? I hope
  My sister Juno has not serv'd me so.

[1] Ingenious device. [2] Entice. [3] Hippolito. [4] Peacocks traditionally
drew Juno's chariot, here represented by the decorated chair or similar
device in which she had been lowered from the superstructure of
the theatre.

Hipp.   Lust and forgetfulness has been amongst us,
         And we are brought to nothing. Some bless'd charity
         Lend me the speeding pity of his sword
         To quench this fire in blood. Leantio's death
         Has brought all this upon us; – now I taste[1] it –
         And made us lay plots to confound each other.
150   The event so proves it, and man's understanding
         Is riper at his fall than all his lifetime.
         She, in a madness for her lover's death,
         Reveal'd a fearful lust in our near bloods,
         For which I am punish'd dreadfully and unlook'd for;
         Prov'd her own ruin too. Veng'ance met veng'ance
         Like a set match,[2] as if the plague[s] of sin
         Had been agreed to meet here altogether.
         But how her fawning partner fell I reach not,
         Unless caught by some springe[3] of his own setting;
160   For on my pain, he never dream'd of dying.
         The plot was all his own, and he had cunning
         Enough to save himself; but 'tis the property
         Of guilty deeds to draw your wise men downward,
         Therefore the wonder ceases. Oh, this torment!
Duke.   Our guard below there!

         Enter a lord *with a guard*

Lord.   My Lord?
Hipp.   Run and meet death then,
         And cut off time and pain.

                                    [*Seizes guard's sword and runs
                                       himself upon it; dies*]

Lord.   Behold, my Lord,
         H'as run his breast upon a weapon's point!
Duke.   Upon the first night of our nuptial honours
         Destruction play her triumph and great mischiefs
170   Mask in expected pleasures! 'Tis prodigious!
         They're things most fearfully ominous; I like 'em not.
         Remove these ruin'd bodies from our eyes.

         [*The bodies of* Isabella, Livia, *and* Hippolito *are removed*]

Bian.   [*Aside*] Not yet? No change? When falls he[4] to the earth?
Lord.   Please but Your Excellence to peruse that paper,
         Which is a brief confesssion from the heart

[1] Realize.   [2] Conspiracy for robbery.   [3] Trap.   [4] The Cardinal.

Of him that fell first,[1] ere his soul departed,
And there the darkness of these deeds speaks plainly.
'Tis the full scope, the manner and intent.
His ward, that ignorantly let him down,
180   Fear put to present flight at the voice of him.
Bian.   [*Aside*] Nor yet?
Duke.   Read, read, for I am lost in sight and strength.

                                              [*Falls*]

Card.   My noble brother!
Bian.   [*Aside*] O the curse of wretchedness!
My deadly hand is fall'n upon my Lord!
Destruction take me to thee, give me way.
The pains and plagues of a lost soul upon him
That hinders me a moment.
Duke.   My heart swells bigger yet. Help here, break't ope!
My breast flies open next.

                                              [*Dies*]

Bian.   Oh, with the poison
That was prepar'd for thee, thee, Cardinal[2]
'Twas meant for thee!
Card.   Poor prince!
190 *Bian.*   Accursed error!
Give me thy last breath, thou infected bosom,
And wrap two spirits in one poison'd vapour.
Thus, thus reward thy murderer, and turn death
Into a parting kiss. My soul stands ready at my lips,
Ev'n vex'd to stay one minute after thee.
Card.   The greatest sorrow and astonishment
That ever struck the general peace of Florence
Dwells in this hour.
Bian.   So my desires are satisfied;
I feel death's power within me.
200   Thou hast prevail'd in something, cursed poison,
Though thy chief force was spent in my lord's bosom.
But my deformity in spirit's more foul;
A blemish'd face best fits a leprous soul.
What make I here? These are all strangers to me,
Not known but by their malice. Now th'art gone,
Nor do I seek their pities.

---

[1] Guardiano. [2] See line 58 above; Ganymede's poisoned cup was intended for the Cardinal.

[Drinks from the poisoned cup]

Card.   Oh, restrain
   Her ignorant, wilful hand!
Bian.   Now do; 'tis done.
   Leantio, now I feel the breach of marriage
   At my heart-breaking. Oh, the deadly snares
210   That women set for women, without pity
   Either to soul or honour! Learn by me
   To know your foes. In this belief I die.
   Like our own sex, we have no enemy.[1]
Lord.   See, my Lord,
   What shift sh'as made to be her own destruction.
Bian.   Pride, greatness, honours, beauty, youth, ambition,
   You must all down together, there's no help for't.
   Yet this my gladness is, that I remove
   Tasting the same death in a cup of love.
Card.   Sin, what thou art these ruins show too piteously.
   Two kings on one throne cannot sit together
   But one must needs down, for his title's wrong;
   So where lust reigns, that prince cannot reign long.

Exeunt.

FINIS

[1] 'We have no enemy other than our own sex.'

THE CHRONICLE HISTORY OF PERKIN WARBECK, A STRANGE TRUTH (c. 1630)

by JOHN FORD
(baptized 17th April 1586-c. 1639)

[Born at Ilsington in Devon. Middle Temple. Few early plays survive, most of them apparently written in collaboration. Best independent plays are tragedies, written c. 1624-c. 1634, *'Tis Pity She's a Whore, The Broken Heart,* and *The Chronicle History of Perkin Warbeck.*]

When John Ford considered the subject of his fifth or sixth play in the late 1620's, history plays had been out of fashion for many years.[1] Perhaps his interest in Perkin Warbeck, a fifteenth-century pretender to the throne of England, was sparked by his reading of Thomas Gainsford's *True and Wonderfull History of Perkin Warbeck* (1618) and Francis Bacon's *Historie of the Raigne of Henry the Seventh* (1622). These books may have stimulated a curiosity about Warbeck's skill, magic or madness that got him some distance along the road to the throne –

No chronicle records his fellow[2]. (V, iii, 209).

Further, John Ford probably recognized an opportunity to draw attention to an earlier, exemplary king of England who had been able to rule his nation firmly and effectively, who was competent to win battles, to detect treachery and fraudulence, to delegate authority to his loyal and efficient noblemen.[3]

Ford's Henry VII provided an implicit ideal for Charles I (reigned 1625-49), who, within three or four years of his accession, was thoroughly disliked by both the English parliament and the aristocracy for his absolutist behaviour, extravagance, repeated irresponsible demands for money, indiscreet partiality[4], and insistence on his divine right to rule. *Perkin Warbeck* includes approving reference to the principle of divine right; however, Henry VII, unlike Charles I, did not rely on it to maintain his position, depending instead on his tactics, strength and shrewdness.

[1] Shakespeare's *Henry VIII* (1613) had been the last of any significance, and *Perkin Warbeck* is Ford's only contribution to the genre. [2] Equal. [3] No other playwright had utilized Henry VII (reigned 1485-1509), whose career came between those of Richard III and Henry VIII. Shakespeare had already written about all the other English kings of interest and importance. (The reign of Elizabeth was evidently felt still to be too close to be handled safely or comfortably by dramatists.) It is evident that Ford was familiar with *2 Henry VI* (c. 1590), *Richard III* (c. 1594) and *Richard II* (1595). [4] Ford has Henry VII say, No undeserving favourite doth boast
His issues from our treasury. (IV, iv, 50-1)

An analysis of *Perkin Warbeck* must necessarily concern itself with three units of history: the times during which the dramatist wrote, the period in which the action took place (1495-9), and events of twenty-five or more years previous to that time, in order to clarify relationships among and allusions to the major figures in the play. (Historical personages of secondary importance are identified when they first appear in the text.)

King Henry VI, the last Lancastrian, reigned from 1422 to 1461 and briefly during 1470 and 1471. He was deposed in 1461 by the Yorkist faction under Richard, Duke of York, who justified his seizure of the throne on the basis of the present ruler's incompetence and his own descent from Edward III. Richard was killed during the Battle of Wakefield (1460), but his son Edward, Earl of March, soon defeated the Lancastrian forces and succeeded to the throne as King Edward IV (reigned 1461-70, 1471-83).

The Lancastrians recaptured the throne in October 1470 and reinstated Henry VI; however, Edward and his supporters finally defeated their enemies at the Battle of Tewkesbury in May 1471. During the battle, Henry's only son, Edward, Prince of Wales, was killed, and within a few days King Henry was murdered in the Tower of London.

Before his death in 1483, King Edward nominated Richard, Duke of Gloucester, as guardian of the young heir, subsequently Edward V (born 1470), and his brother, Richard, Duke of York (born 1473). Edward V reigned from April to June 1483, although the brothers spent most of that period in the Tower, by Gloucester's command, and are believed by many to have been murdered there, at their uncle's instigation, in August 1483. Two bodies, evidently those of the princes, were discovered in the Tower in 1674. (Thus, forty or so years before this discovery, Warbeck's statement that he was the second son of Edward IV had at least a superficial plausibility, although there had been for a century and a half strong suspicions about the fate of the young king and his brother.)

Richard, Duke of Gloucester, seized the throne as Richard III, but was defeated and killed at the Battle of Bosworth Field in 1485 by Henry Tudor's forces.[1] Henry, Earl of Richmond (Richard III's heir, his son Edward, had predeceased him), then ascended the throne as Henry VII with the assent of Parliament. His usurpation was thinly veiled by his descent from John of Gaunt, and by his marriage to Elizabeth, eldest daughter of Edward IV, which finally united the Houses of Lancaster and York.

King Edward IV's brother George, Duke of Clarence, is of interest to readers of *The Chronicle History of Perkin Warbeck*. George was a constant troublemaker and was executed for treason, without real justification, in 1478; his son, Edward, Earl of Warwick, was the major rallying point for Yorkist dissent after the accession of Henry VII and was imprisoned in the Tower from 1486 to 1499, when he was beheaded. It was this young man whom an earlier pretender, Lambert Simnel, had unsuccessfully impersonated[2]

[1]*Perkin Warbeck,* I, i, 33-5.   [2]*Perkin Warbeck,* V, iii, 21-77.

in 1486 and 1487, maintaining that he had escaped from the Tower. Although the true Warwick was shown publicly, many Englishmen briefly supported Simnel, prompted by either genuine belief in him or enmity towards Henry.

Edward IV's sister Margaret married Charles the Bold, Duke of Burgundy, in 1468. After the fall of the House of York in 1485 she remained a thorn in the flesh of the succeeding House of Tudor for many years, encouraging malcontents and pretenders.

The actual history of the second pretender, Perkin Warbeck, is somewhat obscure. He was apparently a native of Tournay in Flanders, named Osbeck,[1] who during the early 1490's lived in the Netherlands, France, Austria, Portugal and Ireland. With the intermittent backing of Margaret, Duchess of Burgundy, Charles VIII of France, the Emperor Maximilian[2], and various English and Irish dissidents, Warbeck impersonated Richard, Duke of York, the younger brother of Edward V, insisting that he had not, like his brother, been murdered in the Tower, but had been smuggled out and had spent his youth in France.

Warbeck's followers invaded England at Deal, Kent, in 1494, where they were defeated. (Warbeck did not himself go ashore.) After an inconclusive sojourn in Ireland, Warbeck received aid in Scotland in 1495. James IV may have been sincere in espousing the pretender's cause, or, like Warbeck's other royal and noble supporters, the Scottish king may have welcomed an excuse to create difficulties for Henry VII.

James apparently urged Warbeck to leave Scotland as soon as it was evident that he had no support in the north of England. Following an unsuccessful effort to recruit new strength in Ireland, Warbeck landed in Cornwall in September 1497. Soon he and his Cornish forces were routed at Taunton, Somerset. Warbeck fled and was taken into custody at Beaulieu Abbey. After two attempts to escape, first from the Palace of Westminster and second from the Tower, he was hanged at Tyburn on 23 November 1499.[3]

John Ford followed the broad outlines of the events summarized here, but he telescoped the passage of time, simplified relationships and created more idealized pictures of both Henry VII and Perkin Warbeck.

Obviously, Ford could not use his characterizations of Henry VII and James IV of Scotland too explicitly to admonish Charles I; he could hardly defend Warbeck's claim to the throne without calling in question the

---

[1] There is no evidence that he was of Jewish descent, as Ford suggested, V, iii, 24.   [2] 1459-1519; born an archduke of Austria, elected King of the Romans in 1486, succeeded as emperor in 1493 on the death of his father Frederick III. In 1477 he married Mary, daughter and heiress of Charles the Bold, Duke of Burgundy. Margaret, Duchess of Burgundy, was his second wife.   [3] The Earl of Warwick was implicated in Warbeck's attempted escape from the Tower; there has been an enduring suspicion that the circumstances of the escape were arranged, to provide the authorities with some justification for ridding themselves of both embarrassments to the state.

legitimacy of the Tudor line of descent; and he could not too assiduously damn the character of James IV, who was one of Charles I's ancestors.

The playwright avoided many difficulties by careful emphasis. He made much of Henry VII's shrewdness and sagacity, and made little of Warbeck's claims to the throne. Henry is invariably calm and confident, Warbeck always rhetorical and impassioned. Indeed, the two men are constantly foils to one another.[1] Ford's sources, Gainsford and Bacon, were, not unnaturally, more sympathetic to Henry than to Warbeck[2], and Ford occasionally modified historical fact in order to make King Henry a more attractive, less suspicious and parsimonious figure than history admits.[3] The play illustrates repeatedly Henry's firm control over the English court and both the supporters of and defectors from it. By contrast to his depiction of Henry's statesmanship, Ford stressed throughout the play Warbeck's charisma, earlier attested to repeatedly, if grudgingly, by Gainsford and Bacon. For example, the former described Warbeck at the beginning of his career, about 1491, as

> a yong man, not fully sixteen, of visage beautiful,
> of countenance majesticall, of wit subtile and craftie;
> in education pregnant, in languages skilfull; of
> behaviour extraordinary, and of manners audacious.
> *The True and Wonderfull History of Perkin Warbeck,* p.31

Ford affirmed Warbeck's plausibility, first by making him believe, apparently unquestioningly, in himself,[4] and second, by characters to believe in him. The most notable of these is, of course, Katherine Gordon, who, in play and history, married the poseur and remained loyal to him even in hardship and defeat.

> I swear
> To die a faithful widow to thy bed,
> Not to be forc'd or won. Oh, never, never:[5] (V, iii, 150-2)

In his interpretation Ford added to Warbeck's magnetism by inventing an earlier suitor for Katherine, the Scottish nobleman Lord Dalyell, to whom she was half committed before Warbeck's appearance in Scotland (I, ii, 159-66).[6]

[1] Headstrong James IV is also a foil to Henry. [2] One of Bacon's sharp references is to 'this little cockatrice of a king'. *The Historie of the Raigne of Henry the Seventh,* p.211. [3] In the dramatized version of events Henry arranged the preliminaries for peace negotiations between England and Scotland *before* the confrontation at Norham Castle (III, iv), making Henry seem the more conciliatory, James the more rash. The Battle of Blackheath is almost irrelevant to the main lines of action, but Ford gave it a central scene (III, i) because of its importance to his theme of stability of the state and its contribution to a favourable impression of Henry and his noblemen. [4] The playwright gave him no self-revealing soliloquies. [5] It is impossible to determine whether or not Ford knew of Katherine's three subsequent marriages. Bacon and Gainsford did not refer to them. [6] Although in the play King James gave Perkin's wooing of Katherine considerable encouragement, it is clear, as in the historical accounts, that she entered into the marriage of her own free will (II, i, 118-20; II, iii, 84-5).

Despite Ford's evident admiration for the dynamism of Perkin Warbeck, the playwright undermined him from the beginning, as he had to do. He allowed Warbeck to appear on stage only after a negative attitude towards him had been established in the English court; he allowed James to adopt Warbeck exceedingly readily and to reject him as casually, when no longer useful; he surrounded the pretender with simple-minded opportunists who provide the only episodes of humour in the play; and he attributed to Warbeck political and military naïveté. Warbeck's self-dramatization and self-delusion reach a climax in his acceptance of 'a martyrdom of majesty' (V, iii, 75).

The facts of history, already familiar to seventeenth-century audiences, gave Ford an inescapable conclusion to Perkin Warbeck's career. The dramatist contributed tragic overtones to the tale by means of tensions between positive and negative elements in events and characterization. Several characters, for a variety of motives, approve of Warbeck and defend him; others are constantly suspicious. These tensions or conflicts are reinforced by Ford's skilful use of language and imagery. In particular, the words Warbeck speaks are invariably regal; he never slips out of his role, even in the depths of despair —

   I am my father's son still ...

       I will be England's king. (IV, ii, 13, 17)

This spirit is maintained even in his final exhortation to his comrades:

     So illustrious mention

  Shall blaze our names, and style us kings o'er death.

           (V, iii, 205-7)

Perkin's belief in himself is echoed in Katherine's admirable loyalty, expressed in a similar apt image:

  You must be king of me, and my poor heart

  Is all I can call mine. (III, ii, 168-9)

Set against the positive tone is the strong, consistent negative imagery used by other characters in their direct or indirect references to the pretender. Imagery of witchcraft appears often, based on the assumption that only sorcery could explain Warbeck's behaviour; metaphorical reference is also frequent to treachery, disease, corruption, tempests, clouds, darkness and animals.[1] As well, a few metaphors of bloodshed provide reminders of the threat to the state that Warbeck represented.

Other accounts of Warbeck's career have emphasized the confession he made near the end of his life. Ford omitted it in order to reinforce Warbeck's absolute self-conviction. This supreme confidence is set sharply in contrast to his abandonment of wife and comrades at Taunton (V, i, 50-7). Yet even after this ignominious circumstance his regal attitude towards himself is unchanged. He speaks later to his captor, Henry VII, as though he were a rival king (V, ii, 53-72), with a dubious claim to the crown; however, Ford's recurrent deflation of Warbeck's pretensions is

---

[1] Cub, mongrel, fox, adder. By contrast, Warbeck repreatedly alludes to himself as a lion (IV, v, 26-9).

climaxed here by Henry's quiet words (which Ford borrowed from Bacon),

    Oh, let him range.
The player's on the stage still; 'tis his part.

                                                                           (V, ii, 67-8)

Much of the pathos that Warbeck's career generates is based on the knowledge that the young man was no more than a pawn to fifteenth-century international dynastic ambitions and military rivalries.

Ford's poetic skill and versatility contribute much to the conviction of the play. The regular flow of the simple, noble poetry is appropriate to the tone of high seriousness and to the vitality of the misguided and ingenuous 'hero'. He can 'utter the language of a king' (II, i, 103-4). As well, tone and language are appropriate to the rank and circumstances of the other characters.

It is easy for a reader of this play to concentrate wholly on Perkin Warbeck, but it is evident that Ford gave much attention to many other characters – the assured Henry, the enthusiastic and youthfully naive James IV, the loyal Katherine, doubly loyal Dalyell (equally faithful in exile to his former loved one and to his erstwhile rival), Katherine's earnest, grieving father, the dignified and clever Bishop Fox, the other honourable Englishmen, and even the mad Irish, celebrating their leader's marital triumph with usquebaugh and bonny-clabber.

The date of the play's composition is unknown, certainly between 1622, when Bacon's book was published, and 1634, the first appearance of the play in print. There are few links with Ford's other plays, but the pathos of the episode in which Warbeck parts for the last time from his wife and other loyal supporters (V, iii, 80-181) is reminiscent of Frank Thorney's farewell to *his* wife and relatives in *The Witch of Edmonton* (V, iii, 53-141).[1]

Perkin Warbeck has interested many twentieth-century critics, although the play has not been performed in modern times. They regard it with much respect for its psychological insights and analysis, and for Ford's dramatic and verbal skills. T.S. Eliot described the play as 'unquestionably Ford's highest achievement and one of the best history plays outside the works of Shakespeare in the whole Elizabethan and Jacobean drama'.[2] Few analysts have quite equalled this ardour, but all have responded with some degree of sympathy to Ford's depiction of a remarkable man in English history, one who has left behind the insoluble mystery of his private thoughts and motivations.

[1] Ford is the likely author of the scene from this early play (1621) in which he collaborated.   [2] *Selected Essays* (1951 [1932]), p. 200.

THE CHRONICLE HISTORY OF PERKIN WARBECK,
A STRANGE TRUTH.
[by John Ford]
[*c.* 1630]

To the rightly honourable William Cavendish, Earl of Newcastle, Viscount Mansfield, Lord Bolsover and Ogle.[1]

My Lord,

Out of the darkness of a former age, enlightened by a late both learned and an honourable pen,[2] I have endeavoured to personate[3] a great attempt and in it a greater danger. In other labours you may read actions of antiquity discoursed; in this abridgement find the actors themselves discoursing, in some kind practised as well what to speak as speaking why to do.[4] Your lordship is a most competent judge in expressions of such credit,[5] commissioned[6] by your known ability in examining and enabled[7] by your knowledge in determining the monuments of time. Eminent titles may indeed inform who their owners are, not often what. To yours the addition of that information in both[8] cannot in any application be observed flattery, the authority being established by truth. I can only acknowledge the errors in writing mine own, the worthiness of the subject written being a perfection in the story and of it. The custom of your lordship's entertainments,[9] even to strangers, is rather an example than a fashion; in which consideration I dare not profess a curiosity,[10] but am only studious that your lordship will please, amongst such as best honour your goodness, to admit into your noble construction[11]

John Ford.

To my own friend, Master John Ford, on his justifiable
      poem of *Perkin Warbeck,* this ode:
  They who do know me know that I,
      Unskill'd to flatter,
  Dare speak this piece in words, in matter,
  A work,[12] without the danger of the lie.
  Believe me, friend, the name of this and thee
      Will live, your story.

---

[1] 1595-1676; poet, scholar, royalist, patron of several poets and playwrights.
[2] Probably an allusion to Sir Francis Bacon (1561-1626); his *Historie of the Raigne of King Henry the Seventh* (1622) provided Ford with much material for this play. [3] Describe. [4] i.e. as offering explanations. [5] Reputation [6] Empowered. [7] Authorized. [8] i.e. who and what you are. [9] Support. [10] Ingenuity. [11] i.e. the noble interpretation you put upon conduct. [12] i.e. a genuine work of art.

Books may want faith, or merit glory;
This neither, without judgment's lethargy.
When the arts dote, then some sick poet may
    Hope that his pen
In new-stain'd paper can find men
To roar, 'He is the wit's.' His noise doth sway.
But such an age cannot be known, for all,
    Ere that time be,
Must prove such truth mortality.[1]
So, friend, thy honour stands too fix'd to fall.

                              George Donne.[2]

To his worthy friend, Master John Ford, upon his
       Perkin Warbeck.
Let men who are writ poets lay a claim
To the Phoebean hill;[3] I have no name
Nor art in verse. True, I have heard some tell
Of Aganippe,[4] but ne'er knew the well;
Therefore, have[5] no ambition with the times
To be in print for making of ill rhymes;
But love of thee and justice to thy pen
Hath drawn me to this bar[6] with other men
To justify, though against double laws,[7] –
Waiving the subtle bus'ness of his cause –
The glorious Perkin and thy poet's art,
Equal with his, in playing the king's part.

                              Ra[lph] Eure.[8]
                        Baronis Primogenitus.

To my faithful, no less deserving friend, the author,
       this indebted oblation.
Perkin is rediviv'd[9] by thy strong hand
And crown'd a king of new; the vengeful wand[10]
Of greatness is forgot. His execution
May rest unmention'd, and his birth's collusion[11]
Lie buried in the story; but his fame

---

[1] A comment on the impermanency of popular literature [2] Conceivably
John Donne's second son, George, a professional soldier. Three verse
tributes, prefacing contemporary plays are the only known works of
George Donne, poet, including Ford's *Lover's Melancholy,* published in
1629 whilst John's son George was a prisoner in France (1628-33). [3] Mount
Helicon, sacred to Phoebus Apollo and the Muses. [4] A spring on Mount
Helicon; its waters were believed to impart poetic inspiration. [5] i.e. I have.
[6] Court of law. [7] Perhaps an allusion to civil and canon law. [8] The eldest
son of William, fourth Baron Eure, who succeeded to the title in 1619.
Ralph predeceased his father. [9] Restored to life. [10] Sceptre. [11] The fraud
concerning his birth.

Thou hast eterniz'd, made a crown his game.[1]
His lofty spirit soars yet. Had he been
Base in his enterprise, as was his sin
Conceiv'd,[2] his title,[3] doubtless prov'd unjust,
Had but for thee been silenc'd in his dust.

George Crymes, miles.[4]

To the author, his friend, upon his Chronicle History.
These[5] are not to express thy wit,
But to pronounce thy judgment fit
In full-fil'd[6] phrase those times to raise
When Perkin ran his wily ways.
Still let the method of thy brain
From error's touch and envy's stain
Preserve thee free, that e'er thy quill
Fair truth may whet and fancy fill.
Thus Graces are with Muses met,
And practic[7] critics on may fret,
For here thou hast produc'd a story
Which shall eclipse their future glory.

John Brograve, Ar[miger].[8]

To my friend and kinsman, Master John Ford, the author.
Dramatic poets, as the times go now,
Can hardly write what others will allow.[9]
The cynic snarls, the critic howls and barks,
And ravens croak to drown the voice of larks.
Scorn those stage-harpies. This I'll boldly say:
Many may imitate, few match thy play.

John Ford, Graiensis.[10]

Prologue
Studies have of this nature been of late
So out of fashion, so unfollow'd, that
It is become more justice[11] to revive

---

[1] Prey. [2] i.e. as he was base in conceiving his sin. [3] Claim. [4] This knight
may be the co-author (with Thomas Crymes) of *Parliamentum Impera-
torium...*, 1654; otherwise unknown. [5] i.e. these lines. [6] Well polished.
[7] Crafty. [8] Evidently a younger son of Sir John Brograve (d. 1613). The
son was a barrister-at-law. An armiger was an esquire, an attendant on a
knight or patron, usually his father. [9] Commend. [10] To his namesake and
cousin of Gray's Inn, the playwright dedicated *The Lover's Melancholy*,
1629, and *Love's Sacrifice*, 1633. [11] Judicious.

The antic follies of the times than strive
To countenance wise industry. No want
Of art doth render wit or[1] lame or scant
Or slothful in the purchase of fresh bays,
But want of truth in them[2] who give the praise
To their self-love, presuming to outdo
10 The writer or, for need, the actors too.
But such this author's silence best befits,
Who bids them be in love with their own wits.
From him to clearer judgments we can say
He shows a history couch'd in a play,
A history of noble mention,[3] known,
Famous, and true; most noble, 'cause our own,
Not forg'd from Italy, from France, from Spain,
But chronicl'd at home; as rich in strain[4]
Of brave attempts as ever fertile rage
20 In action could beget to grace the stage.
We cannot limit[5] scenes, for the whole land
Itself appear'd too narrow to withstand
Competitors for kingdoms. Nor is here
Unnecessary mirth forc'd, to endear[6]
A multitude. On these two rests the fate
Of worthy expectation: truth and state.[7]

---

[1] Either. [2] i.e. critics. [3] Record. [4] Ancestry. [5] Specify. [6] Attract. [7] i.e. matter of state.

The Persons Presented
Henry VII
[Giles, Lord] Daubeney
Sir William Stanley
[Earl of] Oxford
[Earl of] Surrey
[Richard Fox,] Bishop of Durham
[Christopher] Urswick, *chaplain to King Henry*
Sir Robert Clifford
Lambert Simnel
Hialas, *a Spanish agent*
Constable, Officers, Serving-men, *and* Soldiers
James IV, King of Scotland
Earl of Huntly
Early of Crawford
Lord Dalyell
Marchmount, *a herald*
Perkin Warbeck
[Stephen] Frion, *his secretary*
[John a-Water,] Mayor of Cork
[John] Heron, *a mercer*[1]
Skelton, *a tailor*
[Nicholas] Astley, *a scrivener*[2]

WOMEN
Lady Katherine Gordon, *wife to Perkin*
Countess of Crawford
Jane Douglas, *Lady Katherine's maid*

The Scene: the Continent of Great Britain.

[1] A dealer in fabrics. [2] A clerk, secretary, penman.

ACT I SCENE I

[King Henry's *palace, Westminster*]
Enter King Henry, Durham,[1] Oxford,[2] Surrey,[3] Sir William Stanley
(Lord Chamberlain),[4] Lord Daubeney.[5] *The* King *supported to his*
throne by Stanley *and* Durham. *A guard*

Henry.[6]   Still to be haunted, still to be pursued,
Still to be frighted with false apparitions
Of pageant[7] majesty and new-coin'd greatness,
As if we were a mockery king in state,
Only ordain'd to lavish sweat and blood
In scorn and laughter to the ghosts of York,
Is all below our merits; yet, my lords,
My friends and counsellors, yet we sit fast
In our own royal birthright. The rent face
10   And bleeding wounds of England's slaughter'd people
Have been by us, as by the best physician,
At last both throughly cur'd and set in safety,
And yet for all this glorious work of peace
Ourself is scarce secure.
Durham.   The rage of malice
Conjures fresh spirits with the spells of York.
For ninety years ten English kings and princes,
Threescore great dukes and earls, a thousand lords
And valiant knights, two hundred fifty thousand
Of English subjects have in civil wars
20   Been sacrific'd to an uncivil thirst
Of discord and ambition.[8] This hot vengeance
Of the just powers above to utter ruin

---

[1] Richard Fox (*c.* 1448-1528), ecclesiastic, diplomat, Secretary of State,
etc., bishop of several dioceses, including Durham, 1494-1501.   [2] John de
Vere (1442-1513), thirteenth Earl of Oxford. Loyal supporter of Henry
VII, a leader of the forces which defeated the Cornish rebels at the Battle
of Blackheath, 1497.   [3] Thomas Howard (1443-1524), first Earl of Surrey
and second Duke of Norfolk. A long career of service to king and state,
principally in the north of England.   [4] *C.*1435-95. Formerly a Yorkist,
he supported Henry, especially at the Battle of Bosworth Field, 1485.
Henry then created him Lord Chamberlain. Historically, Stanley was
accused of treason and executed in 1495, but with what real justification
is unknown.   [5] One of Henry's principal supporters, even before his
accession to the throne. Succeeded William Stanley as Lord Chamberlain.
Defender of the north against Scottish incursions, an important
commander at Blackheath. Died 1508.   [6] Q identifies the two kings of the
play as *King.* or *K.* and *K. I.* or *Ja.* in speech prefixes. In this edition *Henry.*
and *James.* will be used.   [7] Sham.   [2] It is not necessary to accept literally
Ford's statistics, borrowed from his sources.

And desolation had rain'd on,[1] but that
Mercy did gently sheathe the sword of Justice
In lending to this blood-shrunk commonwealth
A new soul, new birth, in your sacred person.

Daub.   Edward the Fourth, after a doubtful fortune,
Yielded to nature,[2] leaving to his sons,
Edward and Richard, the inheritance
30 Of a most bloody purchase.[3] These young princes
Richard the tyrant, their unnatural uncle,
Forc'd to a violent grave. So just is Heaven,
Him hath Your Majesty| by your own arm,
Divinely strengthen'd, pull'd from his boar's sty[4]
And struck the black usurper to a carcass.
Nor doth the house of York decay in honours,
Though Lancaster doth repossess his right;
For Edward's daughter is King Henry's queen,[5]
A blessed union and a lasting blessing
40 For this poor panting island, if some shreds,
Some useless remnant of the house of York,
Grudge not at this content.

Oxford.   Margaret of Burgundy[6]
Blows fresh coals of division.

Surrey.   Painted fires,
Without or heat to scorch or light to cherish.

Daub.   York's headless trunk, her father; Edward's fate,
Her brother-king; the smothering of her nephews
By tyrant Gloucester, brother to her nature;
Nor Gloucester's own confusion[7] — all decrees
Sacred in Heaven — can move this woman-monster
50 But that she still from the unbottom'd mine
Of devilish policies doth vent the ore
Of troubles and sedition.

Oxford.   In her age —
Great sir, observe the wonder — she grows fruitful,
Who in her strength of youth was always barren;
Nor are her births as other mothers' are,
At nine or ten months' end; she has been with child
Eight or seven years at least. Whose twins[8] being born —

---

[1] i.e. had continued to rain. [2] He died a natural death, in 1483. [3] Seizure
(See Introduction. p.93). [3] A sneering allusion to the white boar, Richard
III's badge, which appeared on his standard. [5] Queen Elizabeth of York,
1465-1503, eldest child of Edward IV. Henry married her in 1486, to unite
the houses of York and Lancaster. [6] 1446-1503; a sister of Edward IV and
Richard III. After Richard's defeat she continued to support the Yorkist
cause in devious ways, especially by her encouragement of Lambert Simnel
(1487) and Perkin Warbeck (1496-7). [7] Overthrow. [8] Simnel and Warbeck.

A prodigy in nature — even the youngest
Is fifteen years of age at his first entrance;
60 As soon as known i' th' world tall striplings, strong
And able to give battle unto kings.
Idols of Yorkish malice!
Daub.[1]   And but idols.
A steely hammer crushes 'em to pieces.
Henry.   Lambert, the eldest, lords, is in our service,
Preferr'd[2] by an officious[3] care of duty
From the scullery to a falc'ner. Strange example!
Which[4] shows the difference between noble natures
And the base-born. But for the upstart duke,
The new-revived York, Edward's second son,
70 Murder'd long since i' th' Tower, he lives again,
And vows to be your king.
Stan.   The throne is fill'd, sir.
Henry.   True, Stanley, and the lawful heir sits on it.
A guard of angèls and the holy prayers
Of loyal subjects are a sure defence
Against all force and counsel of intrusion.[5]
But now, my lords, put case[6] some of our nobles,
Our 'great ones', should give countenance and courage
To trim[7] Duke Perkin, you will all confess
Our bounties have unthriftily been scatter'd
Amongst unthankful men.
80 *Daub.*   Unthankful beasts!
Dogs, villains, traitors!
Henry.   Daubeney, let the guilty
Keep silence. I accuse none, though I know
Foreign attempts against a state and kingdom
Are seldom without some great friends at home.
Stan.   Sir, if no other abler reasons else
Of duty or allegiance could divert
A headstrong resolution, yet the dangers
So lately pass'd[8] by men of blood and fortunes
In Lambert Simnel's party must command
90 More than a fear, a terror to conspiracy.
The high-born Lincoln,[9] son to de la Pole,

---

[1] *Ox.* [Q.]   [2] Promoted. See V, iii, 31-44.   [3] Zealous.   [4] i.e. his acceptance of such a 'promotion'.   [5] Plan of invasion.   [6] Suppose.   [7] Elegant   [8] Endured.
[9] John de la Pole (*c.* 1462-87), Earl of Lincoln, son of John de la Pole, second Duke of Suffolk. The son was loyal to Richard III and a principal supporter of Simnel; Lincoln was killed at the Battle of Stoke, 1487.

The Earl of Kildare,[1] Lord Geraldine,[2]
Francis, Lord Lovell,[3] and the German baron,
Bold Martin Swart,[4] with Broughton[5] and the rest —
Most spectacles of ruin, some of mercy —
Are precedents sufficient to forewarn
The present times, or any that live in them,
What folly, nay, what madness 'twere to lift
A finger up in all defence but yours,
100   Which[6] can be but imposturous in a title.[7]
    Henry.   Stanley, we know thou lov'st us, and thy heart
Is figur'd[8] on thy tongue. Nor think we less
Of any's here. How closely we have hunted
This cub[9] since he unlodg'd,[10] from hole to hole,
Your knowledge is our chronicle. First Ireland,
The common stage of novelty, presented
This gewgaw to oppose us; there the Geraldines
And Butlers[11] once again stood in support
Of this colossic statue.[12] Charles of France
110   Thence call'd him into his protection,
Dissembl'd him[13] the lawful heir of England;
Yet this was all but French dissimulation,
Aiming at peace with us, which being granted
On honourable terms on our part, suddenly
This smoke of straw[14] was pack'd[15] from France again
T'infect some grosser air; and now we learn,
Maugre[16] the malice of the bastard Neville,[17]

---

[1] Gerald Fitzgerald (*c.* 1457-1513), eighth Earl of Kildare; he sided with Simnel, but survived Stoke, and was later reinstated in Henry's favour. [2] Thomas Fitzgerald, younger brother of Gerald, both members of an important Irish family. Thomas was appointed Chancellor of Ireland by Henry VII, but in support of Simnel was killed at Stoke. [3] Francis, first Viscount Lovell, 1454-87(?). Loyal to Richard III until the king's death, supported Simnel at Stoke. [4] Or Schwartz; a mercenary soldier engaged by Margaret of Burgundy to lead a troop of two thousand men in support of Simnel. Swart was killed during the Battle of Stoke. [5] Sir Thomas Broughton of Lancashire, Yorkist and friend of Lovell, believed to have been killed at Stoke. [6] i.e. which defence except yours. [7] Justification. [8] Represented. [9] i.e. Warbeck. [10] Left his hiding place (a hunting term). [11] Another important Irish family, rivals of the Geraldines (see note at I, i, 92); the Butlers remained generally loyal to Henry and took only a small part in Yorkist plotting. [12] An ironic comparison between Warbeck and Chares's 105 ft. bronze statue of Helios, the sun god, at Rhodes. The statue was toppled by an earthquake *c.* 224 B.C. [13] Passed him off as. [14] Ephemera. [15] Sent away. [16] In spite of. [17] Sir George Neville; referred to in Ford's sources as 'the bastard' and a supporter of Warbeck in Flanders; little is known of him.

Sir Taylor[1] and a hundred English rebels,
They're all retir'd to Flanders, to the dam
20 That nurs'd this eager whelp, Margaret of Burgundy.
But we will hunt him there too, we will hunt him,
Hunt him to death even in the beldam's[2] closet,[3]
Though the archduke[4] were his buckler.[5]
Surrey.   She has styl'd him 'the fair white rose of England'.[6]
Daub.   Jolly gentleman! More fit to be a swabber[7]
To the Flemish after a drunken surfeit.

Enter Urswick[8]

Urs.   Gracious sovereign, please you peruse this paper.
Durham.   The king's countenance gathers a sprightly blood.
Daub.   Good news, believe it.
Henry.   Urswick, thine ear.

[They speak apart]

Th'ast lodg'd[9] him?[10]
30 *Urs.*   Strongly safe, sir.
Henry.   Enough. Is Barley[11] come too?
Urs.   No, my Lord.
Henry.   No matter. Phew! He's but a running[12] weed,
At pleasure to be pluck'd up by the roots.
But more of this anon. I have bethought me. —
My lords, for reasons which you shall partake,
It is our pleasure to remove our court
From Westminster to th'Tower.[13] We will lodge
This very night there. Give, Lord Chamberlain,[14]
A present order for it.
Stan.   [Aside]   The Tower! — I shall, sir.
40 *Henry.*   Come, my true, best, fast friends. These clouds will vanish,
The sun will shine at full. The heavens are clearing.

Flourish. Exeunt.

[1] Sir John Taylor; almost unknown apart from his Yorkist sympathies.
[2] Hag's, witch's. [3] Private room. [4] Philip, Duke of Burgundy (1478-1506), son of the Emperor Maximilian I, inherited Burgundy from his mother, Queen Mary. Margaret, widow of Charles the Bold and long-time supporter of Warbeck, was the effective ruler. [5] Shield, protector. [6] The emblem of the house of York. Warbeck claimed to be a son of Edward IV.
[7] Deck cleaner. [8] Christopher Urswick (1448-1522), a supporter of Henry Tudor, sucessively Dean of York, Dean of Windsor, chaplain and almoner to King Henry. [9] Held in custody. [10] i.e. Sir Robert Clifford. See I, iii.
[11] William Barley. Like Clifford, an early supporter of Warbeck. Barley later surrendered and was pardoned. [12] Rapidly spreading. [13] Historically, January 1495. [14] Sir William Stanley.

[ACT I SCENE 2]

[Huntly's *house, Edinburgh*]
Enter Huntly[1] *and* Dalyell[2]

Hunt.   You trifle[3] time, sir.
Dal.   O my noble Lord,
    You conster my griefs to so hard a sense
    That where the text is argument[4] of pity,
    Matter of earnest love, your gloss[5] corrupts it
    With too much ill-plac'd mirth.
Hunt.   Much mirth, Lord Dalyell?
    Not so, I vow. Observe me,[6] sprightly gallant:
    I know thou art a noble lad, a handsome,
    Descended from an honourable ancestry,
    Forward and active, dost resolve to wrestle
10 And ruffle[7] in the world by noble actions
    For a brave mention to posterity.
    I scorn not thy affection for my daughter,
    Not I, by good Saint Andrew; but this bugbear,
    This whoreson[8] tale of honour — honour, Dalyell —
    So hourly chats and tattles in mine ear
    The piece of royalty that is stitch'd up
    In my Kate's blood, that 'tis as dangerous
    For thee, young lord, to perch so near an eaglet
    As foolish for my gravity to admit[9] it.
    I have spoke all at once.
20 *Dal.*   Sir, with this truth
    You mix such wormwood that you leave no hope
    For my disorder'd palate e'er to relish
    A wholesome taste again. Alas, I know, sir,
    What an unequal distance lies between
    Great Huntly's daughter's birth and Dalyell's fortunes.
    She's the king's kinswoman, plac'd near the crown,
    A princess of the blood, and I a subject.
Hunt.   Right; but a noble subject. Put in that too.
Dal.   I could add more; and in the rightest line

---

[1] George Gordon, second Earl of Huntly, d. *c*. 1502. Privy counsellor to
James IV. Huntly's daughter, Lady Katherine, was probably an offspring
of his second marriage (*c*. 1459), to Annabella Stewart, a daughter of
James I of Scotland, 1394-1437; see I, ii, 16-27, 103-4. [2] Not clearly
identifiable; perhaps an invention of Ford's for dramatic interest, but the
Dalyells were a distinguished fifteenth-century Scottish family. [3] Waste.
[4] Evidence. [5] Interpretation. [6] Attend to me. [7] Make a great stir.
[8] Wretched. [9] Permit.

Derive my pedigree from Adam Mure,[1]
A Scottish knight, whose daughter was the mother
To him that first begot the race of Jameses
That sway the sceptre to this very day.
But kindreds are not ours[2] when once the date
Of many years have swallow'd up the memory
Of their originals. So pasture fields
Neighbouring too near the ocean are soop'd up[3]
And known no more. For stood I in my first
And native greatness, if my princely mistress
Vouchsaf'd me not her servant,[4] 'twere as good
I were reduc'd to clownery, to nothing,
As to[5] a throne of wonder.
Hunt.   [*Aside*]   Now, by Saint Andrew,
A spark of mettle! 'A has a brave fire in him.
I would 'a had my daughter, so I knew't not;
But ['t] must not be so, must not. — Well, young lord,
This will not do yet. If the girl be headstrong
And will not hearken to good counsel, steal her
And run away with her; dance galliards, do,
And frisk about the world to learn the languages.
'Twill be a thriving trade. You may set up[6] by't.
Dal.   With pardon, noble Gordon, this disdain
Suits not your daughter's virtue or my constancy.
Hunt.   You are angry. [*Aside*] Would 'a would beat me, I deserve it. —
Dalyell, thy hand; w'are friends. Follow thy courtship;
Take thine own time and speak. If thou prevail'st
With passion more than I can with my counsel,
She's thine. Nay, she is thine. 'Tis a fair match,
Free and allow'd. I'll only use my tongue
Without a father's power;[7] use thou thine.
Self do, self have.[8] No more words. Win and wear her.
Dal.   You bless me. I am now too poor in thanks
To pay the debt I owe you.
Hunt.   Nay, th'art poor
Enough:[9] [*Aside*] I love his spirit infinitely. —
Look ye, she comes. To her now, to her, to her.

Enter Katherine *and* Jane[2]

---

[1] Mure's daughter Elizabeth married, *c.* 1349, Robert II, father of Robert III
and grandfather of James I of Scotland; thus Elizabeth was the great great
great grandmother of the then king of Scotland, James IV (reigned 1488-
1513).   [2] i.e. kinships cannot be claimed.   [3] Swept away.   [4] Lover.   [5] i.e.
as elevated to.   [6] i.e. set up housekeeping.   [7] i.e. without my power to
prohibit.   [8] Proverbial; 'as you do, you shall have.'   [9] i.e. poor in fact, one
of Huntly's objections to the match.   [10] Perhaps one of the several
daughters of Archibald Douglas (1453-1514), fifth Earl of Angus.

Kath.   The king commands your presence, sir.
Hunt.   The gallant,
   This, this, this lord, this servant, Kate, of yours,
   Desires to be your master.
Kath.   I acknowledge him
   A worthy friend of mine.
Dal.   Your humblest creature.
Hunt.   [*Aside*] So, so, the game's afoot. I'm in cold hunting;
   The hare and hounds are parties.[1]
70 *Dal.*   Princely lady,
   How most unworthy I am to employ
   My services in honour of your virtues,
   How hopeless my desires are to enjoy
   Your fair opinion, and, much more, your love,
   Are only matter of despair, unless
   Your goodness give large warrant to my boldness,
   My feeble-wing'd ambition.
Hunt.   [*Aside*]   This is scurvy.
Kath.   My lord, I interrupt you not.
Hunt.   [*Aside*]   Indeed?
   Now, on my life, she'll court him. — Nay, nay, on, sir.
80 *Dal.*   Oft have I tun'd[2] the lesson of my sorrows
   To sweeten discord and enrich your pity,
   But all in vain. Here had my comforts sunk
   And never ris'n again to tell a story
   Of the despairing lover, had not now,
   Even now, the Earl your father, —
Hunt.   [*Aside*]   'A means me, sure.
Dal.   After some fit disputes[3] of your condition,
   Your highness and my lowness, giv'n[4] a licence
   Which did not more embolden than encourage
   My faulting tongue.
Hunt.   How? How? How's that? Embolden?
90   Encourage? I encourage ye? D'ee hear, sir?
   A subtle trick, a quaint[5] one! Will you hear, man?
   What did I say to you? Come, come, to th' point.
Kath.   It shall not need, my Lord.
Hunt.   Then hear me, Kate.
   Keep you on that hand of her, I on this.
   Thou stand'st between a father and a suitor,
   Both striving for an interest in thy heart.
   He courts thee for affection, I for duty;
   He as a servant[6] pleads, but by the privilege
   Of nature, though I might command, my care
100   Shall only counsel what it shall not force.

[1] In league. [2] Modulated. [3] Debates. [4] i.e. has given. [5] Crafty. [6] Lover.

Thou canst but make one choice; the ties of marriage
Are tenures[1] not at will but during life.
Consider whose thou art and who: a princess,
A princess of the royal blood of Scotland,
In the full spring of youth and fresh in beauty.
The king that sits upon the throne is young
And yet unmarried,[2] forward in attempts
On any least occasion to endanger
His person. Wherefore, Kate, as I am confident
10   Thou dar'st not wrong thy birth and education
By yielding to a common servile rage
Of female wantonness, so I am confident
Thou wilt proportion all thy thoughts to side[3]
Thy equals, if not equal thy superiors.
My Lord of Dalyell, young in years, is old
In honours, but nor eminent in titles
Or in estate, that may support or add to
The expectation of thy fortunes. Settle
Thy will and reason by a strength of judgment;
20   For, in a word, I give thee freedom. Take it.
If equal[4] Fates have not ordain'd to pitch
Thy hopes above my height, let not thy passion
Lead thee to shrink mine honour in oblivion.
Thou art thine own. I have done.

Dal.   Oh, y'are all oracle,
The living stock and root of truth and wisdom.

Kath.   My worthiest lord and father, the indulgence[5]
Of your sweet composition[6] thus commands
The lowest of obedience. You have granted
A liberty so large that I want skill
30   To choose without direction of example,
From which I daily learn by how much more
You take off from the roughness of a father
By so much more I am engag'd to tender
The duty of a daughter. For respects
Of[7] birth, degrees of title, and advancement,
I nor admire nor slight them. All my studies
Shall ever aim at this perfection only,
To live and die so that you may not blush
In any course of mine to own me yours.

40 *Hunt.*   Kate, Kate, thou grow'st upon my heart like peace,
Creating every other hour a jubilee.[8]

Kath.   To you, my Lord of Dalyell, I address

---

[1] Claims. [2] James IV married Margaret, daughter of Henry VII, in 1503.
[3] Match. [4] Impartial. [5] Forbearance. [6] Nature. [7] With regard to. [8] An occasion for rejoicing.

Some few remaining words: The general fame
That speaks your merit, even in vulgar[1] tongues
Proclaims it clear; but in the best, a precedent.[2]

Hunt.   Good wench, good girl, i' faith.

Kath.   For my part, trust me,
I value mine own worth at higher rate
'Cause you are pleas'd to prize it. If the stream
Of your protested[3] service, as you term it,
150   Run in a constancy more than a compliment,
It shall be my delight that worthy love
Leads you to worthy actions, and these guide ye
Richly to wed an honourable name;[4]
So every virtuous praise in after ages
Shall be your heir,[5] and I in your brave mention[6]
Be chronicl'd the mother[7] of that issue,
That glorious issue.

Hunt.   Oh, that I were young again!
She'd make me court proud danger and suck spirit[8]
From reputation.[9]

Kath.   To the present motion[10]
160   Here's all that I dare answer: When a ripeness
Of more experience and some use of time
Resolves to treat[11] the freedom of my youth
Upon exchange of troths, I shall desire
No surer credit of a match with virtue
Than such as lives in you. Meantime my hopes are
Preserv'd secure in having you a friend.

Dal.   You are a blessed lady, and instruct
Ambition not to soar a farther flight
Than in the perfum'd air of your soft voice.
170   My noble Lord of Huntly, you have lent
A full extent of bounty to this parley,
And for it shall command your humblest servant.

Hunt.   Enough. We are still friends and will continue
A hearty love. O Kate, thou art mine own —
No more. My Lord of Crawford.[12]

Enter Crawford

Craw.   From the king

---

[1] Vernacular.   [2] Model.   [3] Solemnly affirmed.   [4] i.e. in military or other
fame. These lines are metaphorical.   [5] Shall be descended from you.   [6] In
records of you and your bravery.   [7] i.e. the inspirer.   [8] Vitality.   [9] i.e. a
reputation for valour.   [10] Proposal.   [11] Bargain.   [12] John Lindsay, sixth
Earl of Crawford; married Mariot, a daughter of Alexander, Lord Home,
in 1493. Crawford was killed at the Battle of Flodden, 1513.

                    I come, my Lord of Huntly, who in council
                    Requires your present aid.
Hunt.   Some weighty business?
Craw.   A secretary from a Duke of York,
                    The second son to the late English Edward,
180   Conceal'd I know not where these fourteen years,[1]
                    Craves audience from our master; and 'tis said
                    The Duke himself[2] is following to the court.
Hunt.   Duke upon duke; 'tis well, 'tis well. Here's bustling[3]
                    For majesty. My Lord, I will along with ye.
Craw.   My service, noble lady.
Kath.   [*To* Dalyell]   Please ye walk,[4] sir?
Dal.   [*Aside*]   Times have their changes, sorrow makes men wise;
                    The sun itself must set as well as rise.
                    Then why not I? – Fair madam, I wait on ye.

                                                                Exeunt omnes.

[ACT I SCENE 3]

[The Tower of London]
Enter Durham, Sir Robert Clifford,[5] *and* Urswick   *Lights*

Durham.   You find, Sir Robert Clifford, how securely[6]
                    King Henry, our great master, doth commit
                    His person to your loyalty. You taste
                    His bounty and his mercy even in this,
                    That, at a time of night so late, a place
                    So private as his closet, he is pleas'd
                    To admit you to his favour. Do not falter
                    In your discovery,[7] but as you covet
                    A liberal grace and pardon for your follies,
10   So labour to deserve it by laying open
                    All plots, all persons, that contrive against it.
Urs.   Remember not the witchcraft or the magic,
                    The charms and incantations, which the sorceress
                    Of Burgundy hath cast upon your reason.

---

[1] i.e. since his incarceration in the Tower of London, 1483; more accurately, twelve years have passed.   [2] In fact, Perkin Warbeck.   [3] Contention.   [4] Step in.   [5] Not all of Clifford's activities are known, but he appears to have been a Yorkist sympathizer whom Henry bribed to prove information about rebels and traitors. Clifford may have had private motives for his denunciation of Sir William Stanley (I, iii, 84-122).   [6] Confidently.   [7] Revelation.

Sir Robert, be your own friend now; discharge
Your conscience freely. All of such as love you
Stand sureties for your honesty and truth.
Take heed you do not dally with the king;
He is wise as he is gentle.

Cliff.   I am miserable
If Henry be not merciful.

20 *Urs.*   The king comes.

Enter King Henry

Henry.   Clifford!
Cliff.   Let my weak knees rot on the earth
If I appear as leprous in my treacheries
Before your royal eyes, as to mine own
I seem a monster by my breach of truth.
Henry.   Clifford, stand up. For instance[1] of thy safety,
I offer thee my hand.
Cliff.   A sovereign balm
For my bruis'd soul, I kiss it with a greediness.
Sir, you are a just master, but I –
Henry.   Tell me,
Is every circumstance thou hast set down
30   With thine own hand within this paper true?
Is it a sure intelligence of all
The progress of our enemies' intents
Without corruption?
Cliff.   True, as I wish Heaven,
Or my infected honour white again.
Henry.   We know all, Clifford, fully, since this meteor,[2]
This airy apparition, first discradl'd
From Tournay into Portugal, and thence
Advanc'd his fiery blaze for adoration
To th' superstitious Irish. Since[3] the beard[4]
40   Of this wild comet, conjur'd into France,
Sparkl'd in antic flames in Charles[5] his court,
But, shrunk again from thence and hid in darkness,
Stole into Flanders, flourishing the rags
Of painted[6] power on the shore of Kent,
Whence he was beaten back with shame and scorn,
Contempt, and slaughter of some naked outlaws.
But tell, me, what new course now shapes Duke Perkin?
Cliff.   For Ireland, mighty Henry; so instructed

---

[1]Token.   [2]i.e. Warbeck.   [3]Then.   [4]Tail.   [5]King Charles VIII of France;
see I, i, 109-10.   [6]Pretended.

By Stephen Frion,[1] sometimes[2] secretary
50   In the French tongue unto your sacred excellence,
But Perkin's tutor now.
Henry.   A subtle villain
That Frion! Frion – you, my Lord of Durham,
Knew well the man.
Durham.   French both in heart and actions!
Henry.   Some Irish heads work in this mine of treason.
Speak[3] 'em.
Cliff.   Not any of the best. Your fortune
Hath dull'd their spleens.[4] Never had counterfeit
Such a confus'd rabble of lost bankrupts
For counsellors. First, Heron,[5] a broken mercer;
Then John a-Water,[6] sometimes mayor of Cork;
60   Skelton,[7] a tailor; and a scrivener
Call'd Astley.[8] And whate'er these list of treat of
Perkin must hearken to; but Frion, cunning
Above these dull capacities, still prompts him
To fly to Scotland to young James the Fourth,
And sue for aid to him. This is the latest
Of all their resolutions.
Henry.   Still more Frion!
Pestilent adder, he will hiss out poison
As dang'rous as infections. We must match 'em.
Clifford, thou hast spoke home; we give thee life.
70   But, Clifford, there are people of our own
Remain behind untold.[9] Who are they, Clifford?
Name those, and we are friends, and will to rest.
'Tis thy last task.
Cliff.   Oh, sir, here I must break
A most unlawful oath to keep a just one.[10]
Henry.   Well, well, be brief, be brief.
Cliff.   The first in rank
Shall be John Ratcliffe, Lord Fitzwater,[11] then

[1] French secretary to Henry VII until 1489; in the service of Charles VIII of
France until, with Charles's encouragement, he took up the cause of Warbeck
about 1492.   [2] Sometime, formerly.   [3] Describe.   [4] Mirth.   [5] Fled London
after bankruptcy, joined Warbeck in 1497, but disappeared from history
about the time of Warbeck's capture.   [6] Or John Walters, mayor of Cork
1494-5 and 1499; one of the major manipulators of Warbeck, he was
arrested in 1499 and hanged, with Warbeck, in the same year.   [7] Edward or
Richard Skelton, captured with Warbeck at Beaulieu, but later released.
[8] Nicholas or John Astley; evidently only briefly associated with
Warbeck. Like Skelton, taken at Beaulieu and freed.   [9] Not counted.
[10] i.e. break my oath to the rebels in order to keep my oath of loyalty
to you.   [11] Or Fitzwalter (*c.* 1452-96), High Steward of England
until he joined Warbeck. Captured, then imprisoned in Calais, he was
beheaded after an attempt to escape.

Sir Simon Mountford[1] and Sir Thomas Thwaites,[2]
With William Daubeney,[3] Cressoner,[4] Astwood,[5]
Worsley, the Dean of Paul's,[6] two other friars,
And Robert Ratcliffe.[7]

80 *Henry.*   Churchmen are turn'd devils!
These are the principal?

Cliff.   One more remains
Unnam'd, whom I could willingly forget.

Henry.   Ha, Clifford! One more?

Cliff.   Great sir, do not hear him;[8]
For when Sir William Stanley, your Lord Chamberlain,
Shall come into the list, as he is chief,
I shall lose credit with ye; yet this lord,
Last nam'd, is first against you.

Henry.   Urswick, the light!
View well my face, sirs; is there blood left in it?

Durham.   You alter strangely, sir.

Henry.   Alter, Lord Bishop?
90 Why, Clifford stabb'd me, or I dream'd 'a stabb'd me.
Sirrah, it is a custom with the guilty
To think they set their own stains off by laying
Aspersions on some nobler than themselves.
Lies wait on[9] treasons, as I find it here.
Thy life again is forfeit. I recall
My word of mercy, for I know thou dar'st
Repeat the name no more.

Cliff.   I dare, and once more
Upon my knowledge name Sir William Stanley,
Both in his counsel and his purse, the chief
100 Assistant to the feigned Duke of York.

Durham.   Most strange!

Urs.   Most wicked!

Henry.   Yet again, once more.

Cliff.   Sir William Stanley is your secret enemy,

---

[1] Yorkist, from Staffordshire. Arrested in 1494 and beheaded in January 1495.   [2] Also arrested in 1494 and apparently hanged early in the next year.   [3] Briefly associated with Warbeck, he was captured and beheaded in 1495.   [4] Thomas Cressoner, arrested in 1494, but he seems to have escaped execution by virtue of his youth.   [5] Thomas Astwood, condemned as a traitor in 1494, reprieved because of his youth. Implicated (1499) in an attempted escape of Warbeck and Warwick, he was sentenced to hang, but his fate is unclear.   [6] William Worsley (*c.* 1435-99), arrested as a conspirator against the state in 1494, was pardoned by virtue of his religious status. The friars were also freed.   [7] A little known Yorkist, he was arrested in 1494 and beheaded in 1495. The men whom Clifford named here represent only a partial list of Yorkist or Warbeck sympathizers.   [8] i.e. do not hear him named.   [9] Accompany.

And, if time fit, will openly profess it.
Henry.   Sir William Stanley! Who? Sir William Stanley,
My chamberlain, my counsellor, the love,
The pleasure of my court, my bosom friend,
The charge[1] and the controlment of my person,
The keys and secrets of my treasury,
The all of all I am. I am unhappy.
110   Misery of confidence! Let me turn traitor
To mine own person, yield my sceptre up
To Edward's sister[2] and her bastard duke.
Durham.   You lose your constant temper.
Henry.   Sir William Stanley!
Oh, do not blame me. He, 'twas only he
Who, having rescu'd me in Bosworth Field
From Richard's bloody sword, snatch'd from his head
The kingly crown and plac'd it first on mine.[3]
He never fail'd me. What have I deserv'd
To lose this good man's heart, or he his own?
120   *Urs.*   The night doth waste. This passion ill becomes ye.
Provide against your danger.
Henry.   Let it be so.
Urswick, command straight Stanley to his chamber.
'Tis well we are i' th' Tower. Set a guard on him.
Clifford, to bed; you must lodge here tonight.
We'll talk with you tomorrow. My sad soul
Divines strange troubles.
Daub.   [*Within*]   Ho, the king, the king!
I must have entrance.
Henry.   Daubeney's voice. Admit him.
What new combustions huddle next to keep
Our eyes from rest?

Enter Daubeney

                         The news?
Daub.   Ten thousand Cornish,
Grudging to pay your subsidies,[4] have gather'd

---

[1] i.e. having the responsibility....   [2] Margaret of Burgundy.   [3] Historically,
it was William's brother Thomas, Lord Stanley, who performed this deed,
although, unlike Sir William, he had taken no active part in the battle.
[4] Most of the events in this scene took place in 1495; however, these
special taxes were first imposed on the English people in 1497, prompting
the Cornish uprising in May and June of that year. The rebels were defeated
at the Battle of Blackhealth, near London, 18 June 1497.

            A head.[1] Led by a blacksmith[2] and a lawyer,[3]
        They make for London, and to them is join'd
        Lord Audley.[4] As they march, their number daily
        Increases. They are —
Henry.   Rascals! Talk no more.
        Such are not worthy of my thoughts tonight;
        And if I cannot sleep, I'll wake. To bed.
        When counsels fail, and there's in man no trust,
        Even then an arm from Heaven fights for the just.

                                                              Exeunt.

Finis Actus Primi.

        ACT II SCENE 1

        [*The Great Hall, Stirling Castle*]
        Enter above Countess of Crawford, Katherine, Jane, *with other
        ladies*

Countess.   Come, ladies, here's a solemn preparation
        For entertainment of this English prince.
        The king intends grace more than ordinary;
        'Twere pity now if 'a should prove a counterfeit.
Kath.   Bless the young man, our nation would be laugh'd at
        For honest[5] souls through Christendom. My father
        Hath a weak stomach to the business, madam,

---

[1] Raised a force.   [2] Michael Joseph, of Saint Keverne, Cornwall, 'a notable
talking fellow, and no less desirous to be talked of' (Bacon, p. 187). With
the lawyer (Flammock), Joseph led the Cornish rebels to Wells, where
Lord Audley took over military command, until their defeat and capture
at Blackheath. All three were executed. The bodies of Joseph and Flammock were drawn, quartered and displayed in London. Joseph's divided
remains were also displayed in Devon and Cornwall (see III, i, 99-101).
Joseph's story, in the first person, is one of the moralistic 'Tragedies'
in verse in the 1563 continuation of *The Mirror for Magistrates*, ed. L.B.
Campbell, 1938, pp.402-18. Flammock and Audley are mentioned.
[3] Thomas Flammock, or Flamank, of Bodmin, Cornwall, a persuasive
leader of the rebels.   [4] James Touchet, seventh Baron Audley, *c.* 1463-97;
'an unquiet spirit', convinced that his earlier services to the crown had
been inadequately recognized (Rowse, p. 123). Led approximately 15,000
Cornish miners and peasants to Blackheath, where 5,000 or more
deserted before the battle; captured in the field and beheaded a few days
later.   [5] Ingenuous.

But that the king must not be cross'd.
Countess.   'A brings
A goodly troop, they say, of gallants with him,
10   But very modest people, for they strive not
To fame[1] their names too much. Their godfathers
May be beholding to them, but their fathers
Scarce owe them thanks.[2] They are disguised princes,
Brought up, it seems, to honest trades. No matter;
They will break forth in season.[3]
Jane.   Or break out;[4]
For most of 'em are broken,[5] by report.

                                                              Flourish

The king!
Kath.   Let us observe 'em and be silent.

Enter King James, Huntly, Crawford, *and* Dalyell[*,with other
    noblemen*]

James.   The right of kings, my lords, extends not only
To the safe conservation of their own,
20   But also to the aid of such allies
As change of time and state hath oftentimes
Hurl'd down from careful[6] crowns, to undergo
An exercise of sufferance[7] in both fortunes.[8]
So English Richard, surnam'd Coeur-de-Lion,
So Robert Bruce, our royal ancestor,
Forc'd by the trial[9] of the wrongs they felt,
Both sought and found supplies from foreign kings[10]
To repossess their own. Then grudge not, lords,
A much distressed prince. King Charles of France
30   And Maximilian of Bohemia both
Have ratified his credit by their letters.
Shall we then be distrustful? No. Compassion
Is one rich jewel that shines in our crown,
And we will have it shine there.
Hunt.   Do your will, sir.

[1] Spread abroad.   [2] 'Their godfathers are under obligation to them for not
letting their names be widely known, but their fathers resent their attitude
towards the family name.'   [3] 'They will reveal their true identities in time.'
[4] i.e. break out of gaol.   [5] Bankrupt.   [6] Troubled.   [7] Endurance.   [8] i.e. the
fortunes of time and state.   [9] Undergoing.   [10] Richard I of England
(reigned 1189-99) and Philip II (Philip Augustus) of France (1180-1223)
had a series of agreements for mutual aid. Robert VIII (Robert Bruce,
1304-29) and Philip IV (the Fair) of France (1285-1314) arranged a
short-lived treaty of peace in 1298.

James.   The young duke is at hand. Dalyell, from us
   First greet him, and conduct him on; then Crawford
   Shall meet him next, and Huntly last of all
   Present him to our arms. Sound sprightly music,
   Whilst majesty encounters majesty.

Hautboys[1]. Dalyell *goes out, brings in* Perkin *at the door, where*
   Crawford *entertains*[2] *him, and from* Crawford, Huntly *salutes*
   him and presents him to the King. *They embrace.* Perkin, *in*
   state,[3] *retires some few paces back. During which ceremony*
   the noblemen slightly salute Frion, Heron, *a mercer,* Skelton,
   a tailor, Astley, *a scrivener, with* John a-Water, *all* Perkin's
   followers.[4] *Salutations ended, cease music*

40 *Warb.*   Most high, most mighty king! That now there stands
   Before your eyes, in presence of your peers,
   A subject of the rarest kind of pity
   That hath in any age touch'd noble hearts,
   The vulgar[5] story of a prince's ruin
   Hath made it too apparent. Europe knows,
   And all the western world, what persecution
   Hath rag'd in malice against us, sole heir
   To the great throne of old Plantagenets;
   How from our nursery we have been hurried
50 Unto the sanctuary, from the sanctuary
   Forc'd to the prison, from the prison hal'd
   By cruel hands to the tormentor's fury,
   Is register'd already in the volume[6]
   Of all men's tongues; whose true relation[7] draws
   Compassion, melted into weeping eyes
   And bleeding souls. But our misfortunes since
   Have rang'd a larger progress through strange lands,
   Protected in our innocence by Heaven.
   Edward the Fifth, our brother, in his tragedy
60 Quench'd their hot thirst of blood, whose hire to murder
   Paid them their wages of despair and horror.
   The softness of my childhood smil'd upon
   The roughness of their task and robb'd them farther
   Of hearts to dare or hands to execute.
   Great king, they spar'd my life, the butchers spar'd it,
   Return'd the tyrant, my unnatural uncle,
   A truth[8] of my dispatch; I was convey'd

[1]Oboes. [2]Receives. [3]With formality. [4]It is not known which of
Warbeck's followers in fact accompanied him to Scotland. [5]Commonly
known. [6]Book. [7]i.e. the true relation of this volume or account. [3]An
apparent verification.

With secrecy and speed to Tournay, foster'd
By obscure means, taught to unlearn myself.[1]
70 But as I grew in years I grew in sense
Of fear and of disdain; fear of the tyrant
Whose power sway'd the throne then; when disdain
Of living so unknown, in such a servile
And abject lowness, prompted me to thoughts
Of recollecting who I was, I shook off
My bondage, and made haste to let my aunt
Of Burgundy acknowledge me her kinsman,
Heir to the crown of England, snatch'd by Henry
From Richard's head, a thing scarce known i' th' world.
80 *James.*   My Lord, it stands not with your counsel[2] now
To fly upon invectives. If you can
Make this apparent what you have discours'd
In every circumstance, we will not study
An answer, but are ready in your cause.
   Warb.   You are a wise and just king, by the powers
Above reserv'd beyond all other aids
To plant me in mine own inheritance,
To marry these two kingdoms in a love
Never to be divorc'd while time is time.
90 As for the manner, first of my escape,
Of my conveyance[3] next, of my life since,
The means and persons who were instruments,
Great sir, 'tis fit I overpass in silence,
Reserving the relation to the secrecy
Of your own princely ear, since it concerns
Some great ones living yet, and others dead,
Whose issue might be question'd. For your bounty,
Royal magnificence[4] to him that seeks it,
We vow hereafter to demean[5] ourself
100 As if we were your own and natural brother,
Omitting no occasion in our person
To express a gratitude beyond example.
   James.   He must be more than subject who can utter
The language of a king, and such is thine.
Take this for answer: Be whate'er thou art,
Thou never shalt repent that thou hast put
Thy cause and person into my protection.
Cousin of York, thus once more we embrace thee.
Welcome to James of Scotland. For[6] thy safety,
110 Know such as love thee not shall never wrong thee.
Come. We will taste awhile our court delights,

[1] To forget who I really was. [2] 'It is not appropriate to your design now.'
[3] Transference. [4] Munificence. [5] Conduct. [6] As for.

Dream hence[1] afflictions past, and then proceed
To high attempts of honour. On, lead on.
Both thou and thine are ours, and we will guard ye.
Lead on.

Exeunt. Manent ladies above

Countess.   I have not seen a gentleman
Of a more brave aspect or goodlier carriage.
His fortunes move not him[2] – Madam, y'are passionate.[3]
Kath.   Beshrew me, but his words have touch'd me home,
As if his cause concern'd me. I should pity him
120   If 'a should prove another than he seems.

Enter Crawford

Craw.   Ladies, the king commands your presence instantly
For entertainment of the duke.
Kath.   The duke
Must then be entertain'd, the king obey'd.
It is our duty.
Countess.   We will all wait on him.

Exeunt.

[ACT II SCENE 2]

[*The Tower of London*]
Flourish. Enter King Henry, Oxford, Durham, Surrey

Henry.   Have ye condemn'd my chamberlain?
Durham.   His treasons
Condemn'd him, sir, which were as clear and manifest
As foul and dangerous. Besides, the guilt
Of his conspiracy press'd him so nearly[4]
That it drew from him free confession
Without an importunity.
Henry.   Oh, Lord Bishop,
This argu'd shame and sorrow for his folly,
And must not stand in evidence against
Our mercy and the softness of our nature.
10   The rigour and extremity of law

[1] Away.   [2] His mishaps do not affect him.   [3] Grieved.   [4] Closely.

Is sometimes too, too bitter, but we carry
A chancery[1] of pity in our bosom.
I hope we may reprieve him from the sentence
Of death; I hope we may.
Durham.   You may, you may;
And so persuade your subjects that the title
Of York is better, nay, more just and lawful
Than yours of Lancaster. So Stanley holds;
Which, if it be not treason in the highest,
Then we are traitors all, perjur'd and false,
20   Who have took oath to Henry and the justice
Of Henry's title – Oxford, Surrey, Daubeney,
With all your other peers of state and church,
Forsworn, and Stanley true alone to Heaven,
And England's lawful heir.
Oxford.   By Vere's old honours,
I'll cut his throat dares speak it.
Surrey.   'Tis a quarrel
T'engage a soul in.
Henry.   What a coil is here
To keep my gratitude sincere and perfect!
Stanley was once my friend and came in time
To save my life; yet, to say truth, my lords,
30   The man stay'd[2] long enough t'endanger it.
But I could see no more into his heart
Than what his outward actions did present;
And for 'em have rewarded him so fully,
As that there wanted nothing in our gift
To gratify his merit, as I thought,
Unless I should divide my crown with him
And give him half; though now I well perceive
'Twould scarce have serv'd his turn without the whole.
But I am charitable, lords; let justice
40   Proceed in execution,[3] whiles I mourn
The loss of one whom I esteem'd a friend.
Durham.   Sir, he is coming this way.
Henry.   If 'a speak to me
I could deny him nothing. To prevent it,
I must withdraw. Pray, lords, commend my favours[4]
To his last peace, which I with him will pray for.
That done, it doth concern us to consult
Of other following troubles.

                                              Exit.

---

[1] High court of equity.   [2] Delayed.   [3] 'Let justice be fulfilled.'   [4] Present my
good will.

Oxford.   I am glad
    He's gone. Upon my life, he would have pardon'd
    The traitor had 'a seen him.
Surrey.   'Tis a king
    Compos'd of gentleness.
50 *Durham.*   Rare and unheard of.
    But every man is nearest to himself,[1]
    And that the king observes; 'tis fit 'a should.

    Enter Stanley, *executioner,* Urswick, Daubeney [*,and priest*]

Stan.   May I not speak with Clifford ere I shake
    This piece of frailty off?
Daub.   You shall. He's sent for.
Stan.   I must not see the king?
Durham.   From him, Sir William,
    These lords and I am sent; he bade us say
    That he commends his mercy[2] to your thoughts,
    Wishing the laws of England could remit
    The forfeit of your life as willingly
60 As he would, in the sweetness of his nature,
    Forget your trespass; but howe'er your body
    Fall into dust, he vows — the king himself
    Doth vow — to keep a requiem for your soul,
    As for a friend close treasur'd in his bosom.
Oxford.   Without remembrance of your errors past,
    I come to take my leave and wish you Heaven.
Surrey.   And I. Good angels guard ye.
Stan.   Oh, the king,
    Next to my soul, shall be the nearest subject
    Of my last prayers. My grave Lord of Durham,
70 My Lords of Oxford, Surrey, Daubeney, all,
    Accept from a poor dying man a farewell.
    I was, as you are, once — great, and stood hopeful
    Of many flourishing years, but fate and time
    Have wheel'd about, to turn me into nothing.

    Enter Clifford

Daub.   Sir Robert Clifford comes, the man, Sir William,
    You so desire to speak with.
Durham.   Mark their meeting.
Cliff.   Sir William Stanley, I am glad your conscience
    Before your end hath emptied every burden
    Which charg'd it, as that[3] you can clearly witness

---

[1] i.e. is motivated by self-interest.   [2] Compassion.   [3] Because.

80   How far I have proceeded in a duty
        That both concern'd my truth and the state's safety.
    Stan.   Mercy, how dear is life to such as hug it!
        Come hither. By this token think on me –

    Makes a cross on Clifford's *face with his finger*

    Cliff.   This token? What! I am abus'd!
    Stan.   You are not.
        I wet upon your cheeks a holy sign,
        The cross, the Christian's badge, the traitor's infamy.[1]
        Wear, Clifford, to thy grave this painted emblem.
        Water shall never wash it off; all eyes
        That gaze upon thy face shall read there written
90   A state-informer's character, more ugly
        Stamp'd on a noble name than on a base.
        The heavens forgive thee. Pray, my lords, no change[2]
        Of words; this man and I have us'd too many.
    Cliff.   Shall I be disgrac'd
        Without reply?
    Durham.   Give losers leave to talk;[3]
        His loss is irrecoverable.
    Stan.   Once more
        To all a long farewell; the best of greatness[4]
        Preserve the king. My next suit is, my lords,
        To be remember'd to my noble brother,
100   Derby,[5] my much grieved brother. Oh, persuade him
        That I shall stand no blemish to his house
        In chronicles writ in another age.
        My heart doth bleed for him and for his sighs.
        Tell him he must not think the style[6] of Derby,
        Nor being husband to King Henry's mother,
        The league with peers, the smiles of fortune, can
        Secure his peace above the state of man.[7]
        I take my leave, to travel to my dust.
        Subjects deserve their deaths whose kings are just.

---

[1] Crucifixion was used on occasion in Roman times to punish treason.
[2] Exchange. [3] A proverbial phrase; cf. Middleton, *A Trick to Catch the Old One*, IV, iv, 163. [4] i.e. God. [5] Thomas, Lord Stanley (*c.* 1435-1504), a supporter of Richard III, but abandoned him previous to the Battle of Bosworth Field, 1485. Although Stanley had married Henry Tudor's twice widowed mother, Margaret Beaufort, Countess of Richmond, in 1483, he took no part in the battle, but afterward placed the crown on Henry's head. Stanley was soon created Earl of Derby and held many high offices. [6] Title. [7] Beyond the ordinary state or hopes of man.

110   Come, confessor. On with thy axe, friend, on.[1]

> *Exeunt* [Stanley, *priest, executioner*].

Cliff.   Was I call'd hither by a traitor's breath
       To be upbraided? Lords, the king shall know it.

Enter King Henry *with a white staff*[2]

Henry.   The king doth know it, sir; the king hath heard
       What he or you could say. We have given credit
       To every point of Clifford's information,
       The only evidence 'gainst Stanley's head.
       'A dies for't; are you pleas'd?
Cliff.   I pleas'd, my Lord?
Henry.   No echoes. For your service, we dismiss
       Your more attendance on the court. Take ease
120   And live at home; but, as you love your life,
       Stir not from London without leave from us.
       We'll think on your reward.[3] Away!
Cliff.   I go, sir.

> *Exit.*

Henry.   Die all our griefs with Stanley! Take this staff
       Of office, Daubeney. Henceforth be our chamberlain.
Daub.   I am your humblest servant.
Henry.   We are follow'd
       By enemies at home that will not cease
       To seek their own confusion. 'Tis most true
       The Cornish under Audley are march'd on
       As far as Winchester; but let them come,
130   Our forces are in readiness. We'll catch 'em
       In their own toils.
Daub.   Your army, being muster'd,
       Consist in all, of horse and foot, at least
       In number six and twenty thousand;[4] men
       Daring and able, resolute to fight,
       And loyal in their truths.

---

[1] Sir William Stanley was executed 16 February 1495; the Cornish rebels did not march to Winchester (lines 128-9 below) until June 1497. [2] A symbol of office; see lines 123-4. [3] He received £500. [4] Probably no more than ten thousand of Henry's troops fought at Blackheath.

Henry.   We know it, Daubeney.
   For them we order thus: Oxford in chief,
   Assisted by bold Essex[1] and the Earl
   Of Suffolk,[2] shall lead on the first battalia.[3]
   [*To* Oxford]   Be that your charge.
Oxford.   I humbly thank Your Majesty.
140 *Henry.*   The next division we assign to Daubeney.
   These must be men of action, for on those
   The fortune of our fortunes must rely.
   The last and main ourself commands in person,
   As ready to restore[4] the fight at all times
   As to consummate an assured victory.
Daub.   The king is still oraculous.[5]
Henry.   But, Surrey,
   We have employment of more toil for thee.
   For our intelligence comes swiftly to us
   That James of Scotland late hath entertain'd
150   Perkin the counterfeit with more than common
   Grace and respect; nay, courts him with rare favours.
   The Scot is young and forward; we must look for
   A sudden storm to England from the north,
   Which to withstand, Durham shall post to Norham[6]
   To fortify the castle and secure
   The frontiers against an invasion there.
   Surrey shall follow soon, with such an army
   As may relieve the bishop and encounter
   On all occasions the death-daring Scots.
160   You know your charges all; 'tis now a time
   To execute, not talk. Heaven is our guard still.
   War must breed peace; such is the fate of kings.

                                     Exeunt.

---

[1] Henry Bourchier, second Earl of Essex, d. 1539. Member of Henry's privy council; led a detachment at Blackheath. [2] Edmund de la Pole (1472-1513), brother of John de la Pole, Earl of Lincoln (I, i, 91). Both were Yorkists, but Edmund contributed to Henry's victory at Blackheath; he was later disloyal to Henry VII and was executed by Henry VIII.
[3] A battalion. [4] Renew. [5] Divinely inspired. [6] A town on the English-Scottish border, seven miles south-west of Berwick.

[ACT II SCENE 3]

[Stirling Castle]
Enter Crawford *and* Dalyell

Craw.   'Tis more than strange. My reason cannot answer
Such argument of fine imposture, couch'd
In witchcraft of persuasion, that it[1] fashions
Impossibilities, as if appearance
Could cozen truth itself; this dukeling mushroom
Hath doubtless charm'd[2] the king.
Dal.   'A courts the ladies
As if his strength of language chain'd attention
By power of prerogative.[3]
Craw.   It madded
10   My very soul to hear our master's motion:
What surety both of amity and honour
Must of necessity ensue upon
A match betwixt some noble of our nation
And this brave prince, forsooth!
Dal.   'Twill prove too fatal;
Wise Huntly fears the threat'ning. Bless the lady
From such a ruin!
Craw.   How the council privy
Of this young Phaethon[4] do screw their faces
Into a gravity their trades, good people,
Were never guilty of![5] The meanest of 'em
Dreams of at least an office in the state.
20 *Dal.*   Sure, not the hangman's; 'tis bespoke already
For service to their rogueships. Silence.

Enter King James *and* Huntly

James.   Do not
Argue against our will; we have descended[6]
Somewhat, as we may term it, too familiarly
From justice of our birthright, to examine
The force of your allegiance; sir, we have;
But find it short of duty.
Hunt.   Break my heart,

---

[1] The argument.   [2] Bewitched.   [3] Natural right.   [4] Son of Helios, the sun-god, who allowed him to drive the chariot of the sun for a day. Phaethon lost control of the horses, coming dangerously close to the earth, where-upon Zeus killed him with a thunderbolt.   [5] See II, i, 9-14, above.
[6] Condescended.

Do, do, king. Have my services, my loyalty —
Heaven knows, untainted ever — drawn upon me
Contempt now in mine age, when I but wanted
30   A minute of a peace not to be troubl'd,
My last, my long one? Let me be a dotard,
A bedlam, a poor sot, or what you please
To have me, so you will not stain your blood,
Your own blood, royal sir, though mix'd with mine,
By marriage of this girl to a straggler.[1]
Take, take my head, sir. Whilst my tongue can wag
It cannot name him other.

James.   Kings are counterfeits
In your repute,[2] grave oracle, not presently[3]
Set on their thrones with sceptres in their fists.
40   But use your own detraction.[4] 'Tis our pleasure
To give our cousin[5] York for wife our kinswoman,
The Lady Katherine. Instinct of sovereignty[6]
Designs the honour, though her peevish father
Usurps[7] our resolution.

Hunt.   Oh, 'tis well,
Exceeding well! I never was ambitious
Of using congees[8] to my daughter-queen;
A queen, perhaps a quean.[9] Forgive me, Dalyell,
Thou honourable gentleman. None here
Dare speak one word of comfort?

Dal.   Cruel misery!
50 *Craw.*   The lady, gracious prince, maybe hath settl'd
Affection on some former choice.

Dal.   Enforcement
Would prove but tyranny.

Hunt.   I thank 'ee heartily!
Let any yeoman of our nation challenge
An interest in the girl, then the king
May add a jointure[10] of ascent[11] in titles,
Worthy a free consent. Now 'a pulls down
What old desert hath builded.

James.   Cease persuasions.
I violate no pawns[12] of faiths, intrude not
On private loves. That I have play'd the orator[13]

---

[1] Vagabond.   [2] Opinion.   [3] i.e. if they are not currently.   [4] Disparagement.
[5] A casual, familiar form of address or reference.   [6] i.e. my instinct for
Warbeck's royal blood.   [7] Encroaches upon.   [8] Bows.   [9] Harlot.   [10] Dowry.
[11] A going back in genealogical succession. Huntly bitterly states that the
genealogy of any yeoman after the king has arbitrarily ennobled him might
be more worthy than Warbeck's present claims in prompting Huntly's
consent to Katherine's marriage.   [12] Pledges.   [13] Spokesman.

60 For kingly York to virtuous Kate, her grant[1]
    Can justify, referring her contents[2]
    To our provision. The Welsh Harry[3] henceforth
    Shall therefore know, and tremble to acknowledge,
    That not the painted idol of his policy
    Shall fright the lawful owner from a kingdom.
    We are resolv'd.
Hunt.   Some of thy subjects' hearts,
    King James, will bleed for this.
James.   Then shall their bloods
    Be nobly spent. No more disputes; he is not
    Our friend who contradicts us.
Hunt.   Farewell, daughter.
70 My care by one is lessen'd. Thank the king for't.
    I and my griefs will dance now.

    Enter Warbeck *leading* Katherine, *complimenting;*[4] Countess of
        Crawford, Jane, Frion, Mayor of Cork,[5] Astley, Heron *and* Skelton

                            Look, lords, look;
    Here's hand in hand already.
James.   Peace, old frenzy.
    How like a king 'a looks! Lords, but observe
    The confidence of his aspect. Dross cannot
    Cleave to so pure a metal. Royal youth!
    Plantagenet undoubted!
Hunt.   [*Aside*]   Ho, brave youth![6]
    But no Plantagenet, by'r Lady, yet,
    By red rose or by white![7]
Warb.   An union this way
    Settles possession in a monarchy[8]
80 Establish'd rightly, as is my inheritance.
    Acknowledge me but sovereign of this kingdom,
    Your heart, fair princess, and the hand of Providence
    Shall crown you queen of me and my best fortunes.
Kath.   Where my obedience is, my lord, a duty,
    Love owes true service.
Warb.   Shall I?
James.   Cousin, yes;
    Enjoy her. From my hand accept your bride;

---

[1] Consent. [2] Satisfaction. [3] i.e. Henry VII, grandson of Owen Tudor, a
Welshman. [4] Formally courteous. [5] John a-Water. [6] So other modern
editions; 'Ho brave lady!' Q. [7] i.e. he has no claim to the throne either
through the Lancastrian line (the red rose) or the Yorkist (white). For
the apocryphal episode of the plucking of the roses, see *1 Henry VI*,
II, iv, 30-76. [8] i.e. of romance or love.

And may they live at enmity with comfort
Who grieve at such an equal pledge of troths.
Y'are the prince's wife now.
Kath.   By your gift, sir.
Warb.   Thus I take seizure of mine own.
90 *Kath.*   I miss yet
A father's blessing. Let me find it. Humbly
Upon my knees I seek it.
Hunt.   I am Huntly,
Old Alexander Gordon,[1] a plain subject,
Nor more nor less; and, lady, if you wish for
A blessing, you must bend your knees to Heaven,
For Heaven did give me you. Alas, alas,
What would you have me say? May all the happiness
My prayers ever sued to fall upon you
Preserve you in your virtues. Prithee, Dalyell,
100 Come with me, for I feel thy griefs as full
As mine. Let's steal away and cry together.
Dal.   My hopes are in their ruins.

Exeunt Huntly *and* Dalyell.

James.   Good kind Huntly
Is overjoy'd! A fit solemnity
Shall perfect these delights. Crawford, attend
Our order for the preparation.

Exeunt. Manent Frion, Mayor [of Cork], Astley, Heron *and* Skelton

Frion.   Now, worthy gentlemen, have I not follow'd
My undertakings with success? Here's entrance
Into a certainty above a hope.
Heron.   Hopes are but hopes; I was ever confident, when I traded
110 but in remnants,[2] that my stars had reserved me to the title
of a viscount at least. Honour is honour, though cut out of any stuffs.

Skel.   My brother Heron hath right wisely delivered his opinion
for he that threads his needle with the sharp eyes of industry
shall in time go through-stitch[3] with the new suit of preferment.
preferment.
Astley.   Spoken to the purpose, my fine-witted brother Skelton;

---

[1] In fact, George Gordon. Alexander was his father's name. The error
appeared in Ford's sources. [2] He was formerly a mercer, a dealer in
fabrics. [3] A stitch drawn completely through the material. (Skelton
had been a tailor.)

for as no indenture but has its counterpawn,[1] no *noverint*[2]
but his condition or defeasance,[3] so no right but may have
claim, no claim but may have possession, any act of parliament
to the contrary notwithstanding.

120 *Frion.*   You are all read in mysteries of state,
  And quick of apprehension, deep in judgment,
  Active in resolution; and 'tis pity
  Such counsel should lie buried in obscurity.
  But why in such a time and cause of triumph
  Stands the judicious mayor of Cork so silent?
  Believe it, sir, as English Richard[4] prospers,
  You must not miss employment of high nature.

a-Water.   If men may be credited in their mortality,[5] which
  I dare not peremptorily aver but they may or not be,
130   presumptions by this marriage are then, in sooth, of fruitful
  expectation. Or else I must not justify[6] other men's belief
  more than other should rely on mine.

Frion.   Pith of experience! Those that have borne office
  Weigh every word before it can drop from them.
  But, noble counsellors, since now the present
  Requires in point of honour — pray, mistake not —[7]
  Some service to our lord, 'tis fit the Scots
  Should not engross all glory to themselves
  At this so grand and eminent solemnity.

140 *Skel.*   The Scots! The motion is defied. I had rather, for my
  part, without trial of my country,[8] suffer persecution under
  the pressing-iron of reproach, or let my skin be punched full
  of oylett[9] holes with the bodkin of derision.

Astley.   I will sooner lose both my ears on the pillory of forgery.

Heron.   Let me first live a bankrupt, and die in a lousy Hole[10]
  of hunger, without compounding[11] for sixpence in the pound.

a-Water.   If men fail not in their expectations, there may be
  spirits also that disgest[12] no rude affronts, Master Secretary
  Frion, or I am cozen'd; which is possible, I grant.

150 *Frion.*   Resolv'd like men of knowledge. At this feast, then,
  In honour of the bride, the Scots, I know,
  Will in some show, some masque, or some device,
  Prefer their duties.[13] Now it were uncomely
  That we be found less forward for our prince

---

[1] A contract was cut irregularly so that one part was clearly the counterpart
of the other.   [2] A writ beginning *noverint universi* ('let all know').   [3] Nullifying clause.   [4] i.e. Warbeck, in his role of Richard, Duke of York.   [5] i.e. if
mortal men may be believed.   [6] Defend.   [7] 'Do not take offence at my use
of the word honour.'   [8] i.e. trial by jury.   [9] i.e. eyelet.   [10] A particularly
unpleasant part of the Counter, a debtors' prison, Wood Street, London.
See Middleton, *A Trick to Catch the Old One*, IV, iii, 21-2.   [11] Coming to
terms.   [12] Digest.   [13] Present their respect.

Than they are for their lady; and by how much
We outshine them in[1] persons of account,
By so much more will our endeavours meet with
A livelier applause. Great emperors
Have for their recreations undertook
60   Such kind of pastimes. As for the conceit,[2]
Refer it to my study; the performance
You all shall share a thanks in – 'twill be grateful.
Heron.   The motion is allowed. I have stole to a dancing-school
when I was a prentice.
Astley.   There have been Irish hubbubs, when I have made one too.
Skel.   For fashioning of shapes[3] and cutting a cross-caper, turn
me off to my trade again.
a-Water.   Surely there is, if I be not deceiv'd, a kind of
gravity in merriment; as there is, or perhaps ought to be,
70   respect of persons in the quality of carriage, which is, as it
is construed, either so, or so.[4]
Frion.   Still you come home to me;[5] upon occasion
I find you relish courtship[6] with discretion,
And such[7] are fit for statesmen of your merits.
Pray 'ee wait the prince, and in his ear acquaint him
With this design; I'll follow and direct 'ee.

Exeunt. Manet Frion

Oh the toil
Of humouring this abject scum of mankind!
Muddy-brain'd peasants! Princes feel a misery
180   Beyond impartial sufferance, whose extremes
Must yield to such abettors; yet our tide
Runs smoothly without adverse winds. Run on;
Flow to a full sea. Time alone debates[8]
Quarrels forewritten in the book of fates.

Exit.

---

[1]i.e. in the attitudes of. [2]Device. [3]Designs of garments. [4]Involved
speeches like this characterize Warbeck's comrades, much impressed with
their new status. [5]Understand me. [6]Courtly manners. [7]i.e. such tastes.
[8]Diminishes.

ACT III SCENE 1

[King Henry's *palace, Westminster*]
Enter King Henry, *his gorget*[1] *on, his sword, plume of
feathers, leading-staff, and* Urswick

Henry.   How runs the time of day?
Urs.   Past ten, my Lord.
Henry.   A bloody hour will it prove to some,
        Whose disobedience, like the sons o' th'earth,[2]
        Throw[s] a defiance 'gainst the face of Heaven.
        Oxford, with Essex[3] and stout de la Pole,[4]
        Have quieted the Londoners, I hope,
        And set them safe from fear.
Urs.   They are all silent.
Henry.   From their own battlements they may behold
        St George's Fields[5] o'erspread with armed men;
10   Amongst whom our own royal standard threatens
        Confusion to opposers. We must learn
        To practise war again in time of peace,
        Or lay our crown before our subjects' feet.
        Ha, Urswick, must we not?
Urs.   The powers who seated
        King Henry on his lawful throne will ever
        Rise up in his defence.
Henry.   Rage shall not fright
        The bosom of our confidence. In Kent
        Our Cornish rebels, cozen'd of their hopes,
        Met brave resistance by that country's[5] earl,[6]

[1] Protective device for the throat, sometimes an indication of rank.   [2] The
Titans, who rebelled against their father Uranus, the deity of the sky, and
were eventually consigned to the underworld.   [3] See II, ii, 137.   [4] Edmund
de la Pole, Earl of Suffolk; see II, ii, 137-8.   [5] Then an open area near
present St George's Circus, south-east of Waterloo Station, London.   [6] i.e.
county's.   [7] George Grey (*c.* 1450-1503), second Earl of Kent and Lord
Grey of Ruthin; loyal to Henry over a long period of time, one of the
commanders at the Battle of Blackheath, 1497.

20   George Aberg'enny,[1] Cobham,[2] Poynings,[3] Guildford,[4]
      And other loyal hearts. Now, if Blackheath[5]
      Must be reserv'd the fatal tomb to swallow
      Such stiff-neck'd abjects[6] as with weary marches
      Have travell'd from their homes, their wives and children,
      To pay instead of subsidies[7] their lives,
      We may continue sovereign. Yet, Urswick,
      We'll not abate one penny what in parliament
      Hath freely been contributed. We must not;
      Money gives soul to action. Our competitor,
30   The Flemish counterfeit, with James of Scotland,
      Will prove what courage need and want[8] can nourish
      Without the food[9] of fit supplies; but, Urswick,
      I have a charm in secret that shall loose
      The witchcraft wherewith young King James is bound,
      And free it at my pleasure without bloodshed.
Urs.   Your Majesty's a wise king, sent from Heaven
      Protector of the just.
Henry.   Let dinner cheerfully
      Be serv'd in. This day of the week is ours,
      Our day of Providence, for Saturday
40   Yet never fail'd in all my undertakings
      To yield me rest at night.[10]

                                                A flourish

                        What means this warning?
      Good Fate, speak peace to Henry.

      Enter Daubeney, Oxford, *and attendants*

Daub.   Live the king,
      Triumphant in the ruin of his enemies!
Oxford.   The head of strong rebellion is cut off,

[1] George Neville (c. 1471-1535), third Baron Abergavenny; fought at
Blackheath, and had a distinguished court and military career.   [2] John
Brooke, seventh Lord Cobham, d. 1512; related by marriage to Lord
Abergavenny and cousin of Lord Audley; aided Henry at Blackheath
and elsewhere.   [3] Sir Edward Poynings, 1459-1521; diplomat, soldier,
privy councillor, Governor of Calais, Lord Deputy of Ireland.   [4] Sir
Richard Guildford (c. 1455-1506), one of Henry's most trusted
supporters; soldier, engineer, negotiator, Comptroller of the Royal
Household.   [5] The site of the impending battle was near Greenwich,
about five miles south-east of London.   [6] Outcasts.   [7] See I, iii, 130.
[8] i.e. what sort of courage that need and want.   [9] Sustenance.   [10] Henry
believed Saturday to be his lucky day. The successful Battle of Blackheath began on Saturday, 17 June 1497.

    The body hew'd in pieces.

Henry.   Daubeney, Oxford,
    Minions to noblest fortunes, how yet stands
    The comfort of your wishes?

Daub.   Briefly thus:
    The Cornish under Audley, disappointed
    Of flatter'd[1] expectation from the Kentish,
50   Your Majesty's right-trusty liegemen, flew,
    Feather'd[2] by rage and hearten'd by presumption,
    To take the field even at your palace gates,
    And face you in your chamber-royal. Arrogance
    Improv'd[3] their ignorance, for they, supposing,
    Misled by rumour, that the day of battle
    Should fall on Monday, rather brav'd your forces
    Than doubted any onset;[4] yet this morning,
    When in the dawning I by your direction
    Strove to get Deptford Strand Bridge,[5] there I found
60   Such a resistance as might show what strength
    Could make. Here arrows hail'd in showers upon us
    A full yard long at least,[6] but we prevail'd.
    My Lord of Oxford, with his fellow peers
    Environing the hill, fell fiercely on them
    On the one side, I on the other, till — great sir,
    Pardon the oversight[7] — eager of doing
    Some memorable act, I was engag'd
    Almost a prisoner, but was freed[8] as soon
    As sensible of danger. Now the fight
70   Began in heat, which quenched[9] in the blood of
    Two thousand rebels, and as many more
    Reserv'd to try[10] your mercy, have[11] return'd
    A victory with safety.

Henry.   Have we lost
    An equal number with them?

Oxford.   In the total
    Scarcely four hundred. Audley, Flammock, Joseph,
    The ringleaders of this commotion,
    Railed[12] in ropes, fit ornaments for traitors,
    Wait your determinations.

Henry.   We must pay
    Our thanks where they are only due. Oh, lords,

---

[1] Exaggerated. [2] Winged, speeded. [3] Aggravated. [4] Feared any attack.
[5] A bridge over the Ravensborne, a small tributary on the south side of the
Thames, about four miles east of London. [6] Ford's sources commented,
with some awe, on the Cornish arrows a yard in length. [7] i.e. pardon my
oversight in risking capture. [8] i.e. freed myself. [9] Quenched itself.
[10] Test. [11] i.e. and I have. [12] Tied in a row.

80   Here is no victory, nor shall our people[1]
       Conceive that we can triumph in their falls.
       Alas, poor souls! Let such as are escap'd
       Steal to the country back without pursuit.
       There's not a drop of blood split but hath drawn
       As much of mine. Their swords could have wrought wonders
       On their king's part, who[2] faintly[3] were unsheath'd
       Against their prince, but wounded their own breasts.
       Lords, we are debtors to your care; our payment
       Shall be both sure and fitting your deserts.
90 *Daub.*   Sir, will you please to see those rebels, heads
       Of this wild monster-multitude?
      Henry.   Dear friend,
       My faithful Daubeney, no. On them our justice
       Must frown in terror; I will not vouchsafe
       An eye of pity to them. Let false Audley
       Be drawn upon an hurdle[4] from the Newgate[5]
       To Tower Hill in his own coat of arms
       Painted on paper, with the arms revers'd,
       Defac'd and torn; there let him lose his head.
       The lawyer and the blacksmith[6] shall be hang'd.
100   Quarter'd, their quarters into Cornwall sent,
       Examples to the rest, whom we are pleas'd
       To pardon and dismiss from further quest.[7]
       My Lord of Oxford, see it done.
      Oxford   I shall, sir.
      Henry.   Urswick.
      Urs.   My Lord?
      Henry.   To Dinham, our high treasurer,[8]
       Say we command commissions be new granted
       For the collection of our subsidies
       Through all the west, and that speedily.
       Lords, we acknowledge our engagements[9] due
       For your most constant services.
      Daub.   Your soldiers
110   Have manfully and faithfully acquitted
       Their several duties.
      Henry.   For it we will throw
       A largess free amongst them, which shall hearten
       And cherish up their loyalties. More yet
       Remains of like employment; not a man

---

[1] i.e. my Cornish subjects. [2] i.e. which. [3] Half-heartedly. [4] A sledge.
[5] Then the principal prison in London; near St. Paul's Cathedral. [6] Thomas
Flammock and Michael Joseph; see I, iii, 131, and notes. [7] Inquiry. [8] John,
Lord Dinham, or Dynham, d. 1500. Privy councillor, Treasurer of the
Exhequer 1486-1500; succeeded by the Earl of Surrey. [9] Obligations.

Can be dismiss'd till enemies abroad,
More dangerous than these at home, have felt
The puissance of our arms. Oh happy kings
Whose thrones are raised in their subjects' hearts!

Exeunt omnes.

[ACT III SCENE 2]

[*Stirling Castle*]
Enter Huntly *and* Dalyell

Hunt.   Now, sir, a modest word with you, sad gentleman.
Is not this fine, I trow, to see the gambols,
To hear the jigs, observe the frisks, b'enchanted
With the rare discord of bells, pipes, and tabors,[1]
Hotch-potch of Scotch and Irish twingle-twangles,[2]
Like to so many quiristers[3] of Bedlam,[4]
Trolling a catch?[5] The feasts, the manly stomachs,[6]
The healths in usquebaugh[7] and bonny-clabber,[8]
The ale in dishes never fetch'd from China,
10   The hundred thousand knacks[9] not to be spoken of,
And all this for King Oberon and Queen Mab,[10]
Should put a soul int'ee. Look 'ee, good man,
How youthful I am grown; but, by your leave,
This new queen-bride must henceforth be no more
My daughter; no, by'r lady, 'tis unfit.
And yet you see how I do bear this change,
Methinks courageously. Then shake off care
In such a time of jollity.
Dal.   Alas, sir,
How can you cast a mist upon[11] your griefs?
20   Which, howsoe'er you shadow,[12] but present
To any judging eye the perfect substance
Of which mine are but counterfeits.

---

[1] Small drums. [2] Huntly's interpretation of the sounds made by the
Gaelic harp. [3] Choristers. [4] An asylum, from the Hospital of St Mary
of Bethlehem, near Bishopsgate, London. [5] Singing a round. [6] Dis-
positions. [7] Whisky. [8] Sour milk. [9] Devices. [10] The king and queen
of the fairies, here symbolic of marriage. Katherine Gordon and Perkin
Warbeck were married in January 1496. Mab (*Romeo and Juliet*, I, iv,
53-95), or Maeve, was of Irish origin, but in English folklore was later
succeeded by Titania (*A Midsummer Night's Dream*, II, ii, ff.) [11] Conceal.
[12] Hide.

Hunt.   Foh, Dalyell,
    Thou interrupt[']s[t] the part I bear in music
    To this rare bridal feast. Let us be merry,
    Whilst flattering[1] calms secure us against storms.
    Tempests, when they begin to roar, put out
    The light of peace, and cloud the sun's bright eye
    In darkness of despair; yet we are safe.
Dal.   I wish you could as easily forget
30   The justice of your sorrows as my hopes
    Can yield to destiny.
Hunt.   Pish! Then I see
    Thou dost not know the flexible condition
    Of my apt nature. I can laugh, laugh heartily,
    When the gout cramps my joints; let but the stone
    Stop in my bladder, I am straight a-singing;
    The quartan fever[2] shrinking every limb
    Sets me a-cap'ring straight; do but betray me,
    And bind me a friend ever. What, I trust
    The losing of a daughter, though I doted
40   On every hair that grew to trim[3] her head,
    Admits not any pain like one of these.
    Come, th'art deceiv'd in me. Give me a blow,
    A sound blow on the face, I'll thank thee for't.
    I love my wrongs; still th'art deceiv'd in me.
Dal.   Deceiv'd? O noble Huntly, my few years
    Have learnt experience of too ripe an age
    To forfeit fit credulity. Forgive
    My rudeness; I am bold.
Hunt.   Forgive me first
    A madness of ambition; by example
50   Teach me humility, for patience scorns
    Lectures which schoolmen use to read to boys
    Uncapable of injuries. Though old,
    I could grow tough in fury, and disclaim
    Allegiance to my king, could fall at odds
    With all my fellow peers that durst not stand
    Defendants 'gainst the rape done on mine honour.
    But kings are earthly gods; there is no meddling
    With their anointed bodies; for their actions,
    They only are accountable to Heaven.
60   Yet in the puzzle of my troubl'd brain
    One antidote's reserv'd against the poison
    Of my distractions; 'tis in thee t'apply it.
Dal.   Name it; oh, name it quickly, sir!
Hunt.   A pardon

[1] Deceptive.   [2] A fever that recurs every fourth day.   [3] Adorn.

For my most foolish slighting thy deserts;
I have cull'd out this time to beg it. Prithee,
Be gentle;[1] had I been so, thou hadst own'd
A happy bride, but now a castaway,
And never child of mine more.

Dal.   Say not so, sir;
It is not fault in her.

Hunt.   The world would prate
70   How she was handsome; young I know she was,
Tender and sweet in her obedience;
But lost now. What a bankrupt am I made
Of a full stock of blessings! Must I hope
A mercy from thy heart?

Dal.   A love, a service,
A friendship to posterity.[2]

Hunt.   Good angels
Reward thy charity! I have no more
But prayers left me now.

Dal.   I'll lend you mirth, sir,
If you will be in consort.[3]

Hunt.   Thank ye truly.
I must, yes, yes, I must. Here's yet some ease,
80   A partner in affliction. Look not angry.

Dal.   Good noble sir.

Hunt.   Oh, hark, we may[4] be quiet;
The king and all the others come, a meeting
Of gaudy sights. This day's the last of revels.
Tomorrow sounds of war; then new exchange:
Fiddles must turn to swords. Unhappy marriage!

Flourish
Enter King James, Warbeck *leading* Katherine, Crawford, Countess
[of Crawford] , *and* Jane. Huntly *and* Dalyell *fall among them*

James.   Cousin of York, you and your princely bride
Have liberally enjoy'd such soft delights
As a new-married couple could forethink;
Nor has our bounty shorten'd[5] expectation.
90   But after all those pleasures of repose
Or amorous safety, we must rouse the ease
Of dalliance with achievements of more glory
Than sloth and sleep can furnish. Yet, for farewell,
Gladly we entertain a truce with time

---

[1] Generous.   [2] i.e. extending to succeeding generations.   [3] Harmony.
[4] Must.   [5] Diminished.

    To grace the joint endeavours of our servants.
Warb.   My royal cousin, in your princely favour
    The extent of bounty hath been so unlimited
    As[1] only an acknowledgement in words
    Would breed suspicion in[2] our state and quality.
100   When we shall, in the fulness of our fate,
    Whose minister, necessity, will perfect,
    Sit on our own throne,[3] then our arms, laid open
    To gratitude, in sacred memory
    Of these large benefits, shall twine them close,
    Even to our thoughts and heart, without distinction.
    Then James and Richard, being in effect
    One person, shall unite and rule one people,
    Divisible in titles only.
James.   Seat ye.
    Are the presenters[4] ready?
Craw.   All are ent'ring.
110 Hunt.   Dainty sport toward, Dalyell. Sit; come, sit,
    Sit, and be quiet. Here are kingly bug's-words.[5]

    Enter at one door four Scotch antics,[6] accordingly habited; enter
       at another four wild Irish in trowses,[7] long-haired, and
       accordingly habited. Music. The maskers dance[8]

James.   To all a general thanks.
Warb.   In the next room
    Take your own shapes again; you shall receive
    Particular acknowledgement.

                          [Exeunt maskers.]

James.   Enough
    Of merriments. Crawford, how far's our army
    Upon the march?
Craw.   At Heydonhall,[9] great king;
    Twelve thousand well prepar'd.
James.   Crawford, tonight
    Post thither. We in person, with the prince,
    By four a'clock tomorrow after dinner
    Will be w'ee. Speed away!

[1] To that extent. [2] In regard to. [3] As Richard IV of England. [4] Actors.
[5] Swaggering language (of Warbeck). [6] Clowns. [7] Trews, close-fitting breeches.
[8] The entertainment organized in II,iii, approx. 150-76. [9] Hedon Hall, a
castle about fifteen miles north-west of Berwick-upon-Tweed.

120 *Craw.*   I fly, my Lord

                                                                    [*Exit.*]

   James.   Our business grows to head now. Where's your secretary,
      That he attends 'ee not to serve?
   Warb.   With Marchmount,[1]
      Your herald.
   James.   Good. The proclamation's ready;
      By that it will appear how the English stand
      Affected to your title. Huntly, comfort
      Your daughter in her husband's absence; fight
      With prayers at home for us, who for your honours
      Must toil in fight abroad.
   Hunt.   Prayers are the weapons
      Which men so near their graves as I do use.
      I've little else to do.
130 *James.*   To rest, young beauties!
      We must be early stirring, quickly part;
      A kingdom's rescue craves both speed and art.
      Cousins, good night.

                                                                    Flourish

   Warb.   Rest to our cousin-king.
   Kath.   Your blessing, sir.
   Hunt.   Fair blessings on Your Highness; sure, you need 'em.

   Exeunt omnes; manent Warbeck, Katherine [*, and* Jane]

   Warb.   Jane, set the lights down, and from us return[2]
      To those in the next room this little purse;
      Say we'll deserve their loves.
   Jane.   It shall be done, sir.

                                                                    [*Exit.*]

   Warb.   Now, dearest, ere sweet sleep shall seal those eyes,
140   Love's precious tapers, give me leave to use
      A parting ceremony; for tomorrow
      It would be sacrilege to intrude upon
      The temple of thy peace. Swift as the morning
      Must I break from the down of thy embraces
      To put on steel, and trace the paths which lead

[1] The title of one of the three Scottish heralds (Marchmont, Rothesay and Albany). [2] Take back.

Through various hazards to a careful[1] throne.
Kath. My lord, I would fain go w'ee; there's small fortune
In staying here behind.
Warb. The churlish brow
Of war, fair dearest, is a sight of horror
50 For ladies' entertainment. If thou hear'st
A truth of my sad ending by the hand
Of some unnatural subject, thou withal
Shall hear how I died worthy of my right
By falling like a king; and in the close[2]
Which my last breath shall sound, thy name, thou fairest,
Shall sing a requiem to my soul, unwilling
Only of greater glory 'cause divided
From such a heaven on earth as life with thee.
But these are chimes for funerals; my business
60 Attends on fortune of a sprightlier triumph,
For love and majesty are reconcil'd,
And vow to crown thee empress of the west.
Kath. You have a noble language, sir. Your right
In me is without question, and however
Events of time may shorten my deserts
In others' pity,[3] yet it shall not stagger
Or constancy or duty in a wife.
You must be king of me, and my poor heart
Is all I can call mine.
Warb. But we will live,
70 Live, beauteous virtue, by the lively test
Of our own blood, to let the counterfeit[4]
Be known[5] the world's contempt.
Kath. Pray do not use
That word; it carries fate in't. The first suit
I ever made I trust your love will grant?
Warb. Without denial, dearest.
Kath. That hereafter,
If you return with safety, no adventure
May sever us in tasting any fortune;
I ne'er can stay behind again.
Warb. Y'are lady[6]
Of your desires, and shall command your will.
Yet 'tis too hard a promise.
80 *Kath.* What our destinies
Have rul'd out[7] in their books we must not search,
But kneel to.

[1] i.e. full of care. [2] Cadence. [3] i.e. circumstances may diminish my
deserving the pity of others. [4] King Henry VII, a counterfeit in
Warbeck's view. [5] Be known by. [6] Mistress. [7] Determined.

Warb.   Then to fear when hope is fruitless
Were to be desperately miserable;
Which poverty[1] our greatness dares not dream of,
And much more scorns to stoop to. Some few minutes
Remain yet; let's be thrifty in our hopes.

Exeunt.

[ACT III SCENE 3]

[King Henry's *palace, Westminster.*]
Enter King Henry, Hialas,[2] *and* Urswick

Henry.   Your name is Pedro Hialas, a Spaniard?
Hialas.   Sir, a Castilian born.
Henry.   King Ferdinand,
With wise Queen Isabel, his royal consort,
Writes 'ee a man of worthy trust and candour.
Princes are dear to Heaven who meet with subjects
Sincere in their employments; such I find
Your commendation,[3] sir. Let me deliver
How joyful I repute[4] the amity
With your most fortunate master, who almost
10   Comes near a miracle in his success
Against the Moors,[5] who had devour'd his country,
Entire now to his sceptre.[6] We, for our part,
Will imitate his providence,[7] in hope
Of partage[8] in the use on't. We repute
The privacy of his advisement[9] to us
By you, intended an ambassador
To Scotland, for a peace between our kingdoms,
A policy of love, which well becomes
His wisdom and our care.
Hialas.   Your Majesty
Doth understand him rightly.
20 *Henry.*   Else,[10]
Your knowledge can instruct me; wherein, sir

---

[1] i.e. misery. [2] Pedro de Ayala, Spanish diplomat; came to England to continue negotiations for the marriage of Princess Catherine of Aragon and Arthur, Prince of Wales; also arranged a peace between England and Scotland in 1497. [3] Recommendation. [4] Esteem. [5] Ferdinand II of Aragon drove the Moors out of Granada, their last stronghold in the country, in 1492. [6] i.e. which is now entirely within his rule. [7] Foresight. [8] Share. [9] Counsel. [10] Otherwise.

To fall on ceremony would seem useless,
Which shall not need; for I will be as studious
Of your concealment in our conference
As any counsel shall advise.[1]
Hialas.   Then, sir,
My chief request is that, on notice given
At my dispatch in Scotland, you will send
Some learned man of power and experience
To join in treaty with me.
Henry.   I shall do it,
30   Being that way well provided by a servant[2]
Which may attend 'ee ever.
Hialas.   If King James
By any indirection[3] should perceive
My coming near your court, I doubt the issue
Of my employment.
Henry.   Be not your own herald.
I learn sometimes without a teacher.
Hialas.   Good days
Guard all your princely thoughts.
Henry.   [*To* Urswick]   Urswick, no further
Than the next open gallery attend him. –
A hearty love go with you.
Hialas.   Your vow'd beadsman.

                                        Exeunt Urswick *and* Hialas.

Henry.   King Ferdinand is not so much a fox
40   But that a cunning huntsman may in time
Fall on the scent. In honourable actions
Safe imitation best deserves a praise.

Enter Urswick

What, the Castilian's pass'd away?
Urs.   He is,
And undiscover'd. The two hundred marks[4]
Your Majesty convey'd 'a gently purs'd
With a right modest gravity.
Henry.   What was't
'A mutter'd in the earnest[5] of his wisdom?
'A spoke not to be heard. 'Twas about –

[1] 'I shall be as careful as you advise to conceal our conference.' [2] Agent;
i.e. Richard Fox, Bishop of Durham. [3] Roundabout means. [4] Not a
coin, but a value of two-thirds of a pound; hence approximately £136.
[5] Seriousness.

Urs.   Warbeck.
    How if King Henry were but sure of subjects,[1]
50   Such a wild runagate[2] might soon be cag'd,
    No great ado withstanding.[3]
Henry.   Nay, nay; something
    About my son Prince Arthur's match.
Urs.   Right, right, sir.
    'A humm'd it out, how that King Ferdinand
    Swore that the marriage 'twixt the Lady Catherine
    His daughter and the Prince of Wales your son
    Should never be consummated as long
    As any Earl of Warwick liv'd in England,[4]
    Except by new creation.[5]
Henry.   I remember;
    'Twas so indeed. The king his master swore it?
Urs.   Directly,[6] as he said.
60 *Henry.*   An Earl of Warwick!
    Provide a messenger for letters instantly
    To Bishop Fox. Our news from Scotland creeps,
    It comes so slow. We must have airy spirits;
    Our time requires dispatch. The Earl of Warwick!
    Let him be son to Clarence, younger brother
    To Edward! Edward's daughter is, I think,
    Mother to our Prince Arthur.[7] Get a messenger.

                                         Exeunt.

[ACT III SCENE 4]

[*Before Norham Castle, Scotland*]
Enter King James, Warbeck, Crawford, Dalyell, Heron, Astley,
    Mayor [of Cork], Skelton, *and soldiers*

---

[1] i.e. were certain of the loyalty of his subjects. [2] Vagabond. [3] In
opposition. [4] The reluctance of Ferdinand II of Aragon to permit his
daughter Catherine (1485-1536) to marry Arthur, Henry's eldest son
(1486-1502), was prompted by his fear of Yorkist claims to the
English crown. The Earl of Warwick was the only surviving son of
George, Duke of Clarence (executed 1478), brother to Edward IV;
Warwick's supporters repeatedly urged his right to the throne after the
disappearance in the Tower of Edward's young sons; Warwick was
beheaded in 1499. Arthur and Catherine were married in 1501, but
Arthur died within the year, and Catherine married his younger brother
Henry (later Henry VIII) in 1509. [5] i.e. a newly created title.
[6] Absolutely. [7] 'Let Warwick claim the throne; my wife Elizabeth (a
daughter of Edward IV) is mother to our son and heir.'

James.   We trifle time against these castle walls
        The English prelate[1] will not yield; once more
        Give him a summons.

                              [*A call for*] *parley* [*is sounded*]
        Enter above Durham *armed, a truncheon*[2] *in his hand, and soldiers*

Warb.   See, the jolly clerk[3]
        Appears, trimm'd[4] like a ruffian.
James.   Bishop, yet
        Set ope the ports,[5] and to your lawful sovereign,
        Richard of York, surrender up this castle,
        And he will take thee to his grace; else, Tweed[6]
        Shall overflow his banks with English blood,
        And wash the sand that cements those hard stones
        From their foundation.
10 *Durham.*   Warlike King of Scotland,
        Vouchsafe a few words from a man enforc'd
        To lay his book aside and clap on arms
        Unsuitable to my age or my profession.
        Courageous prince, consider on what grounds
        You rend the face of peace, and break a league
        With a confederate king that courts your amity;
        For whom too? For a vagabond, a straggler,
        Not noted in the world by birth or name,
        An obscure peasant, by the rage of Hell
20   Loos'd from his chains to set great kings at│strife.
        What nobleman, what common man of note,
        What ordinary subject hath come in[7]
        Since first you footed on our territories,
        To only feign a welcome? Children laugh at
        Your proclamations, and the wiser pity
        So great a potentate's abuse by one
        Who juggles merely with the fawns[8] and youth
        Of an instructed[9] compliment. Such spoils,
        Such slaughters as the rapine of your soldiers
30   Already have committed, is enough
        To show your zeal in a conceited justice.
        Yet, great king, wake not yet my master's vengeance,
        But shake that viper off which gnaws your entrails.[10]
        I and my fellow-subjects are resolv'd,

[1] Richard Fox, Bishop of Durham. [2] Baton. [3] Priest. [4] Arrayed.
[5] Gates. [6] Through part of its length, the River Tweed marked the
border between England and Scotland. [7] Joined your forces. [8] Servile
cringes. [9] Taught. [10] The young of the viper or adder were reputed to
eat their way out of the mother's body at birth.

If you persist, to stand your utmost fury
Till our last blood drop from us.

Warb.   [*To* James]   Oh, sir, lend
No[1] ear to this traducer[2] of my honour.
[*To* Durham] What shall I call thee, thou gray-bearded scandal,
That kick'st against the sovereignity[3] to which
40   Thou owest allegiance? Treason is bold-fac'd
And eloquent in mischief. Sacred king,
Be deaf to his known malice.

Durham.   Rather yield
Unto those holy motions which inspire
The sacred heart of an anointed body.
It is the surest policy in princes
To govern well their own than seek encroachment
Upon another's right.

Craw.   The king is serious,
Deep in his meditation.

Dal.   Lift them[4] up
To Heaven, his better genius![5]

Warb.   Can you study[6]
While such a devil raves? O sir!

50 *James.*   Well, – Bishop,
You'll not be drawn to mercy?

Durham.   Conster[7] me
In like case by a subject of your own.
My resolution's fix'd. King James, be counsell'd.
A greater fate waits on thee.

                    Exit Durham *cum suis.*[8]

James.   Forage through
The country; spare no prey of life or goods.

Warb.   Oh, sir, then give me leave to yield to nature;
I am most miserable. Had I been
Born what this clergyman would by defame
Baffle belief with, I had never sought
60   The truth of mine inheritance with rapes
Of women or of infants murder'd, virgins
Deflower'd, old men butcher'd, dwellings fir'd,
My land depopulated, and my people
Afflicted with a kingdom's devastation.
Show more remorse, great king, or I shall never
Endure to see such havoc with dry eyes.

[1]Me [Q.]   [2]Seducer [Q.]   [3]i.e. me, the true king of England.   [4]His
thoughts.   [5]Controlling spirit.   [6]Meditate.   [7]Interpret.   [8]With his own
(men).

Spare, spare my dear, dear England.
James. You fool your piety
Ridiculously, careful of an interest
Another man possesseth. Where's your faction?
70 Shrewdly the bishop guess'd of your adherents,
When not a petty burgess[1] of some town,
No, not a villager hath yet appear'd
In your assistance. That should make 'ee whine,
And not your country's sufferance,[2] as you term it.
Dal. [*To* Crawford] The king is angry.
Craw. [*To* Dalyell] And the passionate duke
Effeminately dolent.[3]
Warb. The experience
In former trials, sir, both of mine own
And other princes cast out of their thrones,
Have so acquainted me how misery
80 Is destitute of friends or of relief,
That I can easily submit to taste
Lowest[4] reproof, without contempt or words.[5]
James. An humble-minded man!

Enter Frion

Now, what intelligence
Speaks Master Secretary Frion?
Frion. Henry
Of England hath in open field[6] o'erthrown
The armies who oppos'd him in the right
Of this young prince.
James. His subsidies,[7] you mean.
More,[8] if you have it.
Frion. Howard, Earl of Surrey,
Back'd by twelve earls and barons of the north,
90 An hundred knights and gentlemen of name,
And twenty thousand soldiers, is at hand
To raise your siege. Brooke,[9] with a goodly navy,
Is admiral at sea, and Daubeney follows
With an unbroken army for a second.[10]

---

[1] Citizen, or official. [2] Suffering. [3] Sad. [4] Basest. [5] Without responding in contempt or words. [6] The Battle of Blackheath III; i, 48-73. [7] The taxes which Henry imposed on the English people (I, iii, 130); King James here corrects Frion's ignorant or prejudiced assumption. [8] i.e. more information. [9] Robert, first Baron Willoughby de Broke (1452-1502), supported Henry at Bosworth Field, Lord Steward of the Household, Admiral of the Fleet from 1490, and other important posts. [10] Reinforcement.

Warb.   'Tis false! They come to side with us.
James.   Retreat.
      We shall not find[1] them stones and walls to cope with.
      Yet, Duke of York, for such thou sayest thou art,
      I'll try thy fortune to the height: To Surrey
100   By Marchmount I will send a brave defiance
      For single combat; once[2] a king will venture
      His person to an earl, with condition[3]
      Of spilling lesser blood.[4] Surrey is bold,
      And James resolv'd.
Warb.   Oh, rather, gracious sir,
      Create me to[5] this glory, since my cause
      Doth interest[6] this fair quarrel. Valu'd least,
      I am his equal.
James.   I will be the man.
      March softly off. Where victory can reap
      A harvest crown'd with triumph, toil is cheap.

                                                        Exeunt omnes.

[ACT IV SCENE 1]

[*Ayton Castle, Scotland[7]*]
Enter Surrey, Durham, *soldiers, with drums and colours*

Surrey.   Are all our braving enemies shrunk back,
      Hid in the fogs of their distemper'd climate,
      Not daring to behold our colours wave
      In spite of this infected air? Can they
      Look on the strength of Cundrestine defac'd,
      The glory of Heydonhall devasted, that
      Of Edington cast down, the pile of Fulden
      O'erthrown? And this the strongest of their forts,
      Old Ayton Castle yielded and demolish'd,
10   And yet not peep abroad? The Scots are bold,
      Hardy in battle, but it seems the cause
      They undertake, considered, appears
      Unjointed in the frame on't.
Durham.   Noble Surrey,

----

[1] Provide. [2] For once. [3] Proviso. [4] i.e. spilling less blood than if the armies met. [5] Invest me with. [6] Have an interest in. [7] Six miles north of Berwick. Surrey's incursion into Scotland took place in July-August 1497. He captured all the border castles named in lines 5-10.

Our royal master's wisdom is at all times
His fortune's harbinger; for when he draws
His sword to threaten war, his Providence
Settles on peace, the crowning of an empire.

Trumpet

Surrey.　　　Rank all in order. 'Tis a herald's sound,
　　　Some message from King James. Keep a fixed station.

Enter Marchmount *and another herald in their coats*

20 *March.*　　From Scotland's awful majesty we come
　　　Unto the English general.
Surrey.　　　　　　　　To me?
　　　Say on.
March.　　　Thus, then: The waste and prodigal
　　　Effusion of so much guiltless blood,
　　　As in two potent armies, of necessity
　　　Must glut the earth's dry womb, his sweet compassion
　　　Hath studied to prevent; for which, to thee,
　　　Great Earl of Surrey, in a single fight
　　　He offers his own royal person, fairly
　　　Proposing these conditions only, that
30　　If victory conclude[1] our master's right,
　　　The Earl shall deliver for his ransom
　　　The town of Berwick to him, with the fishgarths.[2]
　　　If Surrey shall prevail, the king will pay
　　　A thousand pounds down present[3] for his freedom,
　　　And silence further arms. So speaks King James.
Surrey.　　So speaks King James; so like a king 'a speaks.
　　　Heralds, the English general returns
　　　A sensible[4] devotion from his heart,
　　　His very soul, to this unfellow'd[5] grace.
40　　For let the king know, gentle heralds, truly
　　　How his descent from his great throne to honour
　　　A stranger subject, with so high a title
　　　As his compeer in arms, hath conquer'd more
　　　Than any sword could do. For which – my loyalty
　　　Respected[6] – I will serve his virtues ever
　　　In all humility. But Berwick, say,
　　　Is none of mine to part with. In affairs
　　　Of princes, subjects cannot traffic rights

---

[1] Determine.　[2] Enclosures for catching or holding fish. Berwick was noted
for salmon.　[3] Immediately.　[4] Perceptible.　[5] Incomparable.　[6] i.e. if he
will respect my loyalty.

    Inherent to the crown. My life is mine;
50   That I dare freely hazard, and — with pardon
    To some unbrib'd vainglory — if His Majesty
    Shall taste a change of fate,[1] his liberty
    Shall meet no articles.[2] If I fall, falling
    So bravely, I refer me to his pleasure
    Without condition; and for this dear favour,
    Say, if[3] not countermanded, I will cease
    Hostility unless provok'd.
March.   This answer
    We shall relate unpartially.
Durham.   [*To* Marchmount]   With favour,
    Pray have a little patience. [*To* Surrey]   Sir, you find
60   By these gay flourishes how wearied travail
    Inclines to willing rest. Here's but a prologue,[4]
    However confidently utter'd, meant
    For some ensuing acts of peace. Consider
    The time of year, unseasonableness of weather,
    Charge, barrenness of profit; and occasion
    Presents itself for honourable treaty,[5]
    Which we may make good use of. I will back,
    As sent from you in point of noble gratitude,
    Unto King James, with these his heralds. You
70   Shall shortly hear from me, my Lord, for order
    Of breathing[6] or proceeding; and King Henry,
    Doubt not, will thank the service.
Surrey.   To your wisdom,
    Lord Bishop, I refer it.
Durham.   Be it so then.
Surrey.   Heralds, accept this chain[7] and these few crowns.
March.   Our duty, noble general.
Durham.   In part
    Of retribution[8] for such princely love,
    My Lord the general is pleas'd to show
    The king your master his sincerest zeal
    By further treaty, by no common man;
    I will myself return with you.
80 *Surrey.*   Y'oblige[9]
    My faithfullest affections t'ee, Lord Bishop.
March.   All happiness attend Your Worship.

[*Exeunt* Marchmount, *other herald, and* Durham.]

[1]i.e. ill fortune. [2]Conditions. [3]If it is. [4]i.e. James's message.
[5]Negotiation. [6]Pausing. [7]An ornamental chain worn around the neck.
[8]Recompense. [9]Bind.

Surrey.   Come, friends
    And fellow-soldiers; we I doubt shall meet
    No enemies but woods and hills to fight with.
    Then 'twere as good to feed and sleep at home;[1]
    We may be free from danger, not secure.[2]

                                              Exeunt omnes.

[ACT IV SCENE 2]

[*Jedburgh, Scotland*]
Enter Warbeck *and* Frion

Warb.   Frion, oh, Frion, all my hopes of glory
    Are at a stand! The Scottish king grows dull,
    Frosty, and wayward, since this Spanish agent
    Hath mix'd discourses with him. They are private;
    I am not call'd to council now. Confusion
    On all his crafty shrugs! I feel the fabric
    Of my designs are tottering.
Frion.   Henry's policies
    Stir with too many engines.[3]
Warb.   Let his mines,
    Shap'd in the bowels of the earth, blow up
10 Works rais'd for my defence, yet can they never
    Toss into air the freedom of my birth
    Or disavow my blood Plantagenet's.
    I am my father's son still. But, oh, Frion,
    When I bring into count with my disasters
    My wife's compartnership, my Kate's, my life's,
    Then, then my frailty feels an earthquake. Mischief
    Damn Henry's plots! I will be England's king,
    Or let my aunt of Burgundy[4] report
    My fall in the attempt deserv'd[5] our ancestors.
20 *Frion.*   You grow too wild in passion. If you will
    Appear a prince indeed, confine your will
    To moderation.
Warb.   What a saucy rudeness
    Prompts this distrust! If, if I will appear?
    Appear a prince? Death throttle such deceits

[1]i.e. in our camp. [2]Free from care. [3]i.e. Henry's policies are too
devious. [4]Margaret, Duchess of Burgundy; see I, i, 42-62. [5]Was
worthy of.

Even in their birth of utterance! Curs'd cozenage
Of trust! Ye make me mad. 'Twere best, it seems,
That I should turn imposter to myself,
Be mine own counterfeit, belie the truth
Of my dear mother's womb, the sacred bed

30   Of a prince murder'd and a living baffl'd![1]
   Frion.   Nay, if you have no ears to hear, I have
No breath to spend in vain.
   Warb.   Sir, sir, take heed!
Gold and the promise of promotion rarely
Fail in temptation.
   Frion.   Why to me this?
   Warb.   Nothing.
Speak what you will; we are not sunk so low
But your advice may piece[2] again the heart
Which many cares have broken. You were wont
In all extremities to talk of comfort;
Have ye none left now? I'll not interrupt ye.

40   Good, bear with my distractions. If King James
Deny us dwelling here, next whither must I?
I prithee be not angry.
   Frion.   Sir, I told ye
Of letters come from Ireland, how the Cornish
Stomach their last defeat and humbly sue
That with such forces as you could partake[3]
You would in person land in Cornwall, where
Thousands will entertain[4] your title gladly.
   Warb.   Let me embrace thee, hug thee! Th'ast reviv'd
My comforts. If my cousin-king will fail,
Our cause will never.

Enter Mayor [of Cork], Heron, Astley, Skelton

50 |Welcome, my tried friends.
You keep your brains awake in our defence.
Frion, advise with them of these affairs,
In which be wondrous secret. I will listen
What else concerns us here; be quick and wary.

                                 Exit Warbeck.

   Astley.   Ah, sweet young prince! Secretary, my fellow-counsellors
and I have consulted, and jump[5] all in one opinion directly,
that if these Scotch garboils[6] do not fadge[7] to our minds,

---

[1] Disgraced.   [2] Mend.   [3] Get.   [4] Accept.   [5] Coincide.   [6] Brawls.
[7] Succeed.

we will pell-mell run amongst the Cornish choughs[1] presently,
and in a trice.

60 *Skel.*   'Tis but going to sea and leaping ashore, cut ten or
twelve thousand unnecessary throats, fire seven or eight
towns, take half a dozen cities, get into the market place,
crown him Richard the Fourth, and the business is finished.

a-Water.   I grant ye, quoth I, so far forth as men may do, no
more than men may do; for it is good to consider, when
consideration may be to the purpose; otherwise still you shall
pardon me. Little said is soon amended.

Frion.   Then you conclude the Cornish action surest?

Heron.   We do so, and doubt not but to thrive abundantly. Ho, my
70 masters, had we known of the commotion when we set sail out of
Ireland, the land had been ours ere this time.

Skel.   Pish, pish! 'Tis but forbearing being an earl or a duke a
month or two longer. I say, and say it again, if the work go
not on apace, let me never see new fashion more. I warrant
ye, I warrant ye, we will have it so, and so it shall be.

Astley.   This is but a cold, phlegmatic country, not stirring
enough for men of spirit. Give me the heart of England for my
money.

Skel.   A man may batten[2] there in a week only with hot loaves
80 and butter, and a lusty cup of muscadine and sugar at
breakfast, though he make never a meal all the month after.

a-Water.   Surely, when I bore office I found by experience that
to be much troublesome was to be much wise and busy; I have
observed how filching and bragging has been the best service
in these last wars, and therefore conclude peremptorily on the
design in England. If things and things[3] may fall out, as who
can tell what or how, but the end will show it.

Frion.   Resolv'd like men of judgment! Here to linger
More time is but to lose it. Cheer the prince
90 And haste him on to this; on this depends
Fame in success, or glory in our ends.

Exeunt omnes.

---

[1] A variety of jackdaw.   [2] Grow fat.   [3] One thing and another.

[ACT IV SCENE 3]

[*Jedburgh, Scotland*]
Enter King James; Durham *and* Hialas *on either side*

Hialas.   France, Spain, and Germany combine a league
              Of amity with England; nothing wants
              For settling peace through Christendom but love
              Between the British monarchs, James and Henry.
Durham.   The English merchants, sir, have been receiv'd
              With general procession into Antwerp;
              The emperor[1] confirms the combination.[2]
Hialas.   The King of Spain resolves a marriage
              For Catherine his daughter with Prince Arthur.
Durham.   France courts this holy contract.
10 *Hialas.*   What can hinder
              A quietness in England —
Durham.   But your suffrage[3]
              To such a silly creature, mighty sir,
              As is but in effect an apparition,[4]
              A shadow, a mere trifle?
Hialas.   To this union
              The good of both the church and commonwealth
              Invite 'ee.
Durham.   To[5] this unity, a mystery
              Of Providence points out a greater blessing
              For both these nations than our human reason
              Can search into. King Henry hath a daughter,
20   The Princess Margaret. I need not urge
              What honour, what felicity can follow
              On such affinity 'twixt two Christian kings
              Inleagu'd by ties of blood; but sure I am
              If you, sir, ratify the peace propos'd,
              I dare both motion[6] and effect this marriage
              For weal of both the kingdoms.[7]
James.   Dar'st thou, Lord Bishop?
Durham.   Put it to trial, royal James, by sending
              Some noble personage to the English court
              By way of embassy.
Hialas.   Part of the business
              Shall suit my mediation.
30 *James.*   Well, what Heaven
              Hath pointed out to be, must be; you two
              Are ministers, I hope, of blessed fate.

[1] Maximilian of Habsburg.   [2] Alliance.   [3] Support.   [4] Counterfeit.
[5] Besides.   [6] Recommend.   [7] King James married Princess Margaret in 1503.

But herein only I will stand acquitted:
No blood of innocents shall buy my peace.
For Warbeck, as you nick[1] him, came to me
Commended by the states of Christendom,
A prince, though in distress; his fair demeanour,
Lovely[2] behaviour, unappalled spirit,
Spoke him not base in blood, however clouded.
40 The brute beasts have both rocks and caves to fly to,
And men the altars of the church; to us
He came for refuge. Kings come near in nature
Unto the gods in being touch'd with pity.
Yet, noble friends, his mixture with our blood,[3]
Even with our own, shall no way interrupt
A general peace; only[4] I will dismiss him
From my protection, throughout my dominions
In safety, but not ever to return.
Hialas.   You are a just king.
Durham.   Wise and herein happy.
50 *James.*   Nor will we dally in affairs of weight.
Huntly, Lord Bishop, shall with you to England,
Ambassador from us. We will throw down
Our weapons; peace on all sides now. Repair
Unto our council; we will soon be with you.
Hialas.   Delay shall question no dispatch.[5] Heaven crown it!

Exeunt Durham *and* Hialas.

James.   A league with Ferdinand, a marriage
With English Margaret, a free release
From restitution for the late affronts,
Cessation from hostility! And all
60 For Warbeck not deliver'd, but dismiss'd!
We could not wish it better, Dalyell!

Enter Dalyell

Dal.   Here, sir.
James.   Are Huntly and his daughter sent for?
Dal.   Sent for
And come, my Lord.
James.   Say to the English prince
We want his company.

[1] Nickname. [2] Friendly. [3] i.e. his kinship to me. This resulted from
Warbeck's marriage to Katherine Huntly, believed by Ford to be
descended from James I of Scotland. [4] However. [4] 'There shall be no
question of delay in the expedition of any matter.'

Dal.   He is at hand, sir

Enter Warbeck, Katherine, Jane, Frion, Heron, Skelton, Mayor
    [of Cork], Astley

James.   Cousin, our bounty, favours, gentleness,
    Our benefits, the hazard of our person,
    Our people's lives, our land hath evidenc'd
    How much we have engag'd on your behalf.
    How trivial and how dangerous our hopes
70   Appear, how fruitless our attempts in war,
    How windy, rather smoky, your assurance
    Of party[1] shows, we might in vain repeat.
    But now obedience to the mother church,[2]
    A father's care upon his country's weal,
    The dignity of state, directs our wisdom
    To seal an oath of peace through Christendom,
    To which we are sworn already. 'Tis you
    Must only seek new fortunes in the world,
    And find an harbour elsewhere. As I promis'd
80   On your arrival, you have met no usage
    Deserves repentance in your being here;
    But yet I must live master of mine own.
    However, what is necessary for you
    At your departure I am well content
    You be accommodated with, provided
    Delay prove not my enemy.
Warb.   It shall not,
    Most glorious prince. The fame of my designs
    Soars higher than report[3] of ease and sloth
    Can aim at. I acknowledge all your favours
90   Boundless and singular, am only wretched
    In words as well as means to thank the grace
    That flow'd so liberally. Two empires firmly
    You're lord of: Scotland and Duke Richard's heart.
    My claim to mine inheritance shall sooner
    Fail than my life to serve you, best of kings.
    And witness Edward's blood in me, I am
    More loath to part with such a great example
    Of virtue than all other mere respects.[4]
    But, sir, my last suit is, you will not force
100   From me what you have given, this chaste lady,

---

[1] Adherents. [2] James was then considering joining the Holy League,
promoted by Pope Alexander VI to discourage French invasions of Italy.
[3] Rumour. [4] Considerations.

Resolv'd on all extremes.[1]
Kath.   I am your wife;
No human power can or shall divorce
My faith from duty.
Warb.   Such another treasure
The earth is bankrupt of.
James.   I gave her, cousin,
And must avow the gift; will add withal
A furniture[2] becoming her high birth
And unsuspected constancy. Provide
For your attendance. We will part good friends.

Exeunt King *and* Dalyell.

Warb.   The Tudor hath been cunning in his plots;
110   His Fox of Durham would not fail at last.
But what? Our cause and courage are our own.
Be men, my friends, and let our cousin-king
See how we follow fate as willingly
As malice follows us. Y'are all resolv'd
For the west parts of England?
Omnes.   Cornwall! Cornwall!
Frion.   The inhabitants expect you daily.
Warb.   Cheerfully
Draw all our ships out of the harbour, friends.
Our time of stay doth seem too long; we must
Prevent intelligence.[3] About it suddenly.
120 *Omnes.*   A prince, a prince, a prince!

Exeunt Counsellors.

Warb.   Dearest, admit not into thy pure thoughts
The least of scruples, which may charge their softness
With burden of distrust. Should I prove wanting
To noblest courage now, here were the trial.
But I am perfect,[4] sweet; I fear no change,[5]
More than thy being partner in my sufferance.
Kath.   My fortunes, sir, have arm'd me to encounter
What chance soe'er they meet with. Jane, 'tis fit
Thou stay behind, for whither wilt thou wander?
130 *Jane.*   Never till death will I forsake my mistress,
Nor then, in wishing to die with 'ee gladly.
Kath.   Alas, good soul.
Frion.   Sir, to your aunt of Burgundy

[1] Resolved to endure all extremities.   [2] Provision.   [3] 'We must forestall news of our arrival in Cornwall.'   [4] Complete.   [5] i.e. in you.

I will relate your present undertakings;
From her expect on all occasions welcome.
You cannot find me idle in your services.
Warb.   Go, Frion, go. Wise men know how to soothe
Adversity, not serve it. Thou hast waited
Too long on expectation; never yet
Was any nation read of so besotted
140   In reason as to adore the setting sun.
Fly to the archduke's court;[1] say to the duchess,
Her nephew with fair Katherine his wife
Are on their expectation to begin
The raising of an empire. If they fail,
Yet the report[2] will never. Farewell, Frion.

                                        Exit Frion.

This man, Kate, has been true, though now of late
I fear too much familiar with the Fox.[3]

     Enter Huntly *and* Dalyell

Hunt.   I come to take my leave. You need not doubt
My interest in this sometime child of mine.
150   She's all yours now, good sir. O poor lost creature,
Heaven guard thee with much patience![4] If thou canst
Forget thy title to old Huntly's family,
As much of peace will settle in thy mind
As thou canst wish to taste, but in thy grave.
Accept my tears yet, prithee; they are tokens
Of charity, as true[5] as of affection.
Kath.   This is the cruell'st farewell.
Hunt.   Love, young gentleman,
This model[6] of my griefs. She calls you husband;
Then be not jealous of a parting kiss;
160   It is a father's, not a lover's off'ring.
Take it, my last. I am too much a child;

                              [*Kisses her, and weeps*]

Exchange of passion is to little use
So I should grow too foolish.[7] Goodness guide thee!

                                        Exit Huntly.

[1] See note at I, i, 123.   [2] Reputation.   [3] Historically, Frion abandoned
Warbeck in 1497.   [4] 'May you be protected by Heaven with the quality of
patience.'   [5] Surely.   [6] Epitome.   [7] 'If I should grow too irrational.'

Kath.   Most miserable daughter! Have you aught
 To add, sir, to our sorrows?
Dal.   I resolve,
 Fair lady, with your leave, to wait on all
 Your fortunes in my person, if your lord
 Vouchsafe me entertainment.[1]
Warb.   We will be bosom friends, most noble Dalyell;
170 For I accept this tender of your love
 Beyond ability of thanks to speak it.
 Clear thy drown'd eyes, my fairest; time and industry
 Will show us better days or end the worst.

Exeunt omnes.

[ACT IV SCENE 4]

[King Henry's *palace, Westminster*]
Enter Oxford *and* Daubeney

Oxford.   No news from Scotland yet, my Lord?
Daub.   Not any
 But what King Henry knows himself. I thought
 Our armies should have march'd that way; his mind,
 It seems, is alter'd.
Oxford.   Victory attends
 His standard everywhere.
Daub.   Wise princes, Oxford,
 Fight not alone with forces. Providence[2]
 Directs and tutors strength; else elephants
 And barbed horses[3] might as well prevail
 As the most subtle stratagems of war.
10 *Oxford.*   The Scottish king show'd more than common bravery
 In proffer of a combat hand to hand
 With Surrey.
Daub.   And but show'd it; northern bloods
 Are gallant, being fir'd, but the cold climate,
 Without good store of fuel, quickly freezeth
 The glowing flames.
Oxford.   Surrey, upon my life,
 Would not have shrunk an hair's-breadth.
Daub.   May 'a forfeit

[1] Employment. [2] Foresight. [3] With breasts and flanks protected by
barbed armour.

The honour of an English name and nature
Who would not have embrac'd it with a greediness
As violent as hunger runs to food.
20   'Twas an addition[1] any worthy spirit
Would covet, next to immortality,
Above all joys of life. We all miss'd shares
In that great opportunity.

Enter King Henry *and* Urswick, *whispering*

Oxford.   The king!
See, 'a comes smiling.
Daub.   Oh, the game runs smooth
On his side then, believe it. Cards well shuffl'd
And dealt with cunning bring some gamester thrift,[2]
But others must rise losers.
Henry.   The train[3] takes?
Urs.   Most prosperously.
Henry.   I knew it should not miss.
He fondly angles who will hurl his bait
30   Into the water[4] 'cause the fish at first
Plays round about the line and dares not bite.
Lords, we may reign your king[5] yet. Daubeney, Oxford,
Urswick, must Perkin wear the crown?
Daub.   A slave!
Oxford.   A vagabond!
Urs.   A glow-worm![6]
Henry.   Now if Frion,
His practis'd politician, wear a brain
Of proof,[7] King Perkin will in progress ride
Through all his large dominions; let us meet him,
And tender homage! Ha, sirs? Liegemen ought
To pay their fealty.
Daub.   Would the rascal were,
40   With all his rabble, within twenty miles
Of London!
Henry.   Farther off is near enough
To lodge[8] him in his home. I'll wager odds
Surrey and all his men are either idle
Or hasting back; they have not work, I doubt,
To keep them busy.

---

[1] Title, mark of honour. [2] Profit. [3] A lure dragged along the ground to create a scent or trail. [4] i.e. throws it away. [5] i.e. your undisputed king. [6] Fool. [7] i.e. tested. [8] Discover, in his lair (another image from the hunt).

Daub.   'Tis a strange conceit,[1] sir
Henry.   Such voluntary favours as our people
    In duty aid us with, we never scatter'd
    On cobweb parasites, or lavish'd out
    In riot or a needless hospitality.
50   No undeserving favourite doth boast
    His issues[2] from our treasury; our charge
    Flows through all Europe, proving us but steward
    Of every contribution which provides
    Against the creeping canker of disturbance.
    Is it not rare then, in this toil of state
    Wherein we are embark'd, with breach of sleep,
    Cares, and the noise of trouble, that our mercy
    Returns nor thanks nor comfort? Still the west
    Murmur and threaten innovation,[3]
60   Whisper our government tyrannical,
    Deny us what is ours, nay, spurn their lives,
    Of which they are but owners by our gift.[4]
    It must not be.
Oxford.   It must not, should not.

Enter a Post

Henry.   So then.
    To whom?
Post.   This packet to Your Sacred Majesty.
Henry.   Sirrah, attend without.

                         [*Exit* Post.]

Oxford.   News from the north, upon my life.
Daub.   Wise Henry
    Divines aforehand of events; with him
    Attempts and execution are one act.
Henry.   [*To* Urswick] Urswick, thine ear. Frion is caught, the man
70   Of cunning is outreach'd; we must be safe.
    Should Reverend Morton,[5] our archbishop, move
    To a translation higher yet,[6] I tell thee
    My Durham owns a brain deserves that see.[7]
    He's nimble in his industry, and mounting.

---

[1] Fancy. [2] Profits. [3] Insurrection. [4] i.e. by my generosity in not executing rebels. [5] John, Cardinal Morton (*c.* 1420-1500), held several important offices of church and state; Archbishop of Canterbury 1486-1500, succeeded by Bishop Henry Deane. Fox was rewarded with the rich and prestigious bishopric of Winchester, 1501. [6] Die, go to Heaven. [7] Diocese.

Thou hear'st me?

Urs.   And conceive Your Highness fitly.

Henry.   Daubeney and Oxford, since our army stands
Entire, it were a weakness to admit
The rust of laziness to eat amongst them.
Set forward toward Salisbury; the plains
80   Are most commodious for their exercise.
Ourself will take a muster of them there,
And or disband them with reward or else
Dispose as best concerns us.

Daub.   Salisbury?
Sir, all is peace at Salisbury.

Henry.   Dear friend,
The charge must be our own; we would a little
Partake the pleasure with our subjects' ease.[1]
Shall I entreat your loves?

Oxford.   Command our lives.

Henry.   Y'are men know how to do, not to forethink.
My bishop is a jewel tried and perfect,
90   A jewel, lords. The post who brought these letters
Must speed another to the Mayor of Exeter;
Urswick, dismiss him not.

Urs.   He waits your pleasure.

Henry.   Perkin a king! A king!

Urs.   My gracious Lord?

Henry.   Thoughts busied in the sphere of royalty
Fix not on creeping worms without their stings,
Mere excrements of earth. The use of time
Is thriving safety,[2] and a wise prevention
Of ills expected. W'are resolv'd for Salisbury.

Exeunt omnes.

[ACT IV SCENE 5]

[*Near Land's End, Cornwall*]
A general shout within. Enter Warbeck, Dalyell, Katherine, *and* Jane

Warb.   After so many storms as wind and seas
Have threaten'd to our weather-beaten ships,

---

[1] 'We would like to relax briefly with our subjects.'   [2] 'Time can best be
used to make security prosper'.

At last, sweet fairest, we are safe arriv'd
On our dear mother earth, ingrateful only
To Heaven and us in yielding sustenance
To sly usurpers of our throne and right.[1]
These general acclamations are an omen
Of happy process[2] to their welcome lord.
They flock in troops, and from all parts with wings
10 Of duty fly, to lay their hearts before us.[3]
Unequall'd pattern of a matchless wife,
How fares my dearest yet?

Kath.   Confirm'd in health;
By which I may the better undergo
The roughest face of change; but I shall learn
Patience to hope, since silence courts affliction
For comforts, to this truly noble gentleman,[4]
Rare, unexampl'd pattern of a friend;
And my beloved Jane, the willing follower
Of all misfortunes.

Dal.   Lady, I return
20 But barren crops of early[5] protestations,
Frost-bitten in the spring of fruitless hopes.

Jane.   I wait but as the shadow to the body,
For, madam, without you let me be nothing.

Warb.   None talk of sadness; we are on the way
Which leads to victory. Keep cowards' thoughts
With desperate sullenness. The lion faints not
Lock'd in a grate,[6] but loose, disdains all force
Which bars his prey; and we are lion-hearted,
Or else no king of beasts.

Another shout

Hark, how they shout,
30 Triumphant in our cause! Bold confidence

---

[1] Cf. *Richard II*, III, ii, 4-26.   [2] Progress.   [3] After an unsuccessful attempt
to raise support in Ireland, Warbeck and about one hundred followers
landed at Whitesand Bay, Cornwall, on 7 September 1497. Some eight
thousand Cornish malcontents, many of them no doubt survivors of the
defeat at Blackheath in June 1497, joined him, but they failed to capture
Exeter. At Taunton, Somerset, on 21 September Warbeck abandoned his
army, which then scattered. Warbeck feared capture or betrayal, and fled
to Beaulieu Abbey, Hants. There Daubeney and his soldiers persuaded him
to come out of sanctuary, and he was returned as a prisoner to Taunton
(V, ii, 31 ff.).   [4] 'I shall teach patience (i.e. this gentleman, Dalyell) to be
optimistic, since stoicism draws comfort from my afflictions.'
[5] Premature.   [6] Cage.

Marches on bravely, cannot quake at danger.

Enter Skelton

Skel.   Save King Richard the Fourth! Save thee, king of hearts!
The Cornish blades[1] are men of mettle, have proclaim'd through
Bodmin[2] and the whole county my sweet prince monarch of
England. Four thousand tall[3] yeomen, with bow and sword,
already vow to live and die at the foot of King Richard.

Enter Astley

Astley.   The mayor, our fellow counsellor, is servant for an
emperor. Exeter is appointed for the rendezvous, and nothing
wants to victory but courage and resolution. *Sigillatum et*
40   *datum decimo Septembris, anno regni regis primo, et cetera;*
confirmatum est.[4] All's cock-sure.[5]
Warb.   To Exeter, to Exeter! March on!
Commend us to our people. We in person
Will lend them double spirits; tell them so.
Skel. and Astley.   King Richard! King Richard!

                                                      [*Exeunt* Skelton *and* Astley.]

Warb.   A thousand blessings guard our lawful arms!
A thousand horrors pierce our enemies' souls!
Pale fear unedge their weapons' sharpest points,
And when they draw their arrows to the head,
50   Numbness shall strike their sinews. Such advantage
Hath majesty in its pursuit of justice
That on[6] the proppers-up of truth's old throne
It both enlightens counsel and gives heart
To execution, whiles the throats of traitors
Lie bare before our mercy. Oh, divinity
Of royal birth! How it strikes dumb the tongues
Whose prodigality of breath is brib'd
By trains to[7] greatness! Princes are but men,
Distinguish'd by the fineness of their frailty,
60   Yet not so gross in beauty of the mind,

---

[1] A pun on 'good fellows' and 'swords'.   [2] Cornish town, about twenty-
five miles north-west of Plymouth, the home of Michael Joseph (See I,
iii, 129).   [3] Strong.   [4] Sealed and dated 10 September, the first year of the
reign of the king, etc.; it is confirmed.   [5] Absolutely certain.   [6] In regard
to.   [7] Attendants on.

For there's a fire more sacred purifies
The dross of mixture.[1] Herein stands the odds:[2]
Subjects are men on earth; kings, men and gods.

Exeunt omnes.

[ACT V SCENE 1]

[*Near St Michael's Mount, Cornwall*]
Enter Katherine *and* Jane *in riding suits, with one* Servant

Kath.   It is decreed, and we must yield to Fate,
Whose angry justice, though it threaten ruin,
Contempt, and poverty, is all but trial
Of a weak woman's constancy in suffering.
Here in a stranger's and an enemy's land,
Forsaken and unfurnish'd[3] of all hopes
But such as wait on misery, I range
To meet affliction wheresoe'er I tread.
My train and pomp[4] of servants is reduc'd
10   To one kind gentlewoman and this groom.
Sweet Jane, now whither must we?
Jane.   To your ships,
Dear lady, and turn home.
Kath.   Home! I have none.
Fly thou to Scotland; thou hast friends will weep
For joy to bid thee welcome; but, oh, Jane,
My Jane, my friends are desperate of comfort,
As I must be of them. The common charity,
Good people's alms and prayers of the gentle,
Is the revenue must support my state.
As for my native country, since it once
20   Saw me a princess in the height of greatness
My birth allow'd me, here I make a vow
Scotland shall never see me, being fallen
Or lessen'd in my fortunes. Never, Jane,
Never to Scotland more will I return.
Could I be England's queen – a glory, Jane,
I never fawn'd on[5] – yet the king who gave me[6]

[1] i.e. which clears the dross, or refuse, out of the heterogeneity that is the
human state (a metaphor from metallurgy).   [2] Distinction.   [3] Deprived.
[4] Display.   [5] Aspired to.   [6] i.e. gave my hand in marriage to Warbeck.

Hath sent me with my husband from his presence,
Deliver'd us suspected to his nation,[1]
Render'd us spectacles to time and pity.
30   And is it fit I should return to such
As only listen after[2] our descent
From happiness enjoy'd to misery
Expected, though uncertain? Never, never!
Alas, why doest thou weep, and that poor creature
Wipe his wet cheeks too? Let me feel alone
Extremities, who know to give them harbour.
Nor thou nor he has cause; you may live safely.
Jane.   There is no safety whiles your dangers, madam,
Are every way apparent.
Serv.   Pardon, lady;
40   I cannot choose but show my honest heart.
You were ever my good lady.
Kath.   O dear souls,
Your shares in grief are too, too much!

    Enter Dalyell

Dal.   I bring,
Fair princess, news of further sadness yet
Than your sweet youth hath been acquainted with.
Kath.   Not more, my Lord, than I can welcome. Speak it;
The worst, the worst I look for.
Dal.   All the Cornish
At Exeter were by the citizens
Repuls'd, encounter'd by the Earl of Devonshire[3]
And other worthy gentlemen of the country.
50   Your husband march'd to Taunton, and was there
Affronted[4] by King Henry's chamberlain,[5]
The king himself in person, with his army,
Advancing nearer to renew the fight
On all occasions.[6] But the night before
The battles[7] were to join, your husband privately,
Accompanied with some few horse, departed
From out the camp, and posted none knows whither.
Kath.   Fled without battle given?
Dal.   Fled, but follow'd

---

[1] i.e. Warbeck's nation, England. [2] Endeavour to hear of. [3] Edward
Courtenay, d. 1509; loyal to Henry VII, granted extensive lands in Devon,
wounded whilst repelling Warbeck's forces at Exeter, 1497. [4] Confronted.
[5] Giles Daubeney (subsequent to the dismissal of William Stanley, II, ii,
123-4). [6] Historically, King Henry was not personally involved in the
confrontation with the rebels at Exeter. [7] Battalions.

By Daubeney, all his parties[1] left to taste
60 King Henry's mercy – for to that they yielded –
Victorious[2] without bloodshed.

Kath.   Oh, my sorrows!
If both our lives had prov'd the sacrifice
To Henry's tyranny, we had fallen like princes,
And robb'd him of the glory of his pride.

Dal.   Impute it not to faintness or to weakness
Of noble courage, lady, but foresight;
For by some secret friend he had intelligence
Of being bought and sold by his base followers.
Worse yet remains untold.

Kath.   No, no, it cannot!
70 *Dal.*   I fear y'are betray'd. The Earl of Oxford
Runs hot in your pursuit.

Kath.   'A shall not need.
We'll run as hot in resolution gladly
To make the earl our jailor.

Jane.   Madam, madam,
They come, they come!

Enter Oxford *with followers*

Dal.   [*To* Oxford]   Keep back, or he who dares
Rudely to violate the law of honour
Runs on my sword.

Kath.   [*To* Dalyell]   Most noble sir, forbear. –
What reason draws you hither, gentlemen?
Whom seek 'ee?

Oxford.   All stand off. With favour, lady,
From Henry, England's king, I would present
80 Unto the beauteous princess, Katherine Gordon,
The tender of a gracious entertainment.

Kath.   We are that princess, whom your master-king
Pursues with reaching[3] arms to draw into
His power. Let him use his tyranny;
We shall not be his subjects.

Oxford.   My commission[4]
Extends no further, excellentest lady,
Than to a service; 'tis King Henry's pleasure
That you, and all that have relation t'ee,
Be guarded as becomes your birth and greatness.
90 For rest assur'd, sweet princess, that not aught
Of what you do call yours shall find disturbance,
Or any welcome other than what suits

---

[1] Warbeck's adherents.   [2] i.e. Henry's forces.   [3] Far-reaching.   [4] Charge.

          Your high condition.
Kath.   By what title, sir,
     May I acknowledge you?
Oxford.   Your servant, lady,
     Descended from the line of Oxford's earls,
     Inherits what his ancestors before him
     Were owners of.
Kath.   Your king is herein royal,
     That by a peer so ancient in desert
     As well as blood commands us to his presence.
Oxford.   Invites 'ee, princess, not commands.
100 *Kath.*   Pray use
     Your own phrase as you list. To your protection
     Both I and mine submit.
Oxford.   [*Turns to* Dalyell]   There's in your number
     A nobleman whom fame hath bravely spoken.[1]
     To him the king my master bade me say
     How willingly he courts his friendship, far
     From an enforcement more than what in terms
     Of courtesy so great a prince may hope for.
Dal.   My name is Dalyell.
Oxford.   'Tis a name hath won
     Both thanks and wonder, from report, My Lord,
110 The court of England emulates[2] your merit
     And covets to embrace 'ee.
Dal.   I must wait on
     The princess in her fortunes.
Oxford.   Will you please,
     Great lady, to set forward?
Kath.   Being driven
     By Fate, it were in vain to strive with Heaven.

                                                   Exeunt omnes.

[ACT V SCENE 2]

[*Taunton*]
Enter King Henry, Surrey, Urswick, *and a guard of soldiers*

Henry.   The counterfeit, King Perkin, is escap'd.
     Escap'd? So let him. He is hedg'd too fast
     Within the circuit of our English pale

[1] Worthily made known.   [2] Strives to equal.

To steal out of our ports or leap the walls
Which guard our land; the seas are rough and wider
Than his weak arms can tug with. Surrey, henceforth
Your king may reign in quiet. Turmoils past,
Like some unquiet dream, have rather busied
Our fancy than affrighted rest of state.[1]
10   But, Surrey, why, in articling[2] a peace
With James of Scotland, was not restitution
Of losses, which our subjects did sustain
By the Scotch inroads, question'd?
Surrey.   Both demanded
And urg'd, my Lord; to which the king replied
In modest merriment but smiling earnest,
How that our master Henry was much abler
To bear the detriments[3] than he to repay them.
Henry.   The young man, I believe, spake honest truth;
'A studies to be wise betimes![4] Has, Urswick,
20   Sir Rhys ap Thomas[5] and Lord Brooke, our steward,
Return'd the western gentlemen full thanks
From us for their tried loyalties?
Urs.[6]   They have;
Which, as if health and life had reign'd amongst 'em,
With open hearts they joyfully receiv'd.
Henry.   Young Buckingham[7] is a fair-natur'd prince,
Lovely in hopes, and worthy of his father.
Attended by an hundred knights and squires
Of special[8] name, he[9] tender'd humble service,
Which we must ne'er forget. And Devonshire's wounds,
30   Though slight, shall find sound cure in our respect.[10]

Enter Daubeney, *with* Warbeck, Heron, John a-Water, Astley, Skelton

Daub.   Life to the king, and safety fix[11] his throne!
I here present you, royal sir, a shadow
Of majesty, but in effect a substance
Of pity; a young man, in nothing grown
To ripeness but th'ambition of[12] your mercy;
Perkin, the Christian world's strange wonder.

---

[1] The tranquillity of governance. [2] Arranging by treaty. [3] Losses.
[4] Early in life. James IV was then twenty-five years old. [5] Of Carmarthen;
1449-1525. A major landowner and principal Welsh supporter of Henry
from 1485. [6] *Sur*: Q. [7] Edward Stafford, third Duke of Buckingham,
1478-1521; he and his followers aided significantly in the defeat of Warbeck. Buckingham's father, Henry, had rebelled against Richard III, and
was beheaded in 1483. [8] Distinguished. [9] Young Buckingham. [10] Esteem.
[11] Make firm. [12] i.e. the hope to receive.

Henry.   Daubeney,
  We observe no wonder. I behold, 'tis true,
  An ornament of nature, fine and polish'd,
  A handsome youth indeed, but not admire[1] him.
  How came he to thy hands?
40 *Daub.*   From sanctuary
  At Beaulieu,[2] near Southampton, register'd,
  With these few followers, for[3] persons privileg'd.[4]
Henry.   I must not thank you, sir! You were to blame
  To infringe the liberty of houses sacred.
  Dare we be irreligious?
Daub.   Gracious Lord,
  They voluntarily resign'd themselves
  Without compulsion.[5]
Henry.   So? 'Twas very well;
  'Twas very, very well. Turn now thine eyes,
  Young man, upon thyself, and thy past actions.
50   What revels in combustion[6] through our kingdom
  A frenzy of aspiring youth hath danc'd,
  Till, wanting breath, thy feet of pride have slipp'd
  To break thy neck.
Warb.   But not my heart! My heart
  Will mount till every drop of blood be frozen
  By death's perpetual winter. If the sun
  Of majesty be darken'd, let the sun
  Of life be hid from me in an eclipse
  Lasting and universal. Sir, remember
  There was a shooting in of light when Richmond,
60   Not aiming at a crown, retir'd, and gladly,
  For comfort to the Duke of Bretagne's court.[7]
  Richard,[8] who sway'd the sceptre, was reputed
  A tyrant then; yet then a dawning glimmer'd
  To some few wand'ring remnants, promising day
  When first they ventur'd on a frightful shore
  At Milford Haven –[9]
Daub.   Whither speeds his boldness?
  Check his rude tongue, great sir!
Henry.   Oh, let him range.
  The player's on the stage still; 'tis his part;
  'A does but act. What follow'd?

[1] Wonder at.   [2] The Abbey belonged to the Cistercian order.   [3] As.
[4] Claiming the privilege of sanctuary.   [5] Historically, Henry and his
colleagues tricked Warbeck into leaving the Abbey.   [6] Commotion.
[7] Henry Tudor, Earl of Richmond, spent much of his youth in Brittany,
sheltered by Francis II, Duke of Brittany (1435-88).   [8] Richard III.   [9] At
the western extremities of Wales, where Henry first landed in August 1485.

    Warb.   Bosworth Field;
70   Where, at an instant, to the world's amazement,
        A morn to Richmond and a night to Richard
        Appear'd at once.[2] The tale is soon applied:
        Fate, which crown'd these attempts when least assur'd,
        Might have befriended others like resolv'd.
    Henry.   A pretty gallant! Thus your aunt of Burgundy,
        Your duchess-aunt, inform'd her nephew; so
        The lesson, prompted and well-conn'd, was moulded
        Into familiar dialogue, oft rehears'd,
        Till, learnt by heart, 'tis now receiv'd for truth.
80 *Warb.*   Truth in her pure simplicity wants art
        To put a feigned blush on. Scorn wears only
        Such fashion as commends to gazers' eyes
        Sad ulcerated novelty, far beneath
        The sphere of majesty. In such a court
        Wisdom and gravity are proper robes
        By which the sovereign is best distinguish'd
        From zanies[3] to his greatness.
    Henry.   Sirrah, shift[4]
        Your antic pageantry, and now appear
        In your own nature, or you'll taste the danger
        Of fooling out of season.
90 *Warb.*   I expect
        No less than what severity calls justice,
        And politicians safety; let such beg
        As feed on alms. But if there can be mercy
        In a protested[5] enemy, then may it
        Descend to these poor creatures, whose engagements[6]
        To th' bettering of their fortunes have incurr'd
        A loss of all; to them, if any charity
        Flow from some noble orator, in death
        I owe[7] the fee of thankfulness.
    Henry.   So brave!
100   What a bold knave is this! Which of these rebels
        Has been the Mayor of Cork?
    Daub.   This wise formality.[8]
        Kneel to the king, 'ee rascals!
    Henry.   Canst thou hope
        A pardon, where thy guilt is so apparent?
    a-Water.   Under your good favours, as men are men, they may err.

---

[1] Here, twelve miles west of Leicester, Henry defeated Richard III, on
22 August 1485. [2] At one and the same time. [3] Comic servants in
commedia dell'arte. [4] Change (in the sense of change clothing).
[5] Publicly asserted. [6] Involvements. [7] i.e. I owe to the noble orator....
[8] i.e. this wise (intended sarcastically) man who is mannered, self-important.

For I confess, respectively,[1] in taking great parts,[2] the one
side prevailing, the other side must go down. Herein the
point is clear, if the proverb hold, that hanging goes by
destiny,[3] that it is to little purpose to say this thing or
that shall be thus or thus; for as the fates will have it, so

110   it must be, and who can help it?

Daub.   O blockhead, thou a privy councillor?
Beg life and cry aloud, 'Heaven save King Henry!'

a-Water.   Every man knows what is best, as it happens. For my
own part, I believe it is true, if I be not deceived, that
kings must be kings and subjects subjects. But which is which
— you shall pardon me for that; whether we speak or hold our
peace, all are mortal; no man knows his end.

Henry.   We trifle time with follies.

Omnes.[4]   Mercy, mercy!

Henry.   Urswick, command the dukeling and these fellows

120   To Digby,[5] the lieutenant of the Tower.
With safety let them be convey'd to London.
It is our pleasure no uncivil outrage,
Taunts, or abuse be suffer'd to their persons;
They shall meet fairer law than they deserve.
Time may restore their wits, whom vain ambition
Hath many years distracted.

Warb.   Noble thoughts
Meet freedom in capitivity. The Tower!
Our childhood's dreadful nursery!

Henry.   No more.

Urs.   Come, come; you shall have leisure to bethink 'ee.

Exit Urswick *with* Perkin *and his* [comrades].

130 *Henry.*   Was ever so much impudence in forgery?[6]
The custom, sure, of being styl'd a king
Hath fasten'd in his thought that he is such;
But we shall teach the lad another language.
'Tis good we have him fast.

Daub.   The hangman's physic
Will purge this saucy humour.

Henry.   Very likely;
Yet we could temper[7] mercy with extremity,[8]
Being not too far provok'd.

---

[1] Respectfully. [2] Important roles. [3] 'Hanging and wiving go by destiny'
(proverbial). [4] i.e. all the rebels. [5] Most historians refer to Sir John Digby
as Constable of the Tower at this time. [6] Deception. [7] Mix.
[8] Severity.

  Enter Oxford, Katherine, *in her richest attire,* Jane, [Dalyell,]
  and attendants[1]
Oxford.   Great sir, be pleas'd.
  With your accustom'd grace, to entertain
  The Princess Katherine Gordon.
40 Henry.   Oxford, herein
  We must beshrew[2] thy knowledge of our nature.
  A lady of her birth and virtues could not
  Have found us so unfurnish'd of good manners
  As not, on notice given, to have met her
  Half way in point of love.[3] Excuse, fair cousin,
  The oversight. Oh, fie, you may not kneel;
  'Tis most unfitting. First, vouchsafe[4] this welcome,
  A welcome to your own,[5] for you shall find us
  But guardian to your fortune and your honours.
50 Kath. My fortunes and mine honours are weak champions,
  As both are now befriended, sir; however,
  Both bow before your clemency.
Henry.   Our arms
  Shall circle them from malice. A sweet lady!
  Beauty incomparable! Here lives majesty
  At league with love.
Kath.   O sir, I have a husband.
Henry. We'll prove[6] your father, husband, friend, and servant,
  Prove what you wish to grant us.[7] Lords, be careful[8]
  A patent[9] presently be drawn for issuing
  A thousand pounds from our exchequer yearly
60 During our cousin's life. Our queen shall be
  Your chief companion, our own court your home,
  Our subjects all your servants.
Kath.   But my husband?
Henry. [*To* Dalyell] By all descriptions you are noble Dalyell,
  Whose generous truth hath fam'd a rare observance.[10]
  We thank 'ee. 'Tis a goodness gives addition[11]
  To every title boasted from your ancestry,
  In all most worthy.
Dal.   Worthier[12] than your praises,
  Right princely sir, I need not glory in.
Henry. Embrace him, lords. [*To* Katherine] Whoever calls you mistress

---

[1] Historically, Henry first met Katherine at Exeter several days after
dealing with Warbeck at Taunton. [2] Greatly blame. [3] In a matter of
affection. [4] Acknowledge. [5] i.e. exclusively yours. [6] Turn out to be.
[7] 'I'll prove to be whatever you wish me to be.' [8] i.e. be full of care that.
[9] A royal or authoritative document. [10] 'Whose loyalty has been so
notable as to be famous.' [11] An additional mark of honour. [12] i.e.
any title, etc., worthier ....

170   Is lifted in our charge; a goodlier beauty
         Mine eyes yet ne'er encounter'd.
    Kath.   [*Aside*]   Cruel misery
         Of fate, what rests[1] to hope for?
    Henry.   Forward, lords,
         To London. Fair, ere long I shall present 'ee
         With a glad object, peace, and Huntly's blessing.

                                              Exeunt omnes.

    [ACT V SCENE 3]

    [*London*][2]
    Enter Constable *and officers,* Warbeck, Urswick, *and* Lambert
         Simnel,[3] *like a falconer. A pair of stocks.*

    Const.   Make room there! Keep off, I require 'ee, and none come
         within twelve foot of His Majesty's new stocks, upon pain of
         displeasure. Bring forward the malefactor. Friend,[4] you must
         to this gear, no remedy. Open the hole, and in with his legs,
         just in the middle hole,[5] there, that hole. Keep off, or I'll
         commit you all! Shall not a man in authority be obey'd? So,
         so, there; 'tis as it should be. Put on the padlock, and give
         me the key. Off, I say, keep off!
    Urs.   Yet,[6] Warbeck, clear thy conscience; thou hast tasted
10   King Henry's mercy liberally. The law
         Has forfeited[7] thy life. An equal jury[8]
         Have doom'd thee to the gallows; twice, most wickedly,
         Most desperately, hast thou escap'd the Tower,
         Inveigling to thy party with thy witchcraft
         Young Edward, Earl of Warwick, son to Clarence,
         Whose[9] head must pay the price of that attempt.
         Poor gentleman, unhappy in his fate,
         And ruin'd by thy cunning. So a mongrel
         May pluck the true stag down. Yet, yet confess

---

[1] Remains. [2] Historically, successively the yard of Westminster Hall,
Cheapside and Tyburn. [3] After his impersonation of Edward, Earl of
Warwick, and his defeat at the Battle of Stoke, 1487, Simnel was pardoned
and became a minor functionary in Henry's court. [4] i.e. Warbeck. [5] Stocks
were ordinarily designed with leg holes in even numbers, but stocks with
three holes were known (W. Andrews, *Bygone Punishments* 1899). [6] Even
now. [7] Declared forfeit. [8] An impartial jury. Historically Warbeck was not
tried by a jury, but by the king's Marshal and another judge. [9] i.e. young
Edward's. He was beheaded in 1499.

20   Thy parentage, for yet the king has mercy.
  Lamb. You would be Dick the Fourth. Very likely!
  Your pedigree is publish'd;[1] you are known
  For Osbeck's son, of Tournay, a loose runagate,[2]
  A landloper.[3] Your father was a Jew,
  Turn'd Christian merely to repair his miseries.
  Where's now your kingship?
  Warb.   Baited to my death?
  Intolerable cruelty! I laugh at
  The Duke of Richmond's[4] practice[5] on my fortunes.
  Possession of a crown ne'er wanted heralds.
  Lamb. You will not know who I am?
30   *Urs.*   Lambert Simnel,
  Your predecessor in a dangerous uproar;
  But, on submission, not alone[6] receiv'd
  To grace, but by the king vouchsaf'd his service.
  Lamb. I would be Earl of Warwick, toil'd and ruffl'd[7]
  Against my master, leap'd to catch the moon,
  Vaunted my name Plantagenet, as you do.
  An earl, forsooth! Whenas in truth I was,
  As you are, a mere rascal. Yet His Majesty,
  A prince compos'd of sweetness – Heaven protect him –
40   Forgave me all my villainies, repriev'd
  The sentence of a shameful end, admitted
  My surety of obedience to his service;
  And I am now his falconer, live plenteously,
  Eat from the king's purse, and enjoy the sweetness
  Of liberty and favour, sleep securely.
  And is not this now better than to buffet[8]
  The hangman's clutches, or to brave the cordage
  Of a tough halter which will break your neck?
  So then the gallant totters.[9] Prithee, Perkin,
50   Let my example lead thee. Be no longer
  A counterfeit; confess, and hope for pardon.
  Warb. For pardon? Hold, my heart-strings, whiles contempt
  Of injuries,[10] in scorn, may bid defiance
  To this base man's foul language. Thou poor vermin,
  How dar'st thou creep so near me? Thou an earl?
  Why, thou enjoy'st as much of happiness
  As all the swinge[11] of slight ambition flew at.
  A dunghill was thy cradle. So a puddle,
  By virtue of the sunbeams, breathes[12] a vapour.

[1]Warbeck was compelled repeatedly to read his confession in public in
London. [2]Vagabond. [3]Wanderer. [4]i.e. King Henry's. [5]Trickery.
[6]Solely. [7]Struggled. [8]Contend with. [9]Swings to and fro (at the end of
a rope). [10]Affronts. [11]Impetus. [12]Exhales.

60   To infect the purer air, which[1] drops again
      Into the muddy womb that first exhal'd it.
      Bread and a slavish ease, with some assurance[2]
      From the base beadle's whip, crown'd all thy hopes.
      But, sirrah, ran there in thy veins one drop
      Of such a royal blood as flows in mine,
      Thou wouldst not change condition to be second
      In England's state without the crown itself.
      Coarse creatures are incapable of excellence.
      But let the world, as all to whom I am
70   This day a spectacle, to time deliver,
      And by tradition fix[3] posterity,
      Without another chronicle than truth,
      How constantly[4] my resolution suffer'd
      A martyrdom of majesty.
Lamb.   [*To* Urswick]   He's past
      Recovery; a Bedlam cannot cure him.
Urs.   [*To* Lambert Simnel]   Away! – Inform the king of his

                                                      behaviour.

Lamb.   Perkin, beware the rope; the hangman's coming.

                                                      Exit Simnel.

Urs.   If yet thou hast no pity of thy body,
      Pity thy soul.

      Enter Katherine, Jane, Dalyell, *and* Oxford

Jane.   Dear lady!
Oxford.   [*To* Katherine]   Whither will 'ee,
      Without respect of[5] shame?
80 *Kath.*   Forbear me, sir,
      And trouble not the current of my duty.
      O my lov'd lord! Can any scorn be yours
      In which I have no interest? Some kind hand
      Lend me assistance, that I may partake
      Th'infliction of this penance.[6] My life's dearest,
      Forgive me; I have stay'd too long from tend'ring
      Attendance on reproach,[7] yet bid me welcome.
Warb.   Great miracle of constancy! My miseries
      Were never bankrupt of their confidence,
90   In worst afflictions, till this;[8] now I feel them.
      Report[9] and thy deserts, thou best of creatures,

[1] i.e. which vapour. [2] Security. [3] Make firm to. [4] Steadfastly. [5] Regard
to. [6] Warbeck's punishment. [7] i.e. one who has been reproached.
[8] This moment. [9] i.e. thy reputation.

Might to eternity have stood a pattern
For every virtuous wife without this conquest.
Thou hast outdone belief; yet may their ruin
In after-marriages be never pitied
To whom thy story shall appear a fable.[1]
Why wouldst thou prove so much unkind to greatness[2]
To glorify thy vows by such a servitude?[3]
I cannot weep, but trust me, dear, my heart

100   Is liberal of passion. Harry Richmond,
A woman's faith hath robb'd thy fame of triumph.

Oxford.   Sirrah, leave off your juggling, and tie up
The devil that ranges in your tongue.

Urs.   Thus witches,
Possess'd, even [to] their deaths deluded, say
They have been wolves and dogs, and sail'd in egg-shells
Over the sea, and rid on fiery dragons,
Pass'd in the air more than a thousand miles
All in a night; the enemy of mankind[4]
Is powerful but false, and falsehood confident.

110 *Oxford.*   Remember, lady, who you are. Come from
That impudent imposter.

Kath.   You abuse us,
For when the holy churchman join'd our hands,
Our vows were real then; the ceremony
Was not in apparition,[5] but in act.
Be[6] what these people term thee, I am certain
Thou art my husband. No divorce in Heaven
Has been sued out[7] between us; 'tis injustice
For any earthly power to divide us.
Or we will live, or let us die together.
There is a cruel mercy.

120 *Warb.*   Spite of tyranny,
We reign in our affections, blessed woman.
Read in my destiny the wrack of honour;
Point out, in my contempt of death, to memory
Some miserable happiness, since herein,
Even when I fell, I stood enthron'd a monarch
Of one chaste wife's troth, pure and uncorrupted.
Fair angel of perfection, immortality
Shall raise thy name up to an adoration,
Court every rich[8] opinion of true merit,

130   And saint it in the calendar of virtue,

---

[1] 'May people who participate in later marriages which fail, and who believe your story only a legend, never be pitied.' [2] i.e. to your own rank. [3] Service to me. [4] Satan. [5] Illusion. [6] Though you (Warbeck) may be. [7] Put in suit. [8] Powerful.

When I am turn'd into the self-same dust
Of which I was first form'd.
Oxford.   The Lord Ambassador,
Huntly, your father, madam, should 'a look on
Your strange subjection in a gaze so public,
Would blush on your behalf and wish his country
Unleft for entertainment[1] to such sorrow.
Kath.   Why art thou angry, Oxford? I must be
More peremptory in my duty. [*To* Warbeck] Sir,
Impute it not unto immodesty
140   That I presume to press you to[2] a legacy
Before we part for ever.
Warb.   Let it be, then,
My heart, the rich remains of all my fortunes.
Kath.   Confirm it with a kiss, pray.
Warb.   Oh, with that
I wish to breathe my last! Upon thy lips,
Those equal twins of comeliness, I seal
The testament of honourable vows.
Whoever be that man that shall unkiss[3]
This sacred print[4] next,[5] may he prove more thrifty[6]
In this world's just applause, not more desertful.
150 *Kath.*   By this sweet pledge of both our souls, I swear
To die a faithful widow to thy bed,
Not to be forc'd or won. Oh, never, never![7]

Enter Surrey, Daubeney, Huntly, *and* Crawford

Daub.   Free[8] the condemned person, quickly free him.
What has 'a yet confess'd?
Urs.   Nothing to purpose;
But still 'a will be king.
Surrey.   Prepare your journey
To a new kingdom then. Unhappy madam,
Wilfully foolish! See, my Lord Ambassador,
Your lady daughter will not leave the counterfeit
In this disgrace of fate.[9]
Hunt.   I never pointed[10]
160   Thy marriage, girl, but yet, being married,
Enjoy thy duty to a husband freely.
The griefs are mine. I glory in thy constancy,
And must not say I wish that I had miss'd

---

[1] Experience.   [2] For.   [3] Cancel.   [4] Impress.   [5] Cf. *Richard II*, V, i, 74-5.
[6] Prosperous.   [7] Katherine was subsequently married thrice more before
her death in 1537.   [8] Release to us.   [9] This adverse fortune.
[10] Appointed, prescribed.

Some partage[1] in these trials of a patience.
Kath.   You will forgive me, noble sir?
Hunt.   Yes, yes.
In every duty of a wife and daughter
I dare not disavow thee. To your husband –
For such you are, sir – I impart a farewell
Of manly pity. What your life has pass'd through
170   The dangers of your end will make apparent,
And I can add, for comfort to your sufferance,
No cordial but the wonder of your frailty,
Which keeps so firm a station.[2] We are parted.
Warb.   We are. A crown of peace renew thy age,
Most honourable Huntly. Worthy Crawford,
We may embrace; I never thought[3] thee injury.
Craw.   Nor was I ever guilty of neglect
Which might procure such thought. I take my leave, sir.
Warb.   To you, Lord Dalyell, what? Accept a sigh;
'Tis hearty and in earnest.
180   *Dal.*   I want utterance.
My silence is my farewell.
Kath.   Oh, oh, –
Jane.   Sweet madam,
What do you mean? [*To* Dalyell] My Lord, your hand.
Dal.   Dear lady,
Be pleas'd that I may wait 'ee to your lodging.

                                        Exeunt Dalyell, Katherine, Jane.
Enter Sheriff *and officers,* Skelton, Astley, Heron, *and*
Mayor [of Cork], *with halters about their necks*

Oxford.   Look 'ee. Behold your followers, appointed
To wait on 'ee in death.[4]
Warb.   Why, peers of England,
We'll lead 'em on courageously. I read
A triumph over tyranny upon
Their several foreheads. Faint not in the moment
Of victory! Our ends and Warwick's head,
190   Innocent Warwick's head – for we are prologue
But to his tragedy – conclude the wonder
Of Henry's fears; and then the glorious race
Of fourteen kings, Plantagenets, determines[5]

---

[1] Share.   [2] 'The wonder is that a frail mortal can stand so firmly.'   [3] i.e.
thought to do thee.   [4] Only a-Water and his son (who does not appear in
this play) were in fact hanged at the same time as Warbeck (23 November
1499); Warwick was beheaded at Tower Hill five days later.   [5] Concludes.

In this last issue male.[1] Heaven be obey'd.
Impoverish time of its amazement, friends,
And we will prove as trusty in our payments
As prodigal to nature in our debts.[2]
Death? Pish! 'Tis but a sound, a name of air,
A minute's storm, or not so much. To tumble
200   From bed to bed, be massacr'd[3] alive
By some physicians for a month or two,
In hope of freedom from a fever's torments,
Might stagger manhood; here the pain is past
Ere sensibly[4] 'tis felt. Be men of spirit;
Spurn coward passion! So illustrious mention
Shall blaze our names, and style us kings o'er death.
Daub.   Away! Imposter beyond precedent!
No chronicle records his fellow.

Exeunt all officers and prisoners.

Hunt.   I have
Not thoughts left. 'Tis sufficient in such cases
Just laws ought to proceed.

Enter King Henry, Durham, *and* Hialas

210 *Henry.*   We are resolv'd.
Your business, noble lords, shall find success
Such as your king importunes.
Hunt.   You are gracious.
Henry.   Perkin, we are inform'd, is arm'd to die.
In that we'll honour him. Our lords shall follow
To see the execution; and from hence
We gather this fit use:[5] that public states,
As our particular bodies, taste[6] most good
In health when purged of corrupted blood.

Exeunt omnes.

[1] i.e. in me.   [2] 'Let us not give time a short period to be amazed by us; we will prove as dependable in our payments to fame as we are generous in our debt to nature (i.e. life).'   [3] Mangled.   [4] Consciously.   [5] Benefit. [6] Experience.

Epilogue

Here has appear'd, though in a several[1] fashion,
The threats of majesty, the strength of passion,
Hopes of an empire, change of fortunes; all
What can to theatres of greatness fall,[2]
Proving their weak foundations. Who will please,
Amongst such several sights, to censure these,[3]
No births abortive, nor a bastard brood,
Shame to a parentage or fosterhood,
May warrant by their loves all just excuses,[4]
And often find a welcome to the Muses.

FINIS.

---

[1] Distinct.   [2] i.e. everything that can happen in the realm of greatness.
[3] i.e. to pass judgment on these sights or events.   [4] i.e. may justify by their
affection or loyalty all legitimate excuses (for this work of art).

THE CARDINAL (1641)

by JAMES SHIRLEY
(1596-1666)

[Born in London and baptized on 7 September 1596. Educated at
Merchant Taylors', Oxford and Cambridge Universities (B.A. 1617).
Anglican holy orders, became a Roman Catholic *c.* 1623. Headmaster
St Alban's Grammar School, 1621-*c.* 1624. Playwright from *c.* 1625;
wrote for Queen's men, Ogliby's Theatre, Dublin, *c.* 1636-*c.* 1640, King's
men, *c.* 1640-2. Royalist soldier, schoolmaster in London. Poetry, masques
and more than thirty plays: comedies, notably *Hyde Park* (1632), *The
Lady of Pleasure* (1635), tragicomedies and one tragedy, *The Cardinal*
(1641). Shirley and his wife died (of exposure) during the Great Fire of
London].

Was the title figure of Shirley's only tragedy produced entirely from his
imagination or modelled, in whole or part, on a real person? Certainly,
Shirley's Cardinal owes something to biographies, folk-lore and other plays
about high ranking Roman Catholic and English churchmen, traditionally
thought to be Machiavellian in their drive for personal power, greedy for
physical gratification (especially sexual), manipulative behind the scenes,
éminences rouges.

Shirley's ambiguous pointing in the Prologue is of great interest. Here
the author urged viewers or readers not to identify the title character with
Cardinal Richelieu.[1] Shirley continued:

> A poet's art is to lead on your thought
> Through subtle paths and workings of a plot ...
> I will say nothing positive; you may
> Think what you please ...   (7-12)

These and other words of the Prologue may be regarded as an
invitation to make an alternative identification. Shirley may have had in
mind William Laud, Archbishop of Canterbury from 1633 to 1641, when
he was impeached.[2] *The Cardinal* was written and produced later in the
same year, although not published until 1653.

Archbishop Laud had a reputation for ambition and ruthlessness. He
was falsely accused of having pro-Catholic sympathies, and indisputably
he manipulated James I and Charles I.[3] There is, as well, the story that

[1] 1585-1642; chief minister to Louis XIII of France for over twenty
years, Cardinal from 1622 until his death from overwork.   [2] Laud was
tried and beheaded in 1645.   [3] Aspects of their characters may be
incorporated in the unnamed, pliant king of the play.

William Laud had hindered Shirley's early career in the Anglican Church, when Laud was President of St John's College, Oxford, where Shirley was apparently a student briefly. He evidently became a Roman Catholic about 1623, and may have suffered from or resented the Archbishop's persecution of Catholics during the 1630's.

One may see parallels between Cardinal Wolsey (*c.* 1475-1530) and the Cardinal of Shirley's play, but in 1641 Archbishop Laud was much more in the public consciousness. One aspect of Laud's ascetic life did not conform to the popular view of contemporary churchmen: there was not a hint of the sexual misdemeanours reputedly characteristic of self-indulgent prelates of the time.

Shirley's Cardinal seems, then, to be a composite figure, particularly since no clearly identifiable sources for the action of the play are evident. It belongs to an enduring tradition of plays about corrupt churchmen, thwarted romantic love linked with illicit sexual ambitions and the inevitably associated revenge motif. The lineage of the play may be traced from Kyd's *Spanish Tragedy* (1592), through Tourneur's *Revenger's Tragedy* (*c.* 1606),[1] Webster's *White Devil* (*c.* 1610) and *The Duchess of Malfi* (*c.* 1613), Middleton's *Women Beware Women* (*c.* 1621), Middleton and Rowley's *Changeling* (1622), Ford's *'Tis Pity She's a Whore* (*c.* 1630) and other related plays.

James Shirley is more notable as a clever adaptor and assimilator than as an original playwright. In particular, it is possible to trace many echoes and influences from *The Duchess of Malfi*. Shirley's Cardinal and his nephew Columbo share with Webster's Ferdinand and his brother (another Aragonian Cardinal) a concern that the duchess should marry only as commanded, if at all. Both Webster and Shirley's widowed duchesses marry, for love, a man of lower rank. In both plays the secretary is named Antonio; in Hernando, Columbo and D'Alvarez are interwoven elements from Webster's Bosola, Antonio and Ferdinand. Several verbal parallels are referred to in the footnotes to this edition of *The Cardinal*.

Like *The Duchess of Malfi*, *The Cardinal* contains much comedy.[2] The play includes several episodes of domestic intrigue, and there is much teasing and levity, with sexual overtones, particularly in the scenes involving Valeria, Celinda and Placentia. The men-servants' amusing preparations to stage their comedy (written by the chaplain!) have ironic overtones in relation to the serious scenes which precede and succeed III, ii.

Although the play has a clear, straight-line plot, interest is divided amongst several characters. By one reading, the Cardinal is the central figure, the arch-manipulator; by another it is Duchess Rosaura, who is repeatedly the object of the Cardinal's scheming, the victim of Columbo's wounded vanity and the unsuccessful revenger of her own wrongs.

---

[1] Sometimes credited to Middleton.   [2] Shirley devoted most of his professional career to writing comedies.

Columbo himself occupies a crucial role as ambitious militarist, as tricked
or rejected lover, as activator of the Cardinal's schemes. Hernando too
takes centre stage on occasion; he is the man whose military judgment
and courage are questioned, the man who would heroically rescue the
duchess. Although Valeria, Celinda and Placentia are deftly characterized
and individualized, they make only small contributions to the action.

The initial impression of the Cardinal is of deviousness:

> [He] holds intelligence
> With every bird i' th'air.   (I, i, 20-1)

His preoccupation is arranging the marriage of his nephew Columbo and
Duchess Rosaura. Her intuition warns her of his true character:

> Do not I walk upon the teeth of serpents
> And ... play with their stings?   (II, ii, 18-21)

The Cardinal's essential hypocrisy is in the foreground of the
duchess's bold criticism of the man who has the temerity to judge her
actions:

> |My fame, Lord Cardinal?
> It stands upon an innocence as clear
> As the devotions you pay to Heaven.   (II, iii, 114-6)
> 'Cause
> You dare do worse than marriage, must not I
> Be admitted what the church and law allows me?
>
> (II, iii, 121-3)

Such insights into the spirit of the Cardinal prepare one for his subsequent cruelty and violence, masked by his concern for the duchess's
welfare – 'He carries angels in his tongue and face' (V, ii, 89).

The final Machiavellian irony of the play centres on the Cardinal's
determination to carry Rosaura with him to death after he believes himself mortally wounded. In the complex effort to bring about the
duchess's death he becomes the author of his own demise. Despite the
title of the play, a twentieth-century reader may not regard the Cardinal
as either the primary or even a tragic figure in the play. Rather, it is the
destruction of the duchess's innocence and beauty that arouses pity.

Shirley's dramatic skill ensures sympathetic responses to the duchess
from the opening moments of the play: she was widowed before the
consummation of her first marriage, her sincere love for D'Alvarez was
condemned by the Cardinal and she is now betrothed unwillingly to the
rough-edged warrior, Columbo. The duchess's conflicts with Columbo and
the Cardinal create the primary tensions of the play, and her naive efforts
to obtain a release from the distasteful engagement precipitate the
tragedy.

Duchess Rosaura, like the Duchess of Malfi, is attractive for her
candour, courage, intelligence and vitality. One of the rewards of the
play is observing her development in strength of character as the dog-
matic Columbo and the ambitious Cardinal attempt to overwhelm her.
She must, of necessity, use a trick to end the involuntary betrothal, and
she seems, at first consideration, to act precipitously to achieve this

objective. Shirley has, however, incorporated a scene break, implying the passage of time, at an important point. The interval occurs between Rosaura's receipt of Columbo's letter, which terminates the engagement as she had requested (II, ii), and her seeking the king's permission to marry D'Alvarez (II, iii). Rosaura does not now tell the king why Columbo has released her, and Shirley does not reveal the text of her ambiguous letter until D'Alvarez has been barbarously murdered, moments after the marriage ceremony (III, ii, 147-52). Soon, desperate to achieve revenge on those responsible for her lover's death, the duchess joins forces with Hernando, who has his own reasons to be angry with both the Cardinal and Columbo.[1] Shirley could not allow her overtly to offer herself to Hernando, as the conventional reward for an avenger, without making her disloyal to D'Alvarez. She states that her lover's ashes can be appeased only by Hernando's taking revenge on Columbo, then continues cautiously:

> Yet if ever
> I entertain a thought of love hereafter
> Hernando from the world shall challenge[2] it.   (IV, ii, 186-8)

Qualifications of the same kind dominate Rosaura's subsequent comments to Hernando on the subject of his reward:

> [If thou shouldst die] thy memory
> Shall have a shrine, the next within my heart
> To my Alvarez'.   (IV, ii, 195-7)

> I do love
> *No man alive*[3] so well as you.   (V, iii, 26-7)

Several modern editors have assumed that Duchess Rosaura becomes genuinely distracted subsequent to her pretended madness, adopted, like that of Hamlet, for self-protection (IV, ii, 316-21). Although she encourages Hernando's assumption that she is mad (V, iii, 43-5), everything she says makes good sense –

> I can understand, although they say
> I have lost my wits   (V, iii, 12-3)

She is capable of plotting shrewdly the downfall of the Cardinal and defending herself verbally as he aggressively approaches her (V, iii, 128-69).

The basic theme which dominates the entire play is the search for justice. The duchess, D'Alvarez and Hernando all suffer an injustice initiated either by the Cardinal or Columbo. Halfway through the play Shirley uses the device of false hope – 'This shows like justice' (III, ii 247) – by the punishment of Columbo for his murder of D'Alvarez. This optimism is quickly qualified by the weakness of the king, who releases Columbo almost immediately, but hope for justice is revived by the

---

[1] Columbo had earlier found a flimsy pretext to dismiss Hernando from military service (II, i, 35-36). Columbo needed no advice about attacking the beseiged city, for he had already learned privately that it was vulnerable and could easily be captured (II, i, 77-80). [2] Claim. [3] Editor's italics.

confrontation which follows between Hernando and the Cardinal.

Inevitably, Shirley's imagery centres on the two subjects which dominate the play: justice and sexuality. The dramatist made little effort to develop elaborate patterns of imagery. Most of the images, usually in the form of metaphors, occur in isolation, arising out of the context as appropriate.

Not unnaturally, military images occur frequently, as do metaphors of death, poison and corruption. Some of these are related to surgery; for example,

> I have brought a lancet wi' me
> Shall open your hot veins and cool your fever.
>
> (V, iii, 175-6)

Shirley alluded repeatedly, often with heavy sarcasm, to the Cardinal's symbol of office, his red robes. The author referred, for instance, to 'the red cock' (V, iii, 54) and 'the o'ergrown lobster' (V, ii, 114). On occasion he used blood and passion metaphorically, creating sometimes an implicit link with the Cardinal's red.[1]

Nautical imagery is used frequently. The Cardinal 'sits at helm of state' (I, i, 40), making the lovers (Rosaura and D'Alvarez) 'fear a shipwreck on the coast' (II, iii, 69). Whilst he is dying the Cardinal utters his most sustained, though conventional, nautical speech:

> ... waft me with a little prayer;
> My wings that flag may catch the wind. But 'tis
> In vain; the mist is risen, and there's none
> To steer my wandering bark.   (V, iii, 282-5)

The need for clear vision or insight is alluded to at times, in terms of optical devices. This metaphor is used subtly to give force to the moralistic admonition that ends the play:

> None have more need of perspectives than kings.
>
> (V, iii, 299)

It may be that Shirley's fifteen years of writing comedies contributed to the rapid pace of *The Cardinal* and to the facile poetry, often genuinely conversational in tone. *Sententiae* rarely slow the play, although on occasion the convoluted syntax impedes the usually smooth flow of the verse. Infrequently Shirley established an emphasis with a short line or an extra stress, but apart from the one comic scene (III, ii), the play has in it very little prose.

James Shirley incorporated in *The Cardinal* much that is skilful in plot, characterization and themes; yet the play fails to reach the first rank of tragedy, perhaps because it inherited rather than innovated a tradition; it is too deeply immersed in its own conventions. Although each scene has a fundamental validity, the play has an atmosphere of unreality.

Like many other seventeenth-century tragedies, *The Cardinal* cannot inspire. Sordidness dominates, and no fully satisfying catharsis occurs

---

[1] See, for example, V, iii, 190.

at the end of the play. *The Cardinal* does not lead beyond itself; there are no survivors of the action to carry the torch.

Samuel Pepys saw the play in 1662, 1667 and 1668, with increasing enthusiasm; it was revived repeatedly until 1682, but seems not to have been performed since. The earliest edition (1653) is a satisfactory text, with few errors and inconsistencies.[1]

[1] The lack of a stage direction in the quarto at V, iii, 181, creates a possible misunderstanding of Hernando's character. Here he wounds the Cardinal, whereupon Antonelli and several servants rush in to defend their master, and Hernando challenges them all. Within moments, overwhelmed by numbers, he has received a fatal wound and dies. All editors since Gifford include the direction *Stabs himself* (at line 181); however, it seems altogether implausible, in view of his declared intention to defend himself to the death (V, iii, 65-79), that he should take his own life at the moment of possible victory over the Cardinal.

THE CARDINAL
by James Shirley
1641

To my worthily honoured friend, G.B.,[1] Esquire:

Sir,

I did suffer at the first some contention within me, and, looking upon myself, was inclined to stifle my ambitious thoughts in this dedication, but when some time and a happy conversation had preferred me to more acquaintance with you, which was more argument[2] to me than the fame[3] I had heard of your reputation with the most temperate and ingenious men, I found you not only an excellent judge, but a good man. At this, my modesty took full encouragement to make this offering, which as I conceive to be the best of my flock, I knew not a better altar whereon to make it a sacrifice, with this protestation, that it comes, and that is it only, which makes all devotions acceptable, from the heart, and your candid acceptance will bind me with all my services and remembrance to merit a reception with you, in the quality and honour of,

        Sir,

           Your most humble and devoted servant,

               Ja. Shirley.

---

[1] Perhaps George Buck, a descendant of Sir George Buck, Master of the Revels. The younger Buck wrote a conventional poetic tribute for Shirley's *Poems* (1646). [2] Proof. [3] Report.

To the surviving honour and ornament of the English scene,
                    James Shirley:
As Fate, which doth all human matters sway,
Makes proudest things grow up into decay,
And when they are to envied greatness grown
She wantonly falls off and throws them down,
So when our English drama was at height,
And shin'd and rul'd with majesty and might,
A sudden whirlwind[1] threw it from its seat,
Deflower'd the groves and quench'd the Muses' heat.
Yet, as in saints and martyr'd bodies, when
They cannot call their blessed souls again
To earth, relics and ashes men preserve
And think they do but what, blest, they deserve,
So I, by my devotion led, aspire
To keep alive your noble vestal fire,
Honour this piece which shows, sir, you have been
The last supporter of the dying scene,
And though I do not tell you how you dress
Virtue in glories and bold vice depress,[2]
Nor celebrate your lovely duchess' fall
Or the just ruin of your Cardinal,
Yet this I dare assert: When men have nam'd
Jonson, the nation's laureate, the fam'd
Beaumont and Fletcher, he that wo' not see
Shirley the fourth[3] must forfeit his best eye.

                                                    HALL.[4]

Prologue.[5]
The Cardinal! 'Cause we express no scene
We do believe most of you, gentlemen,
Are at this hour in France[6] and busy there
Though you vouchsafe to lend your bodies here;
But keep your fancy active till you know
By th' progress of our play 'tis nothing so.
A poet's art is to lead on your thought
Through subtle paths and workings of a plot,
And where your expectation does not thrive,

[1] One of several allusions to the troubled times in which the play was first
produced (1641). See also the Epilogue and the Alternate Prologue (p. 263).
[2] Disparage. [3] i.e. in stature. [4] Probably John Hall, of Durham, 1627-56,
author of *Horae Vacivae or Essayes* (1646), to which Shirley contributed
a brief prefatory poem. John Hall was also the author of a poetic tribute
attached to Brome's *A Jovial Crew* (published 1652). [5] Shirley's alternative
prologue is printed as an appendix at the end of this play, p.   . [6] i.e.
imaginatively, busy with the assumption that Cardinal Richelieu is the
real subject of the play.

If things fall better, yet you may forgive.
I will say nothing positive; you may
Think what you please — we call it but a play.
Whether the comic Muse or ladies' love,
Romance, or direful tragedy it prove
The bill[1] determines not; and would you be
Persuaded, I would have't a comedy,
For all[2] the purple[3] in the name and state
Of him that owns it; but 'tis left to fate.
Yet I will tell you ere you see it play'd
What the author — and he blush'd too, when he said,
Comparing with his own, for 't had been pride,
He thought, to build his wit a pyramid
Upon another's wounded fame, this play
Might rival with his best, and dar'd to say —
Troth, I am out! He said no more. You, then,
When 'tis done, may say your pleasures, gentlemen.

---

[1] Play advertisement. [2] In spite of. [3] This word described many shades of red, hence the allusion to the crimson robes of a cardinal.

Persons

King of Navarre
Cardinal
Columbo, *the Cardinal's nephew*
D'Alvarez
Hernando, *a colonel*
Alphonso
Lords
[Antonio,] *secretary to the duchess*
Colonels [, other officers, *and* Soldier]
Antonelli, *the Cardinal's servant*
Surgeon
Guard
Gentlemen-Usher
Attendants, etc.
Duchess Rosaura
Valeria, ⎫
Celinda, ⎭ *ladies*
Placentia, *a lady that waits upon the duchess*
[Jacques, Pedro, Rogero, and other servants]

Scene: Navarre.

ACT I SCENE 1

[The royal palace]
Enter two Lords *at one door,* Antonio[1] *at the other*

1 Lord.	Who is that?
2 Lord.	The duchess's secretary.
1 Lord.	[*To* Antonio] Signior.
Ant.	Your lordship's servant.
1 Lord.	How does Her Grace, since she left her mourning
	For the young Duke Mendoza,[2] whose timeless[3] death
	At sea left her a virgin and a widow?
2 Lord.	She's now inclining to a second bride.[4]
	When is the day of mighty marriage

10   To our great Cardinal's nephew, Don Columbo?

Ant.	When they agree; they wo' not steal to church.
	I guess the ceremonies will be loud and public.
	Your lordships will excuse me.

Exit.

1 Lord.	When they agree? Alas, poor lady, she
	Dotes not upon Columbo, when she thinks
	Of the young Count D'Alvarez, divorc'd from her
	By the king's power.
2 Lord.	And counsel of the Cardinal, to advance
	His nephew to the duchess' bed. 'Tis not well.

20 *1 Lord.*   Take heed. The Cardinal holds intelligence[5]

	With every bird i' th'air.
2 Lord.	Death on his purple pride!
	He governs all, and yet Columbo is
	A gallant gentleman.
1 Lord.	The darling of the war, whom victory
	Hath often courted; a man of daring
	And most exalted spirit. Pride in him
	Dwells like an ornament, where so much honour
	Secures[6] his praise.
2 Lord.	This is no argument
	He should usurp, and wear Alvarez' title

30   To the fair duchess. Men of coarser blood[7]

	Would not so tamely give this treasure up.
1 Lord.	Although Columbo's name is great in war,
	Whose glorious art and practice is above
	The greatness of Alvarez, yet he[8] cannot

---

[1]Q has Secretary or Sec. throughout.   [2]Not identifiable.   [3]Untimely.
[4]Bridegroom.   [5]Communication.   [6]Ensures.   [7]Inferior birth.   [8]Alvarez.

Want soul,[1] in whom alone survives the virtue
Of many noble ancestors, being the last
Of his great family.
2 Lord.   'Tis not safe, you'll say, to wrastle with the king.
1 Lord.   More danger if the Cardinal be displeas'd,
40   Who sits at helm of state. Count D'Alvarez
Is wiser to obey the stream than, by
Insisting on his privilege to her love,
Put both their fates upon a storm.
2 Lord.   If wisdom, not inborn fear, make him compose,[2]
I like it. How does the duchess bear herself?
1 Lord.   She moves by the rapture[3] of another wheel[4]
That must be obey'd, like some sad passenger
That looks upon the coast his wishes fly to,
But is transported by an adverse wind,
50   Sometimes a churlish pilot.
2 Lord.   She has a sweet and noble nature.
1 Lord.   That
Commends Alvarez! Hymen[5] cannot tie
A knot of two more equal hearts and blood.

Enter Alphonso

2 Lord.   Alphonso?
Alph.   My good Lord.
1 Lord.   What great affair
Hath brought you from the confines?[6]
Alph.   Such as will
Be worth your counsels, when the king hath read
My letters from the governor. The Aragonians,
Violating their confederate oath and league,
Are now in arms. They have not yet march'd towards us,
60   But 'tis not safe to expect[7] if we may timely
Prevent invasion.
2 Lord.   Dare they be so insolent?
1 Lord.   This storm I did foresee.
2 Lord.   What have they but the sweetness[8] of the king
To make a crime?
1 Lord.   But how appears the Cardinal
At this news?
Alph.   Not pale, although
He knows they have no cause to think him innocent,
As by whose counsel they were once surpris'd.

---

[1]Spirit.   [2]Agree.   [3]Momentum.   [4]i.e. an agency of movement.   [5]The
Greek god of marriage.   [6]Frontier (between Navarre and Aragon).   [7]Defer
action, wait.   [8]Mildness.

1 Lord.   There is more
                   Than all our present art can fathom in
70   This story, and I fear I may conclude
                   This flame has breath at home to cherish[1] it.
                   There's treason in some hearts, whose faces are
                   Smooth[2] to the state.
Alph.   My lords, I take my leave.
2 Lord.   Your friends, good captain.

                                                                    Exeunt.

[ACT I SCENE 2]

[*The duchess's house*]
Enter Duchess, Valeria, Celinda

Val.   Sweet madam, be less thoughtful. This obedience[3]
                   To passion will destroy the noblest frame
                   Of beauty that this kingdom ever boasted.
Cel.   This sadness might become your other habit[4]
                   And ceremonious black for him that died.
                   The times of sorrow are expir'd, and all
                   The joys that wait upon the court, your birth,
                   And a new hymen[5] that is coming towards you
                   Invite a change.
Duch.   Ladies, I thank you both.
10   I pray excuse a little melancholy
                   That is behind.[6] My year of mourning hath not
                   So clear'd my account with sorrow but there may
                   Some dark thoughts stay, with sad reflections,
                   Upon my heart for him I lost. Even this
                   New dress and smiling garment, meant to show
                   A peace concluded 'twixt my grief and me,
                   Is but a sad remembrance. But I resolve
                   To entertain more pleasing thoughts, and if
                   You wish me heartily to smile, you must
20   Not mention grief, not in advice to leave it.
                   Such counsels open but afresh the wounds
                   Ye would close up, and keep alive the cause
                   Whose bleeding you would cure. Let's talk of something
                   That may delight. You two are read in all
                   The histories of our court; tell me, Valeria,

---

[1]Encourage.   [2]Bland.   [3]Yielding.   [4]Apparel.   [5]Marriage.   [6]i.e. remains.

Who has thy vote for the most handsome man?[1]
[*Aside*] Thus I must counterfeit a peace, when all
Within me is at mutiny.
Val.   I have examin'd
All that are candidates for the praise of ladies,
30   But find — may I speak boldly to Your Grace,
And will you not return it in your mirth,
To make me blush?
Duch.   No, no; speak freely.
Val.   I wo' not rack[2] your patience, madam, but
Were I a princess, I should think Count D'Alvarez
Had sweetness to deserve me from the world.
Duch.   [*Aside*] Alvarez! She's a spy upon my heart.
Val.   He's young and active, and compos'd most sweetly.
Duch.   I have seen a face more tempting.
Val.   It had then
Too much of woman in't. His eyes speak movingly,
40   Which may excuse his voice, and lead away
All female pride his captive. His hair black,
Which naturally falling into curls —
Duch.   Prithee, no more. Thou art in love with him.
The man in your esteem, Celinda, now?
Cel.   Alvarez is, I must confess, a gentleman
Of handsome composition, but with
His mind,[3] the greater excellence, I think
Another may delight a lady more,
If man be well consider'd. That's Columbo,
Now, madam, voted[4] to be yours.
50 *Duch.*   [*Aside*]   My torment!
Val.   [*Aside*] She affects[5] him not.
Cel.   He has person[6] and a bravery beyond
All men that I observe.
Val.   He is a soldier,
A rough-hewn man, and may show well at distance.
His talk will fright a lady. War and grim-
Fac'd honour are his mistresses.[7] He raves[8]
To hear a lute. Love meant him not his priest.
Again your pardon, madam; we may talk,
But you have art to choose and crown affection.

[Valeria *and* Celinda *move aside and talk*]

---

[1]Cf., *Two Gentlemen of Verona*, I, ii, 1-6; *The Merchant of Venice*, I, ii,
35-132.   [2]Strain.   [3]i.e. with reference to his intellect.   [4]Assigned by a
vow.   [5]Fancies.   [6]A bearing.   [7]Cf. Hotspur, *1 Henry IV*, I, iii, 201-7;
II, iii, 31-112; IV, i, 76-82, etc.   [8]Goes mad.

60 *Duch.*   What is it to be born above these ladies,
                And want their freedom? They are not constrain'd
                Nor slav'd by their own greatness[1] or the kings's,
                But let their free hearts look abroad and choose
                By their own eyes to love. I must repair
                My poor afflicted bosom and assume
                The privilege I was born with, which now prompts me
                To tell the king he hath no power nor art
                To steer a lover's soul.

          Enter Antonio

                                      What says Count D'Alvarez?
     Ant.   Madam, he'll attend you.
70 *Duch.*   Wait you, as I directed. When he comes
                Acquaint me privately.
     Ant.   Madam, I have news;
                'Tis now arriv'd the court, we shall have wars.
     Duch.   I find an army here of killing thoughts.
     Ant.   The king has chosen Don Columbo general,
                Who is immediately to take his leave.
     Duch.   [*Aside*] What flood is let into my heart! — How far
                Is he to go?
     Ant.   To Aragon.
     Duch.   That's well
                At first. He should not want a pilgrimage
                To the unknown world[2] if my thoughts might convey him.
80 *Ant.*   'Tis not impossible he may go thither.
     Duch.   How?
     Ant.   To the unknown other world.[3] He goes to fight;
                That's in his way. Such stories are in nature.[4]
     Duch.   Conceal this news.
     Ant.   He wo' not be long absent.
                The affair will make him swift to kiss Your Grace's hand.

                                                                    [*Exit.*]

     Duch.   He cannot fly
                With too much wing to take his leave.
                             [*To* Celinda *and* Valeria] I must
                Be admitted to your conference. Ye have
                Enlarg'd my spirits; they shall droop no more.
90 *Cel.*   We are happy if we may advance one thought
                To Your Grace's pleasure.

[1] Rank. [2] i.e. to some very distant place. [3] Death. [4] i.e. death is in the
natural way of things in war.

Val.   Your eye before was in eclipse. These smiles
      Become you, madam.
Duch.   [*Aside*] I have not skill to contain myself.

Enter Placentia

Plac.   The Cardinal's nephew, madam, Don Columbo.
Duch.   Already? Attend him.

Exit Placentia.

Val.   Shall we take our leave?
Duch.   He shall not know, Valeria, how you prais'd him.[1]
Val.   If he did, madam, I should have the confidence
      To tell him my free thoughts.

Enter Columbo

100 *Duch.*   My lord, while I'm in study to requite
      The favour you ha' done me, you increase
      My debt to such a sum, still[2] by a new honouring
      Your servant, I despair of my own freedom.
Col.   Madam, he kisseth your white hand, that[3] must
      Not surfeit in this happiness; and, ladies,
      I take your smiles for my encouragement.
      I have not long to practise these court tactics.

[*Kisses* Celinda *and* Valeria]

Cel.   [*Aside*] He has been taught to kiss.
Duch.   There's something, sir,
      Upon your brow I did not read before.
Col.   Does the character[4] please you, madam?
110 *Duch.*   More,
      Because it speaks you cheerful.
Col.   'Tis for such
      Access[5] of honour, as must make Columbo
      Worth all your love. The king is pleas'd to think
      Me fit to lead his army.
Duch.   How! An army?
Col.   We must not use the priest till I bring home
      Another triumph, that now stays for me
      To reap it in the purple[6] field of glory.
Duch.   But do you mean to leave me, and expose

---

[1] The duchess speaks ironically; see I, ii, 52-6.   [2] Always.   [3] i.e. he who.
[4] Appearance.   [5] Increase.   [6] Bloody.

Yourself to the devouring war? No enemy
120 Should divide us; the king is not so cruel.
Col.   The king is honourable, and this grace[1]
More answers my ambition than his gift
Of thee and all thy beauty, which I can
Love as becomes thy soldier, and fight
To come again,[2] a conqueror of thee.

She weeps

Then[3] I must chide this fondness.[4]

Enter Antonio

Ant.   Madam, the king and my Lord Cardinal.

[*Exit.*]
Enter King, Cardinal, *and lords*

King.   Madam, I come to call a servant[5] from you
And strengthen his excuse. The public cause
130 Will plead for your consent. At his return
Your marriage shall receive triumphant ceremonies;
Till then you must dispense.[6]
Card.   [*Aside*]   She appears sad
To part with him. [*To* Columbo] I like it fairly, nephew.

[Celinda *and* Valeria *talk apart*]

Cel.[7]   Is not the general a gallant man?
What lady would deny him a small courtesy?
Val.   Thou hast converted me, and I begin
To wish it were no sin.
Cel.   Leave that to narrow consciences.
Val.   You are pleasant.[8]
Cel.   But he would please one[9] better. Do such men
Lie with their pages?
140 *Val.*   Wouldst thou make a shift?[10]
Cel.   He is going to a bloody business;
'Tis pity he should die without some heir.
That lady were hard-hearted now that would

---

[1] Favour.   [2] i.e. to return to once more.   [3] In addition.   [4] Foolishness.
[5] Lover.   [6] Forgo.   [7] Celinda and Valeria's speech prefixes have been erroneously transposed in Q, lines 134-46.   [8] Facetious.   [9] i.e. Valeria.
[10] 'Would you change places with Columbo's page?'

Not help posterity, for the mere good[1]
O' th' king and commonwealth.
Val.   Thou art wild. We may be observ'd.
Duch.   [*To* King] Your will must guide me. Happiness and
                              conquest
Be ever waiting on his sword!
Col.   Farewell.

                    Exeunt King, Columbo, Cardinal, Lords.

Duch.   Pray give leave to examine a few thoughts.
Expect me in the garden.
Ladies.   We attend.

                              Exeunt Ladies.

Duch.   This is above all expectation happy.
Forgive me, Virtue, that I have dissembled,
And witness with me I have not a thought
To tempt or to betray him, but secure[2]
The promise I first made to love and honour.

    Enter Antonio

Ant.   The Count D'Alvarez, madam.
Duch.   Admit him,
And let none interrupt us.

                         [*Exit.* Antonio.]

                    How shall I
Behave[3] my looks? The guilt of my neglect,
Which had no seal from hence,[4] will call up blood
160   To write upon my cheeks the shame and story
In some red letter.

    Enter D'Alvarez

D'Alv.   Madam, I present
One that was glad to obey Your Grace, and come
To know what your commands are.
Duch.   Where I once
Did promise love, a love that had the power
And office of a priest to chain my heart

---

[1] If for nothing more than the good.   [2] To reinforce her relationship with
D'Alvarez.   [3] Discipline.   [4] i.e. which had no warrant from me.

To yours, it were injustice to command.

D'Alv.   But I can look upon you, madam, as
Becomes a servant; with as much humility,
In tenderness[1] of your honour and great fortune,
70   Give up, when you call back your bounty, all that
Was mine, as I had pride to think them[2] favours.

Duch.   Hath love taught thee no more assurance in
Our mutual vows, thou canst suspect it possible
I should revoke a promise made to Heaven
And thee so soon? This must arise from some
Distrust of thy own faith.

D'Alv.   Your Grace's pardon.
To speak with freedom, I am not so old
In cunning to betray, nor young in time
Not to see when and where I am at loss,
180   And how to bear my fortune and my wounds,
Which, if I look for health, must still bleed inward,
A hard and desperate condition.
I am not ignorant your birth and greatness
Have plac'd you to grow up with the king's grace
And jealousy,[3] which to remove, his power
Hath chosen a fit object for your beauty
To shine upon, Columbo, his great favourite.
I am a man on whom but late the king
Has pleas'd to cast a beam, which was not meant
190   To make me proud, but wisely to direct
And light me to my safety. Oh, dear madam,
I will not call more witness of my love,
If you will let me still give it that name,
Than this, that I dare make myself a loser,
And to your will give all my blessings up.
Preserve your greatness and forget a trifle,
That shall at best, when you have drawn me up,
But hang about you like a cloud, and dim
The glories you were born to.

Duch.   Misery
200   Of birth and state! That I could shift into
A meaner blood or find some art to purge
That part which makes my veins unequal.[4] Yet
Those nice[5] distinctions have no place in us;
There's but a shadow difference, a title.
Thy stock partakes as much of noble sap
As that which feeds the root of kings, and he
That writes[6] a lord hath all the essence of

[1] Consideration.   [2] i.e. your bounties.   [3] Vigilance.   [4] i.e. unequal to yours.
[5] Subtle.   [6] Designates himself.

Nobility.

D'Alv.   'Tis not a name that makes
Our separation; the king's displeasure

210   Hangs a portent to fright us, and the matter
That feeds this exhalation[1] is the Cardinal's
Plot to advance his nephew. Then Columbo,
A man made up for some prodigious[2] act,
Is fit to be consider'd. In all the three
There is no character[3] you fix upon
But has a form of ruin to us both.

Duch.   Then you do look on these with fear?

D'Alv.   With eyes
That should think tears a duty, to lament
Your least unkind fate; but my youth dares boldly

220   Meet all the tyranny o' th' stars, whose black
Malevolence but shoot my single tragedy.
You are above the value of many worlds
Peopled with such as I am.

Duch.   What if Columbo,
Engag'd to war in his hot thirst of honour,
Find out the way to death?

D'Alv.   'Tis possible.

Duch.   Or say, no matter by what art[4] or motive,
He gives his title[5] up and leave[s] me to
My own election?[6]

D'Alv.   If I then be happy
To have a name within your thought, there can

230   Be nothing left to crown me with new blessing.
But I dream thus of Heaven, and wake to find
My amorous soul a mockery. When the priest
Shall tie you to another, and the joys
Of marriage leave no thought at leisure to
Look back upon Alvarez, that must wither
For loss of you, yet then I cannot lose
So much of what I was, once in your favour,
But in a sigh pray still you may live happy.

Exit.

Duch.   My heart is in a mist.[7] Some good star smile

240   Upon my resolution, and direct
Two lovers in their chaste embrace to meet.
Columbo's bed contains my winding sheet.

Exit.

[1] Meteor.   [2] Portentous.   [3] Face.   [4] Stratagem.   [5] Claim.   [6] Preference.
[7] A cloud, i.e. confused.

[ACT II SCENE 1]

[*In* Columbo's camp]
Enter General Columbo, Hernando, *two* Colonels, Alphonso, *two*
Captains, *and other officers, as at a council of war*

Col.   I see no face in all this council that
Hath one pale fear upon't, though we arriv'd not
So timely[1] to secure[2] the town, which gives
Our enemy such triumph.
1 Colonel.   'Twas betray'd.
Alph.   The wealth of that one city
Will make the enemy glorious.[3]
1 Colonel.   They dare
Not plunder it.
Alph.   They give fair quarter[4] yet.
They only seal up men's estates,[5] and keep
Possession for the city's use. They take up[6]
No wares without security, and he
Whose single[7] credit will not pass[8] puts in[9]
Two lean[10] comrades, upon whose bonds 'tis not
Religion[11] to deny 'em.
Col.   To repair this[12]
With honour, gentlemen?
Hern.   My opinion is
To expect awhile.
Col.   Your reason?
Hern.   Till their own
Surfeit betray 'em; for their soldier,
Bred up with coarse and common bread, will show
Such appetites on the rich cates they find,
They will spare our swords a victory, when their own
Riot and luxury destroys 'em.
20 *1 Colonel.*   That
Will show our patience too like a fear.
With favour of his excellence,[13] I think
The spoil of cities takes not off the courage,

[1] Opportunely.   [2] Protect.   [3] Vainglorious.   [4] Offer fair terms.   [5] Claim
private property.   [6] Seize.   [7] Individual.   [8] Is not acceptable.   [9] Offers as
security.   [10] Ill-provided.   [11] A matter of principle.   [12] i.e. the disgrace of
this defeat.   [13] i.e. with permission of Hernando.

But doubles it on soldiers. Besides,
While we have tameness to expect, the noise[1]
Of their success and plenty will increase
Their army.

Hern.   'Tis considerable, we do not
    Exceed in foot or horse,[2] our muster not
    'Bove sixteen thousand both; and the infantry
    .Raw and not disciplin'd to act.

30 *Alph.*   Their hearts,
    But with[3] a brave thought of their country's honour,
    Will teach 'em how to fight, had they not seen
    A sword. But we decline[4] our own too much;
    The men are forward[5] in their arms, and take
    The use with avarice of fame.[6]

                        They[7] *rise and talk privately*

Col.   Colonel,
    I do suspect you are a coward.

Hern.   Sir!

Col.   Or else a traitor. Take your choice. No more.
    I call'd you to a council, sir, of war,
    Yet keep your place.

Hern.   I have worn other names.

40 *Col.*   Deserve 'em. Such
    Another[8] were enough to unsoul an army.
    Ignobly talk of patience till they drink
    And reel to death? We came to fight and force 'em
    To mend their pace. Thou hast no honour in thee,
    Not enough noble blood to make a blush
    For thy tame eloquence.

Hern.   My lord, I know
    My duty to a general; yet there are
    Some that have known me here. Sir, I desire
    To quit my regiment.

Col.   You shall have licence.

50   [*Calls*] Ink and paper!

    Enter [*servant*] *with paper and standish;*[9] *exit.*

1 Colonel.   The general's displeas'd.
2 Colonel.   How is't, Hernando?

---

[1] Report.   [2] 'It is a consideration that we do not exceed the enemy in strength.'   [3] i.e. with only.   [4] Disparage.   [5] Eager.   [6] i.e. they use their arms as if greedy for fame.   [7] Columbo and Hernando.   [8] i.e. as you.   [9] A stand containing ink, pens, etc.

Hern.   The general has found out employment for me;
    He is writing letters back.
Alph., [1] Capt.   To his mistress?
Hern.   Pray do not trouble me; yet prithee speak,
    And flatter not thy friend. Dost think I dare
    Not draw my sword and use it when cause
    With honour calls to action?
Alph., [1] Colonel.   With the most valiant man alive!
Hern.   You'll do me some displeasure in your loves.[1]
60   Pray, to your places.
Col.   [*To* Hernando] So, bear those letters to the king.
    It[2] speaks my resolution before
    Another sun decline to charge the enemy.
Hern.   [*Aside*] A pretty court way·
    Of dismissing an officer! – I obey. Success
    Attend your councils.

                                      Exit.

Col.   If here be any dare not look on danger
    And meet it like a man, with scorn of death,
    I beg his absence, and a coward's fear
    Consume him to a ghost.
70 *1 Colonel.*   None such here.
Col.   Or if in all your regiments you find
    One man that does not ask to bleed with honour,
    Give him a double pay to leave the army.
    There's service to be done will call the spirits
    And aid of men.
1 Colonel.   You give us all new flame.
Col.   I am confirm'd, and you must lose no time.
    The soldier that was took last night to me
    Discover'd[3] their whole strength, and that we have
    A party[4] in the town, the river that
80   Opens the city to the west unguarded.
    We must this night use art and resolutions;
    We cannot fall ingloriously.
1 Capt.   That voice is every man's.

    Enter Soldier, *and* Antonio *with a letter*

Col   What now?
Sold.   Letters.
Col.   Whence?

---

[1] i.e. I shall be in trouble (with Columbo) as a result of your affection.
[2] This communication.   [3] Disclosed.   [4] Partisans.

Sold.   From the duchess.
Col.   They are welcome.
          Meet at my tent again this evening.
90   Yet stay. Some wine. The duchess' health!
          See it go round.

                              [*Moves apart and reads a letter*]

Ant.   It wo' not please His Excellence.
1 Colonel.   The duchess' health!
2 Capt.   To me! More wine!
Ant.   The clouds are gathering, and his eyes shoot fire;
          Observe what thunder follows.
2 Capt   The general has but ill news. I suspect
          The duchess sick, or else the king,
1 Capt.   Maybe
          The Cardinal.
2 Capt.   His soul has long been look'd for.[1]
Col.   [*Aside*] She dares not be so insolent! It is
100   The duchess' hand. How am I shrunk in fame
          To be thus play'd withall! She writes and counsels
          Under my hand[2] to send her back a free
          Resign of all my interest to her person,
          Promise, or love; that there's no other way,
          With safety of my honour, to revisit her.
          The woman is possess'd with some bold devil,
          And wants an exorcism; or I am grown
          A cheap, dull, phlegmatic fool, a post that's carv'd
          I th' common street,[3] and holding out my forehead
110   To every scurril[4] wit to pin disgrace
          And libels on't. [*To* Antonio] Did you bring this to me,
                                                                sir?
          My thanks shall warm your heart.

                                        Draws a pistol[5]

Ant.   Hold, hold, my lord.
          I know not what provokes this tempest, but
          Her Grace ne'er show'd more freedom from a storm
          When I receiv'd this paper. If you have
          A will to do an execution,
          Your looks, without that engine, sir, may serve.
          I did not like the employment.

---

[1] Expected (in Heaven).   [2] In my own writing.   [3] A post utilized for putting
up messages and notices.   [4] Scurrilous.   [5] Cf. *Antony and Cleopatra*,
II, v, 60-7.

Col.   Ha! Had she
          No symptom, in her eye or face, of anger
          When she gave this[1] in charge?
120 *Ant.*   Serene as I
          Have seen the morning rise upon the spring,
          No trouble in her breath, but such a wind
          As came to kiss and fan the smiling flowers.
     Col.   No poetry![2]
     Ant.   By all the truth in prose,
          By honesty, and your own honour, sir,
          I never saw her look more calm and gentle.
     Col.   I am too passionate; you must forgive me.
          [*Aside*] I have found it out: The duchess loves me dearly;
          She express'd a trouble in her when I took
130   My leave, and chid me with a sullen eye.
          'Tis a device to hasten my return.
          Love has a thousand arts; I'll answer it
          Beyond her expectation, and put
          Her soul to a noble test. – Your patience, gentlemen;
          The king's health will deserve a sacrifice of wine.

                                        [*Writes at standish*]

     Ant.   [*Aside*] I am glad to see this change, and thank my wit
          For my redemption.
     1 Colonel.   Sir, the soldiers' curse on him loves not our master.
     2 Colonel.   And they curse loud enough to be heard.
140 *2 Capt.*   Their curse has the nature of gunpowder.
     Ant.   They do not pray with half the noise.
     1 Colonel.   Our general is not well mix'd.[3]
          He has too great a portion of fire.[4]
     2 Colonel.   His mistress cool him – her complexion[5]
          Carries some phlegm[6] – when they two meet in bed?
     2 Capt.   A third[7] may follow.
     1 Capt.   'Tis much pity
          The young duke liv'd not to take the virgin off.[8]
     1 Colonel.   'Twas the king's act to match two rabbit-suckers.[9]
150 *2 Colonel.*   A common trick of state.
          The little great man marries, travels then

---

[1]i.e. this letter.   [2]'Don't use poetic description.'   [3]i.e. he does not have
within him equal proportions of the four elements.   [4]An excess of fire
was believed to create a choleric temperament, hot and dry, making the
person proud, quick to anger, revengeful.   [5]Temperament.   [6]It had the
character of being cold and moist.   [7]i.e. an offspring.   [8]i.e. remove her
from the state of virginity. The following line suggests an arranged child-
marriage.   [9]Suckling rabbits, i.e. children.

Till both grow up, and dies when he should do
The feat. These things are still[1] unlucky
On the male side.
Col.   This to the duchess' fair hand.

                                        [*Gives* Antonio *a letter*]

Ant.   She will think
Time hath no wing till I return.

                                                      [*Exit.*]

Col.   Gentlemen,
Now each man to his quarter, and encourage
The soldier. I shall take a pride to know
Your diligence, when I visit all your
Several commands.
160 *Omnes.*   We shall expect.
2 Colonel.   And move by your directions.
Col.   Y'are all noble.

                                              Exeunt.

[ACT II SCENE 2]

[*The duchess's house*]
Enter Cardinal, Duchess, Placentia

Card.   I shall perform a visit daily, madam,
In th'absence of my nephew, and be happy
If you accept my care.
Duch.   You have honour'd me,
And if your entertainment[2] have not been
Worthy Your Grace's person, 'tis because
Nothing can reach it in my power; but where
There is no want of zeal, other defect
Is only a fault to exercise[3] your mercy.
Card.   You are bounteous in all. I take my leave,
10   My fair niece, shortly,[4] when Columbo has
Purchas'd[5] more honours to prefer[6] his name

---

[1] Always.   [2] The welcome I have shown you.   [3] i.e. only a fault in me upon
which you may exercise...   [4] i.e. whom you shall be shortly.   [5] Acquired.
[6] Advance.

And value to your noble thoughts. Meantime,
Be confident you have a friend, whose office
And favour' with the king shall be effectual
To serve Your Grace.
Duch.   Your own good deeds reward you,
Till mine rise equal to deserve their benefit.[1]

Exit Cardinal.

Leave me awhile.

Exit Placentia.

Do not I walk upon the teeth of serpents
And, as[2] I had a charm against their poison,
20   Play with their stings? The Cardinal is subtle,
Whom 'tis not wisdom to incense, till I
Hear to what destiny Columbo leaves me.
Maybe the greatness of his soul will scorn
To own what comes with murmur,[3] if he can
Interpret me so happily.[4]

Enter Antonio *with a letter*

Art come?
Ant.   His Excellence salutes Your Grace.
Duch.   Thou hast
A melancholy brow. How did he take my letter?
Ant.   As he would take a blow, with so much sense
Of anger his whole soul boil'd in his face,
30   And such prodigious flame in both his eyes
As they had been th'only seat of fire, and at
Each look a salamander[5] leaping forth,
Not able to endure the furnace.
Duch.   Ha! Thou dost
Describe him with some horror.
Ant.   Soon as he
Had read again and understood your meaning,
His rage had shot me with a pistol, had not
I us'd some soft and penitential language
To charm the bullet.
Duch.   Wait at some more distance.

[1] 'May your good deeds reward you until mine equal them, to deserve their beneficent influence.'   [2] i.e. as if.   [3] Discontent.   [4] Fortunately.   [5] An animal reputed to be able to live in fire. Cf. a similar but less extravagant image to describe Ferdinand in Webster, *The Duchess of Malfi,* III, iii, 49-50.

[Antonio *moves aside*]

My soul doth bathe itself in a cold dew.
40   Imagine I am opening of a tomb;
Thus I throw off the marble to discover

[*Opens* Columbo's *letter*]

What antic[1] posture death presents in this
Pale monument to fright me. Ha!
My heart, that call'd my blood and spirits to
Defend it from the invasion of my fears,
Must keep a guard about it still, lest this
Strange and too mighty joy crush it to nothing!
Antonio.
Ant.   Madam.
Duch.   Bid my steward give thee
Two thousand ducats.[2] Art sure I am awake?
50 *Ant.*   I shall be able to resolve[3] you, madam,
When he has paid the money.
Duch.   Columbo now is noble.

Exit Duchess.

Ant.   This is better
Than I expected, if my lady be
Not mad, and live to justify[4] her bounty.

Exit.

[ACT II SCENE 3]

[*The royal palace*]
Enter King, D'Alvarez, Hernando, Lords

King.   The war is left to him,[5] but we must have
You reconcil'd, if that be all your difference.
His rage flows like a torrent when he meets
With opposition. Leave[6] to wrastle with him,
And his hot blood retreats into a calm,
And then he chides his passion. You shall back[7]

[1] Grotesque.   [2] The equivalent of about £750 in seventeenth-century
terms.   [3] Assure.   [4] Make good.   [5] i.e. Columbo.   [6] Cease.   [7] i.e. go back.

With letters from us.

Hern.   Your commands are not
      To be dispúted.

King.   Alvarez.

                                        [*They talk aside*]

1 Lord.   [*To* Hernando]   Lose not
      Yourself[1] by cool submission. He[2] will find
10   His error and the want of such a soldier.

2 Lord.   Have you seen the Cardinal?

Hern.   Not yet.

1 Lord.   He wants no plot —

Hern.   The king I must obey;
      But let the purple gownman place his engines
      I' th' dark, that wounds me.[3]

2 Lord.   Be assur'd
      Of what we can to friend you, and the king
      Cannot forget your service.

Hern.   I am sorry
      For that poor gentleman.[4]

D'Alv.   [*To* King]   I must confess, sir,
      The duchess has been pleas'd to think me worthy
      Her favours, and in that degree of honour[5]
20   That has oblig'd my life to make the best
      Return of service, which is not, with bold
      Affiance[6] in her love, to interpose
      Against her happiness and your election.[7]
      I love so much her honour I have quitted[8]
      All my desires, yet would not shrink to bleed
      Out my warm stock of life, so the last drop
      Might benefit her wishes.

King.   I shall find
      A compensation for this act, Alvarez.
      It hath much pleas'd us.

      Enter Duchess *with a letter* [, *attended by a*] *Gentleman-Usher*

Duch.   Sir, you are the king,
30   And in that sacred title[9] it were sin
      To doubt a justice. All that does concern

---

[1]'Do not lose your integrity.'   [2]Columbo.   [3]'The Cardinal, who would in-
jure me, must set up his snares in darkness (to escape my vigilance).'   [4]i.e.
Alvarez.   [5]In honouring me so much.   [6]Trust.   [7]Choice.   [8]Renounced.
[9]i.e. of king, by divine right. Perhaps the allusion is evidence of Shirley's
royalist sympathies.

My essence[1] in this world and a great part
Of the other bliss[2] lives in your breath.[3]
King.   What intends the duchess?
Duch.   That will instruct you, sir. Columbo has,

                        [*Gives* King *the letter*]

Upon some better choice or discontent,
Set my poor soul at freedom.
King.   'Tis his character.[4]

                               Reads

"Madam, I easily discharge all my pretensions[5] to your love
and person. I leave you to your own choice, and in what
you have obliged yourself to me, resume[6] a power to cancel
40   if you please.   Columbo."
This is strange.
Duch.   Now do an act to make
Your chronicle[7] belov'd and read for ever.
King.   Express youself.[8]
Duch.   Since by divine infusion,[9]
For 'tis no art could force the general to
This change[10] – second this justice and bestow
The heart you would have given from me, by
Your strict commands to love Columbo, where
'Twas meant by Heaven, and let your breath return
Whom you divorc'd, Alvarez, mine.
Lords.   This is
But justice, sir.
50 *King.*   It was decreed above,
And since Columbo has releas'd his interest
Which we had wrought[11] him, not without some force
Upon your will, I give you your own wishes.
Receive your own Alvarez; when you please
To celebrate your nuptial, I invite
Myself your guest.
Duch.   Eternal blessings crown you!
Omnes.   And every joy your marriage.

   Exit King, *who meets the* Cardinal. *They confer.*

[1] Existence. [2] i.e. the bliss of the other world, Heaven. [3] Utterance.
[4] Handwriting. [5] Claims. [6] i.e. you resume. [7] History. [8] State yourself
explicitly. [9] Inspiration. [10] The Duchess, in her haste to make her point,
leaves the phrases dangling. Words like 'this has come to pass' might follow
"change." [11] Fashioned for.

D'Alv.   I know not whether I shall wonder[1] most
           Or joy to meet this happiness.
Duch.   Now the king
60   Hath planted us, methinks we grow already,
       And twist our loving souls above the wrath
       Of thunder to divide us.[2]
D'Alv.   Ha! The Cardinal
       Has met the king. I do not like this conference.
       He looks with anger this way; I expect
       A tempest.
Duch.   Take no notice of his presence.
       Leave me to meet and answer it. If the king
       Be firm in's royal word, I fear no lightning.
       Expect me in the garden.
D'Alv.   I obey,
       But fear a shipwreck on the coast.

       Exeunt D'Alvarez [, Hernando, Lords, Gentleman-Usher].

Card.   Madam.
70 *Duch.*   My Lord.
   Card.   The king speaks of a letter that has brought
           A riddle in't.
Duch.   'Tis easy to interpret.
Card.   From my nephew? May I deserve the favour?[3]
Duch.   [*Aside*] He looks as though his eyes would fire the paper.
       They are a pair of burning glasses,[4] and
       His envious[5] blood doth give 'em flame.
Card.   [*Aside*] What lethargy could thus unspirit him?
       I am all wonder. – Do not believe, madam,
       But that Columbo's love is yet more sacred
80   To honour and yourself than thus to forfeit
       What I have heard him call the glorious wreath
       To all his merits[6] given him by the king,
       From whom he took you with more pride than ever
       He came from victory. His kisses hang
       Yet panting on your lips, and he but now
       Exchang'd religious[7] farewell to return
       But with more triumph to be yours.
Duch.   My Lord,
       You do believe your nephew's hand was not
       Surpris'd[8] or strain'd[9] to this?

---

[1] Be surprised. [2] i.e. which might attempt to divide us. [3] 'May I have the privilege (of reading my nephew's letter)?' [4] Lenses to concentrate the rays of the sun. [5] Spiteful. [6] Rewards. [7] Devout. [8] Taken unawares. [9] Forced.

90 *Card.*   Strange arts and windings in the world, most dark
       And subtle progresses! Who brought this letter?
   Duch.   I inquir'd not his name. I thought it not
       Considerable[1] to take such narrow[2] knowledge.
   Card.   Desert[3] and honour urg'd it here, nor can
       I blame you to be angry; yet his[4] person
       Oblig'd you should have given a nobler pause
       Before you made your faith and change[5] so violent,
       From his known worth into the arms of one,
       However fashion'd to your amorous wish,
100   Not equal to his cheapest fame, with all
       The gloss[6] of blood[7] and merit.
   Duch.   This comparison,
       My good Lord Cardinal, I cannot think
       Flows from an even justice; it betrays
       You partial where your blood[8] runs.
   Card.   I fear, madam,
       Your own[9] takes too much licence, and will soon
       Fall to the censure of unruly tongues.
       Because Alvarez has a softer cheek,
       Can, like a woman, trim his wanton[10] hair,
       Spend half a day with looking in the glass
110   To find a posture to present himself,
       And bring more effeminacy than man[11]
       Or honour to your bed, must he supplant him?
       Take heed; the common murmur, when it catches
       The scent of a lost fame —
   Duch.   My fame, Lord Cardinal?
       It stands upon an innocence as clear
       As the devotions you pay to Heaven.
       I shall not urge,[12] my Lord, your soft indulgence[13]
       At my next shrift.
   Card.   You are a fine court lady!
   Duch.   And you should be a reverend churchman.
   Card.   One
120   That, if you have not thrown off modesty,
       Would counsel you to leave Alvarez.
   Duch.   'Cause
       You dare do worse than marriage[14] must not I
       Be admitted what the church and law allows me?
   Card.   Insolent! Then you dare marry him?
   Duch.   Dare?

[1]Worthy of consideration. [2]Precise. [3]Worth. [4]Columbo's. [5]i.e. change
of faith. [6]Appearance. [7]Lineage. [8]Kinship. [9]Blood, i.e. passion.
[10]Unrestrained. [11]Manliness. [12]Solicit. [13]Dispensation. [14]The playwright's anticipation of the Cardinal's actions, V, iii, 127-71.

Let your contracted flame and malice, with
Columbo's rage higher than that, meet us
When we approach the holy place clasp'd hand
In hand, we'll break through all your force, and fix
Our sacred vows together there.

Card.   I knew

130   When, with as chaste a brow, you promis'd fair
To another. You are no dissembling lady!

Duch.   Would all your actions had no falser lights
About 'em!

Card.   Ha?

Duch.   The people would not talk and curse so loud.[1]

Card.   I'll have you chid into a blush for this.

Duch.   Begin at home, great man; there's cause enough.
You turn the wrong end of the perspective[2]
Upon your crimes, to drive them to a far

140   And lesser sight; but let your eyes look right,[3]
What giants would your pride and surfeit seem,
How gross your avarice, eating up whole families!
How vast are your corruptions and abuse
Of the king's ear? At which you hang[4] a pendant,
Not to adorn but ulcerate, while the honest
Nobility, like pictures in the arras,[5]
Serve only for court ornament. If they speak,
'Tis when you set their tongues, which you wind up
Like clocks, to strike at the just[6] hour you please.

150   Leave, leave, my Lord, these usurpations,
And be what you were meant, a man to cure,
Not let in, agues to religion.
Look to the church's wounds.

Card.   You dare presume,
In your rude spleen[7] to me, to abuse the church?

Duch.   Alas, you give false aim, my Lord; 'tis your
Ambition and scarlet[8] sins that rob
Her altar of the glory, and leave wounds
Upon her brow, which fetches grief and paleness
Into her cheeks, making her troubl'd bosom

160   Pant with her groans, and shroud her holy blushes
Within your reverend purples.[9]

Card.   Will you now take breath?

---

[1] Here and below, Shirley, writing in 1641, apparently voices some sharp criticism of the established Church in England. Cf. Milton, *Lycidas*, 113-31.   [2] Telescope.   [3] Correctly, normally.   [4] i.e. hang like.   [5] A hanging tapestry.   [6] Exact.   [7] Passion.   [8] A *double entendre,* implying both bloody and the colour of the Cardinal's robes.   [9] Cf. Webster, *The Duchess of Malfi,* I, i, 574, and Middleton and Rowley, *The Changeling,* III, iv, 168.

Duch.   In hope, my Lord, you will behold yourself
    In a true glass,[1] and see those unjust acts
    That so deform you, and by timely cure
    Prevent a shame, before the short-hair'd men[2]
    Do crowd and call for justice. I take leave.

                                       Exit.

Card.   This woman has a spirit that may rise
    To tame the devil's. There's no dealing with
    Her angry tongue; 'tis action and revenge
170   Must calm her fury. Were Columbo here
    I could resolve,[3] but letters shall be sent
    To th'army, which may wake him into sense
    Of his rash folly, or direct his spirit
    Some way to snatch his honour from this flame.
    All great men know, the soul of life is fame.

                                       Exit.

[ACT III SCENE 1]

[The royal palace]
Enter Valeria, Celinda

Val.   I did not think, Celinda, when I prais'd
    Alvarez to the duchess, that things thus
    Would come about. What does your ladyship
    Think of Columbo now?[4] It staggers all
    The court he should forsake his mistress; I
    Am lost with wonder yet.
Cel.   'Tis very strange
    Without a spell.[5] But there's a fate[6] in love;
    I like him ne'er the worse.

    Enter two Lords

1 Lord.   Nothing but marriages and triumph[7] now.
10 *Val.*   What new access of joy makes you, my Lord,
    So pleasant?

---

[1] Mirror. Cf. *Hamlet,* III, iv, 20-1. [2] i.e. the Puritans. [3] Settle the matter.
[4] Celinda had earlier praised Columbo — I, ii, 48-53. [5] Unless there has
been some magic force. [6] Destiny. [7] Festivity.

1 Lord.   There's a packet[1] come to court
 Makes the king merry. We are all concern'd in't.
 Columbo hath given the enemy a great
 And glorious defeat, and is already
 Preparing to march home.
Cel. He thriv'd the better for my prayers.
2 Lord. You have been his great admirer, madam.
1 Lord. The king longs to see him.
Val. This news exalts[2] the Cardinal.

 Enter Cardinal

1 Lord. [*To his companions*] |He's here!
20 He appears with discontent; the marriage
 With Count D'Alvarez hath a bitter taste,
 And not worn off his palate. But let us leave him.
Ladies. [*Aside*] We'll to the duchess.

      Exeunt [Lords, Valeria, Celinda]; *manet* Cardinal.

Card. He has not won so much upon the Aragon
 As he has lost at home, and his neglect
 Of what my studies had contriv'd, to add
 More lustre to our family by the access[3]
 Of the great duchess' fortune, cools his triumph
 And makes me wild.

 Enter Hernando

Hern.   My good Lord Cardinal.
30 *Card.* You made complaint to th' king about your general.
 Hern. Not a complaint, my Lord; I did but satisfy
 Some questions o' the king's.
Card.   You see he[4] thrives
 Without your personal valour or advice,
 Most grave and learned in the wars.[5]
Hern.   My Lord,
 I envy not his fortune.
Card.   'Tis above
 Your malice, and your noise[6] not worth his anger.
 'Tis barking 'gainst the moon.
Hern.   More temper[7] would
 Become that habit.[8]
Card. The military thing would show some spleen.

---

[1] Parcel of letters. [2] Elates. [3] Addition. [4] Columbo. [5] A sarcastic description of Hernando. [6] Outcry. [7] Calmness. [8] i.e. your Cardinal's robes.

40   I'll blow an army of such wasps[1] about
        The world! Go look[2] your sting you left i' th' camp, sir.

        Enter King *and* lords

Hern.   The king! [*To* Cardinal] This may be one day counted for.[3]

                                                                        Exit.

King.   All things conspire, my Lord, to make you fortunate.
        Your nephew's glory, –
Card.   'Twas your cause and justice
        Made him victorious. Had he been so valiant
        At home, he had had another conquest to
        Invite, and bid her welcome to new wars.[4]
King.   You must be reconcil'd to Providence, my Lord.
        I heard you had a controversy with
50   The duchess; I will have you friends.
Card.   I am not angry.
King.   For my sake then
        You shall be pleas'd, and with me grace the marriage.
        A churchman must show charity and shine
        With first example. She's a woman.
Card.   You shall prescribe in all things. Sir, you cannot
        Accuse[5] my love, if I still wish my nephew
        Had been so happy to be constant to
        Your own and my election.[6] Yet my brain
        Cannot reach[7] how this comes about; I know
60   My nephew lov'd her with a near affection.

        Enter Hernando

King.   He'll give you fair account at his return.
        [*To* Hernando] Colonel, your letters may be spar'd;[8] the
                                                                        general
        Has finish'd, and is coming home.
Hern.   I am glad on't, sir.

                                                                [*Exit* King.]

                        My good Lord Cardinal,
        'Tis not impossible but some man provok'd
        May have a precious mind[9] to cut your throat.
Card.   You shall command me, noble colonel.

[1] i.e. as you.   [2] Look for.   [3] Answerable.   [4] i.e. the wars of love.   [5] Censure.
[6] Preference.   [7] Understand.   [8] Saved.   [9] Fine intention.

I know you wo' not fail to be at th' wedding.
Hern.   'Tis not Columbo that is married, sir.
70 *Card.*   Go teach the postures[1] of the pike and musket;
Then drill your myrmidons[2] into a ditch,
Where starve and stink in pickle. You shall find
Me reasonable. You see the king expects me.
Hern.   So does the devil.
Some desperate hand may help you on your journey.

Exeunt.

[ACT III SCENE 2]

[*The duchess's house*]
Enter Antonio, Pedro, Jaques, *and other* servants[3]

Ant.   Here, this, ay, this will fit your part. You shall wear the
slashes[4] because you are a soldier. Here's for the blue mute.[5]

[*Gives out costumes*]

1 Serv.   This doublet will never fit me. Pox on't! Are these
breeches good enough for a prince too? Pedro plays but a
lord, and he has two laces more in a seam.
Ant.   You must consider Pedro is a foolish lord; he may wear
what lace he please.
2 Serv.   Does my beard fit my clothes well, gentlemen?
Ant.   Pox o' your beard!
10 *3 Serv.*   That will fright away the hair.[6]
1 Serv.   This fellow plays but a mute, and he is so troublesome
and talks.
3 Serv.   Master Secretary might have let Jaques play the soldier;
he has a black patch already.[7]
2 Serv.   By your favour, Master Secretary, I was ask'd who writ
this play for us.

---

[1] Handling.   [2] Ruffians; from the reputation of the men of Thessaly who
fought fiercely under Achilles at Troy.   [3] Lines 1-80 of this scene represent
the only comic episode in the play. Similar situations are developed in *A
Midsummer Night's Dream*, I, ii; III, i, 1-108; IV, ii, etc. and Rowley, *et al.
The Witch of Edmonton,* II, i, 37-95; III, i; III, iv, 14-70.   [4] Slits in the
material of a doublet or jacket to expose a coloured lining, and a pun on
'wounds'.   [5] A non-speaking role performed by a servant in blue livery.
[6] Loss of hair frequently characterizes one phase of the development of the
pox (syphilis).   [7] i.e. over a missing eye.

Ant.　For us? Why, art thou any more than a blue mute?
2 Serv.　And, by my troth, I said I thought it was all your own.
Ant.　Away, you coxcomb!
20 *4 Serv.*　[*To* other servants] Dost think he has no more wit than
　　to write a comedy? My lady's chaplain made the play,
　　though he[1] is content, for the honour and trouble of the
　　business, to be seen in't.[2]

Enter Fifth Servant

Rogero.　Did anybody see my head,[3] gentlemen? 'Twas here but now.
　　I shall have never a head to play my part in.
Ant.　Is thy head gone? 'Tis well thy part was not in't. Look,
　　look about. Has not Jaques it?
Jaques.　I his head? 'T wo' not come on upon my shoulders.[4]
Ant.　Make haste, gentlemen. I'll see whether the king has
30　　supp'd. Look every man to his wardrop[5] and his part.

Exit [, *with* Rogero].

2 Serv.　Is he gone? In my mind a masque had been fitter for a
　　marriage.
Jaques.　Why, mute? There was no time for't, and the scenes[6]
　　are troublesome.
2 Serv.　Half a score deal[7] tack'd together in the clouds,[8]
　　what's that? A throne to come down, and dance. All the
　　properties have been paid forty times over and are in the
　　court stock; but the secretary must have a play to show his
　　wit!
40 *Jaques.*　Did not I tell thee 'twas the chaplain's? Hold your
　　tongue, mute.
1 Serv.　Under the rose[9] and would this cloth-of-silver doublet might
　　never come off again, if there be any more plot than you see
　　in the back of my hand.
2 Serv.　You talk of a plot! I'll not give this[10] for the best
　　poet's plot in the world[11] and if it be not well carried.[12]
Jaques.　Well said, mute.

---

[1] Antonio. [2] i.e. to play one of the roles. [3] Head dress or wig. [4] i.e. it
would not fit on my shoulders. [5] Costume. [6] Scenery. [7] Planks. [8] Above
the stage. [9] In confidence. [10] Perhaps snaps his fingers. [11] This may be
an allusion to Sir John Suckling's effort, regarded as treasonous by the
House of Commons, to raise a troop of soldiers in support of Charles I. If
so, at least this part of the play must have been written after 6 May 1641,
when Suckling fled to Paris, where he died shortly after. [12] Performed.

3 Serv.   Ha, ha! Pedro[1] since he has put on his doublet has
    repeated but three lines, and he has broke five buttons!
50 *2 Serv.*   I know not, but by this false beard — and here's hair
    enough to hang a reasonable honest man — I do not remember
    to say a strong line[2] indeed in the whole comedy, but when
    the chambermaid kisses the captain.
3 Serv.   Excellent, mute![3]

Enter another Servant

Rogero.   They have almost supp'd, and I cannot find my head yet.
Jaques.   Play in thine own.
Rogero.   Thank you for that! So I may have it made a property!
    If I have not a head found me, let Master Secretary play my
    part himself without it.

Enter Antonio

60 *Ant.*   Are you all ready, my masters? The king is coming through
    the gallery. Are the women[4] dress'd?
1 Serv.   Rogero wants a head.
Ant.   Here, with a pox to you, take mine! You a player? You a
    puppy-dog! Is the music ready?

Enter Gentleman-Usher

Gent.-Usher.   Gentlemen, it is my lady's pleasure that you
    expect till she call for you. There are a company of
    cavaliers in gallant equipage, newly alighted, have offered
    to present their revels[5] in honour of this hymen,[6] and 'tis
    Her Grace's command that you be silent till their entertain-
70   ment be over.
1 Serv.   Gentlemen?
2 Serv.   Affronted!
Rogero.   Master Secretary, there's your head again. A man's a
    man![7] Have I broken my sleep to study fifteen lines for an
    ambassador, and after that a constable,[8] and is it come to
    this?
Ant.   Patience, gentlemen, be not so hot. 'Tis but deferr'd, and
    the play may do well enough cold.

---

[1] Presumably the second servant (since he replies below to the criticism),
but Shirley's links between Christian names and the numbers in speech
heads are not clear or consistent.   [2] i.e. that I say a sententious, convoluted line.   [3] 'Well done for a mute!'   [4] i.e. the boys who were to play
the female roles.   [5] Entertainment.   [6] Marriage.   [7] 'One can take only so
much!'   [8] Court dignitary.

Jaques. If it be not presented, the chaplain will have the
80 greatest loss: he loses his wits.

Hoboys[1]

Ant. This music speaks the king upon entrance. Retire, retire,
and grumble not.

Exeunt.

Enter King, Cardinal, Alvarez, Duchess, Celinda, Valeria,
Placentia, Lords, Hernando. *They being set, enter* Columbo *and
five more in rich habits, vizarded;*[2] *between every two a torch-
bearer. They dance, and after beckon to* Alvarez *as desirous
to speak with him*

D'Alv. With me?

They embrace and whisper

King. Do you know the masquers, madam?
Duch. Not I, sir.
Card. [*Aside*] There's one, but that my nephew is abroad
And has more soul than thus to jig upon
Their hymeneal night, I should suspect
'Twere he.

The masquers lead in D'Alvarez[3]

Duch. Where's my lord D'Alvarez?

Recorders

90 *King.*   Call in the bridegroom.

Enter Columbo.[4] *Four masquers bring in* Alvarez *dead, in one of
their habits, and, having laid him down, exeunt.*[5]

Duch. What mystery is this?
Card. We want the bridegroom still.
King.   Where is Alvarez?

Columbo *points to the body; they unvizard it and find*
Alvarez *bleeding*

[1] Oboes. [2] Masked. [3] The masquers evidently surround D'Alvarez before
pushing him offstage. [4] Still masked. [5] Cf. Tourneur, *The Revenger's
Tragedy,* V, i.

Duch.   Oh, 'tis my lord! He's murder'd!
King.   Who durst commit this horrid act?
Col.   I, sir.

                                                    [*Removes his mask*]

King.   Columbo? Ha!
Col.   Yes, Columbo, that dares stay
      To justify that act.
Hern.   Most barbarous!
Duch.   Oh, my dearest lord!
King.   Our guard seize on them all! This sight doth shake
100   All that is man within me. Poor Alvarez,
      Is this thy wedding day?

      Enter Guard. [*Some exit, to pursue the masquers.*]

Duch.   If you do think there is a Heaven, or pains
      To punish such black crimes i' th'other world,
      Let me have swift and such exemplar justice
      As shall become this great assasinate.[1]
      You will take off[2] our faith else, and if here
      Such innocence must bleed and you look on,[3]
      Poor men that call you gods on earth will doubt[4]
      To obey your laws; nay, practise to be devils,
110   As fearing, if such monstrous sins go on,
      The saints will not be safe in Heaven.
King.   You shall,
      You shall have justice.
Card.   [*Aside*]   Now to come off were brave.[5]

      Enter Servant

Serv.   The masquers, sir, are fled; their horse,[6] prepar'd
      At gate, expected to receive 'em, where
      They quickly mounted. Coming so like friends,
      None could suspect their haste, which is secur'd
      By advantage of the night.

                                                    [*Exit.*]

Col.   I answer for 'em all — 'tis stake enough
      For many lives — but if that poniard
120   Had voice it would convince they were but all

---

[1] Assassin.   [2] Kill.   [3] i.e. merely look on.   [4] Fear.   [5] 'To win our cause now would be a distinguished achievement.'   [6] i.e. horses.

Spectators of my act,[1] and now, if you
Will give your judgments leave, though at the first
Face of this object[2] your cool bloods were frighted,
I can excuse this deed and call it justice,
An act your honours and your office, sir,[3]
Is bound to build a law upon for others
To imitate. I have but took his life
And punish'd her with mercy, who had both
Conspir'd to kill the soul[4] of all my fame.

130   Read there, and read an injury as deep

[*Gives* duchess's *letter*[5] *to* king]

In my dishonour as the devil knew
A woman had capacity or malice
To execute. Read there how you were cozen'd, sir,
Your power affronted and my faith; her smiles
A juggling witchcraft to betray, and make
My love her horse[6] to stalk withal, and catch
Her curled minion.[7]

Card.   Is it possible
The duchess could dissemble so, and forfeit
Her modesty[8] with you and to us all?

140   Yet I must pity her. My nephew has
Been too severe, though this affront would call
A dying man from prayers and turn him tiger,
There being nothing dearer than our fame,
Which, if a common man, whose blood has no
Ingredient of honour, labour to
Preserve, a soldier, by his nearest tie
To glory,[9] is above all others bound
To vindicate; and yet it might have been less bloody.

Hern.   [*Aside*] Charitable devil!

150 *King.*   *Reads* " I pray, my lord, release under your hand[10] what you
dare challenge[11] in my love or person as a just forfeit to
myself. This act will speak you honourable to my thoughts,
and when you have conquered thus yourself you may proceed
to many victories, and after, with safety of your fame,
visit again.

                          The lost Rosaura."
    To this your answer was a free resign?

Col.   Flatter'd[12] with great opinion of her faith

---

[1] The killing of D'Alvarez. [2] Purpose. [3] The king. [4] Essential element.
[5] See II, ii, 101 ff. [6] i.e. a stalking-horse; a horse or an imitation of one
used to conceal a hunter. [7] Lover. [8] Good character. [9] i.e. his life.
[10] In your own handwriting. [11] Claim. [12] Beguiled.

And my desert[1] of her, with thought that she,
Who seem'd to weep and chide my easy will
160   To part with her,[2] could not be guilty of
A treason or apostasy so soon,
But rather meant[3] this a device to make
Me expedite the affairs of war, I sent
That paper, which her wickedness, not justice,
Applied[4] – what I meant trial[5] – her divorce.[6]
I lov'd her so, I dare call Heaven to witness,
I knew not whether[7] I lov'd most; while she,
With him whose crimson penitence[8] I provok'd,
Conspir'd my everlasting infamy.
Examine but the circumstance.[9]
170 *Card.*   'Tis clear,
This match[10] was made at home before she sent
That cunning writ in hope to take him off,[11]
As knowing his impatient soul would scorn
To own a blessing came on crutches to him.
It was not well to raise his expectation, –
[*To* King] Had you, sir, no affront? – to ruin him
With so much scandal and contempt.
King.   We have
Too plentiful a circumstance to accuse
You, madam, as the cause of your own sorrows,
180   But not without an accessory more
Than[12] young Alvarez.
Card.   Any other instrument?[13]
King.   Yes, I am guilty, with herself and Don
Columbo, though our acts look'd several ways,
That[14] thought a lover might so soon be ransom'd,[15]
And did exceed the office of a king
To exercise dominion over hearts
That owe to the prerogative of Heaven
Their choice or separation. You must, therefore,
When you kneel for justice and revenge,
190   Madam, consider me a lateral agent
In poor Alvarez' tragedy.
1 Lord.   It was your love to Don Columbo, sir.
Hern.   [*Aside*] So, so. The king is charm'd.[16] Do you observe
How, to acquit Columbo, he would draw

---

[1] Sense of her merit.   [2] i.e. 'to chide the apparent ease of my departure.'
[3] i.e. rather thinking that she meant.   [4] Put into operation as.   [5] A test.
[6] i.e. breaking the engagement.   [7] Which.   [8] Repentance through bloodshed.
[9] Facts.   [10] The relationship between the duchess and D'Alvarez.
[11] Remove.   [12] i.e. with only one accessory.   [13] Agent.   [14] i.e. I who.
[15] Set free.   [16] Bewitched.

     Himself into the plot. Heaven, is this justice?
Card.   Your judgment is divine in this.
King.   And yet
     Columbo cannot be secure[1] and we
     Just in his pardon, that[2] durst make so great
     And insolent a breach of law and duty.
2 Lord.   [*Aside*] Ha, will he turn again?
200 *King.*   And should we leave
     This guilt of blood to Heaven, which[3] cries and strikes
     With loud appeals the palace of eternity;
     Yet here is more to charge Columbo than
     Alvarez' blood, and bids[4] me punish it
     Or be no king.
Hern.   [*Aside*] 'Tis come about, my lords.
King.   And if I should forgive
     His timeless death, I cannot the offence,
     That with such boldness struck at me. Has my
     Indulgence to your merits – which are great –
210   Made me so cheap[5] your rage could meet no time
     Nor place for your revenge but where my eyes
     Must be affrighted and affronted with
     The bloody execution? This contempt
     Of majesty transcends my power to pardon,
     And you shall feel my anger, sir.
Hern.   [*Aside*] Thou[6] shalt have one short prayer more for that.[7]
Col.   Have I i' th' progress of my life
     No actions to plead me up deserving,
     Against this ceremony?[8]
Card.   Contain yourself.
220 *Col.*   I must be dumb then. Where is honour
     And gratitude of kings, when they forget
     Whose hand secur'd their greatness? Take my head off;
     Examine then which of your silken lords,
     As I have done, will throw himself on dangers,
     Like to a floating island[9] move in blood,
     And where your great defence calls him to stand
     A bulwark, upon his bold breast to take
     In death that you may live. But soldiers are
     Your valiant fools whom, when your own securities
230   Are bleeding, you can cherish, but when once
     Your state and nerves are knit, not thinking when
     To use their surgery again, you cast

[1] Without care. [2] i.e. he [Columbo] who. [3] i.e. which blood. [4] i.e. and it bids. [5] Despised. [6] i.e. the king. [7] A sarcastic remark, meaning 'I shall offer up one extra prayer for you in commendation of your offer to punish Columbo'. [8] Rite. [9] A whale.

Them off and let them hang in dusty armouries,
Or make it death to ask for pay.
King.   No more.
We thought to have put your victory and merits
In balance with Alvarez' death, which, while
Our mercy was to judge, had been your safety;
But the affront to us, made greater by
This boldness to upbraid our royal bounty,
Shall tame or make you nothing.
240 [1] *Lord.*   [*Aside*]   Excellent!
Hern.   [*Aside*] The Cardinal is not pleas'd.
Card.   [*To* Columbo]   Humble yourself
To th' king.
Col.   And beg my life? Let cowards do 't
That dare not die. I'll rather have no head
Than owe it to his charity.
King.   To th' castle with him!

                    [*Guard escort* Columbo *out*]

Madam, I leave you to your grief, and what
The king can recompense to your tears or honour
Of your dead lord expect.
Duch.   This shows like justice.

                                        Exeunt.

[ACT IV SCENE 1]

[*The royal palace*]
Enter two Lords, Hernando

1 Lord.   This is the age of wonders.
2 Lord.   Wondrous mischiefs!
Hern.   Among those guards, which some call tutelar angels,
Whose office is to govern provinces,
Is there not one will undertake Navarre?[1]
Hath Heaven forsook us quite?
1 Lord.   Columbo at large!
2 Lord.   And grac'd now more than ever.
1 Lord.   He was not pardon'd;
That word was prejudicial to his fame.

[1] Reprove the king.

Hern.   But, as the murder done had been a dream
    Vanish'd to memory, he's courted as
10 Preserver of his country. With what chains
    Of magic does this Cardinal hold the king?
2 Lord.   What will you say, my lord, if they enchant
    The duchess now, and by some impudent art
    Advance a marriage to Columbo yet?
Hern.   Say? I'll say no woman can be sav'd, nor is't
    Fit indeed any[1] should pretend to[2] Heaven
    After one such impiety in their sex,
    And yet my faith has been so stagger'd since
    The king restor'd Columbo I'll be now
    Of no religion.
20 *1 Lord.*   'Tis not possible
    She can forgive the murder; I observ'd
    Her tears.
Hern.   Why, so did I, my Lord,
    And if they be not honest, 'tis to be
    Half damn'd to look upon a woman weeping.
    When do you think the Cardinal said his prayers?
2 Lord.   I know not.
Hern.   Heaven forgive my want of charity,
    But if I were to kill him he should have
    No time to pray.[3] His life could be no sacrifice
    Unless his soul went too.
1 Lord.   That were too much.[4]
30 *Hern.*   When you mean to dispatch him you may give
    Time for confession. They[5] have injur'd me
    After another rate.[6]
2 Lord.   You are too passionate, cousin.[7]

    Enter Columbo, Colonels, Alphonso, *courtiers. They
    pass over the stage.*

Hern.   How the gay men do flutter to congratulate
    His gaol delivery! There's one honest man.[8]
    What pity 'tis a gallant fellow should
    Depend on knaves for his preferment.
1 Lord.   Except this cruelty upon Alvarez,
    Columbo has no mighty stain upon him;
    But for his uncle –
Hern.   If I had a son
40 Of twelve years old that would not fight with him,

[1] i.e. any woman. [2] Make claim to deserve. [3] Cf. *Hamlet*, III, iii, 84-6.
[4] i.e. too much punishment. [5] Columbo and the Cardinal. [6] More severely.
[7] A casual, familiar form of address. [8] i.e. Columbo.

And stake his soul against his Cardinal's cap,
I would disinherit him. Time has took a lease
But for three lives[1] I hope; a fourth may see
Honesty walk without a crutch.
2 Lord.   This is
But air and wildness.
Hern.   I'll see the duchess.
[*1 Lord.*] You may do well to comfort her.[2]
We must attend the king.
Hern.   Your pleasures.

                                                              Exit Hernando.

        Enter King *and* Cardinal

1 Lord.   [*To* 2 Lord] A man[3] of a brave soul.
2 Lord.   [*To* 1 Lord]   The less his safety –
The king and Cardinal in consult.

                                                    [*The* lords *move aside*]

50 *King.*   Commend us to the duchess, and employ
What language you think fit and powerful
To reconcile her to some peace. My Lords.
Card.   Sir, I possess[4] all for your sacred uses.

                                                              Exeunt severally.

        [ACT IV SCENE 2]

        [*The duchess's house*]
        Enter Antonio *and* Celinda

Ant.   Madam, you are the welcom'st lady living.
Cel.   To whom, Master Secretary?
Ant.   If you have mercy
To pardon so much boldness, I durst say,
To me. I am a gentleman –
Cel.   And handsome.
Ant.   But my lady has much wanted you.
Cel.   Why, Master Secretary?

[1] A three-party lease was sometimes terminated by the death of the longest-lived signatory.   [2] Q gives this line to Hernando, all mod. eds. to 1 Lord, who has next line in Q and all later eds.   [3] i.e. Hernando.   [4] Control.

Ant. You are the prettiest, –
Cel. So.
Ant. The wittiest, –
10 *Cel.* So.
Ant. The merriest lady i' th' court.
Cel. And I was wish'd to make the duchess pleasant?[1]
Ant. She never had so deep a cause of sorrow;
 Her chamber's but a coffin of a larger
 Volume, wherein she walks so like a ghost,
 'Twould make you pale to see her.
Cel.   Tell Her Grace
 I attend[2] here.
Ant.   I shall most willingly.
 [*Aside*] A spirited lady! Would I had her in my closet.[3]
 She is excellent company among the lords.
20 Sure she has an admirable treble. – Madam.

               Exit.

Cel. I do suspect this fellow would be nibbling,
 Like some whose narrow fortunes will not rise
 To wear things when the invention's rare and new,
 But, treading on the heel of pride, they hunt
 The fashion when 'tis crippled, like fell tyrants.
 I hope I am not old yet! I had the honour
 To be saluted[4] by our Cardinal's nephew
 This morning. There's a man!

 Enter Antonio

Ant.   I have prevail'd.
 Sweet madam, use what eloquence you can
30 Upon her, and if ever I be useful
 To your ladyship's service, your least breath commands me.

              [*Exit.*]

 Enter Duchess

Duch. Madam, I come to ask you but one question.
 If you were in my state, my state of grief,
 I mean an exile from all happiness
 Of this world and almost of Heaven – for my
 Affliction is finding[5] out despair –
 What would you think of Don Columbo?
Cel.   Madam?

[1] Cheerful. [2] Await. [3] Private room. [4] Greeted. [5] Searching.

Duch.   Whose bloody hand wrought all this misery.
            Would you not weep as I do, and wish rather
40   An everlasting spring of tears to drown
            Your sight than let your eyes be curs'd to see
            The murderer again, and glorious?[1]
            So careless of his sin that he is made
            Fit for new parricide, even while his soul
            Is purpl'd o'er and reeks with innocent blood.
            But do not, do not answer me. I know
            You have so great a spirit — which I want,
            The horror of his fact[2] surprising[3] all
            My faculties — you would not let him live;
50   But I, poor I, must suffer more. There's not
            One little star in Heaven will look on me,
            Unless to choose me out the mark on whom
            It may shoot down some angry influence.[4]

            Enter Placentia

Plac.   Madam, here's Don Columbo says he must
            Speak with Your Grace.
Duch.   ⎪But he must not, I charge you.
            None else wait? Is this well done,
            To triumph in his tyranny? Speak, madam,
            Speak but your conscience.

                                                    [*Exit* Placentia.]

            Enter Columbo *and* Antonio

Ant.   Sir, you must not see her.
Col.   Not see her? Were she cabl'd up[5] above
60   The search of bullet or of fire, were she
            Within her grave, and that the toughest mine
            That ever Nature teem'd[6] and groan'd withal,
            I would force some way to see her.

                                                    [*Exit* Antonio]

                                    Do not fear
            I come to court you, madam; y'are not worth
            The humblest of my kinder thoughts. I come
            To show the man you have provok'd and lost,
            And tell you what remains of my revenge.

---

[1] Proud. [2] Deed. [4] Overpowering. [4] Cf. I, ii, 219-21, 239-41, above.
[5] Fastened. [6] Gave birth to.

Live, but never presume again to marry.[1]
I'll kill the next at th'altar and quench all
70   The smiling tapers with his blood. If after[2]
You dare provoke[3] the priest and Heaven so much
To take another, in thy bed I'll cut him from
Thy warm embrace, and throw his heart to ravens.
Cel.   This will appear an unexampl'd cruelty.
Col.   Your pardon, madam;[4] rage and my revenge
Not perfect[5] took away my eyes. You are
A noble lady; this[6] not worth your eye-beam,[7]
One of so slight a making and so thin,
An autumn leaf is of too great a value
80   To play,[8] which shall be soonest lost i' th'air.
Be pleas'd to own me by some name in your
Assurance.[9] I despise to be receiv'd
There.[10] Let her witness that I call you mistress.
Honour me to make these pearls your carcanet.[11]
Cel.   My lord, you are too humble in your thoughts.[12]
Col.   [*Aside*] There's no vexation too great to punish her.[13]

                                                              Exit.

Enter Antonio

Ant.   Now, madam?
Cel.   Away, you saucy fellow! Madam, I
Must be excus'd if I do think more honourably
Than you have cause of this great lord.
90 *Duch.*   Why, is not
All womankind concern'd to hate what's impious?
Cel.   For my part –
Duch.   Antonio, is this a woman?
Ant.   I know not whether she be man or woman;
I should be nimble to find out[14] the experiment.
She look'd with less state[15] when Columbo came.
Duch.   [*To* Celinda] Let me entreat your absence.
                     |[*Aside*] I am cozen'd in her. –
I took you for a modest, honest lady.
Cel.   Madam, I scorn any accuser, and,
Deducting the great title of a duchess,
100   I shall not need one grain of your dear honour

---

[1] Cf. Webster, *The Duchess of Malfi,* I, i, 320-6. [2] Hereafter. [3] Call forth.
[4] i.e. Celinda. [5] Not yet complete. [6] i.e. Duchess Rosaura. [7] Glance.
[8] To dally with.   [9] Trust. [10] i.e. by Duchess Rosaura. [11] A gold necklace,
usually jewelled. [12] 'You humble yourself too much in considering me.'
[13] Duchess Rosaura. [14] Study. [15] Less dignity, i.e. more flustered.

To make me full weight.[1] If Your Grace be jealous,
I can remove.[2]

Exit.

Ant.   She is gone.
Duch.   Prithee remove
My fears of her return.

Exit Antonio.

                          She is not worth
Considering; my anger's mounted higher.
He need not put in[3] caution for my next
Marriage. Alvarez, I must come to thee
Thy virgin wife and widow, but not till
I ha' paid those tragic duties to thy hearse
Become[4] my piety and love; but how?
Who shall instruct a way?

Enter Placentia

110 *Plac.*   Madam, Don
Hernando much desires to speak with you.
Duch.   Will not thy own discretion think I am
Unfit for visit?
Plac.   Please Your Grace, he brings
Something he says imports[5] your ear and love
Of the dead Lord Alvarez.
Duch.   Then admit him.

[*Exit* Placentia.]

Enter [Placentia *and*] Hernando

Hern.   I would speak, madam, to yourself.
Duch.   [*To* Placentia]   Your absence.

[*Exit* Placentia.]

Hern.   I know not how Your Grace will censure so
Much boldness, when you know the affairs I come for.
Duch.   My servant has prepar'd me to receive it,
If it concern my dead lord.
120 *Hern.*   Can you name

[1] Of great importance.   [2] Withdraw.   [3] Introduce.   [4] Are appropriate to.
[5] Concerns.

So much[1] of your Alvarez in a breath
Without one word of your revenge? Oh, madam,
I come to chide you, and repent my great
Opinion of your virtue,[2] that[3] can walk
And spend so many hours in naked[4] solitude,
As if you thought that no arrears were due
To his death when you had paid his funeral charges,
Made your eyes red, and wept a handkercher.[5]
I come to tell you that I saw him bleed;
130   I that can challenge[6] nothing in his name
And honour saw his murder'd body warm
And panting with the labour of his spirits,[7]
Till my amaz'd soul shrunk and hid itself,
While barbarous Columbo, grinning, stood
And mock'd the weeping wounds. It is too much
That you should keep your heart[8] alive so long
After this spectacle, and not revenge it.
Duch.   You do not know the business of my heart,
That censure me so rashly. Yet I thank you,
140   And if you be Alvarez' friend, dare[9] tell
Your confidence that I despise my life,
But know not how to use it in a service
To speak[10] me his revenger. This will need
No other proof than that to you, who may
Be sent with cunning to betray me, I
Have made this bold confession. I so much
Desire to sacrifice to that hovering ghost
Columbo's life that I am not ambitious
To keep my own two minutes after it.
150 *Hern.*   If you will call me coward, which is equal
To think I am a traitor, I forgive it
For this brave resolution, which time
And all the destinies must aid. I beg
That I may kiss your hand for this, and may
The soul of angry honour guide it.
Duch.   Whither?
Hern.   To Don Columbo's heart.
Duch.   It[11] is too weak, I fear, alone.
Hern.   Alone? Are you in earnest? Why, will it not
Be a dishonour to your justice, madam,
160   Another arm should interpose? But that
It were a saucy act to mingle[12] with you,

---

[1] 'Can you refer to so much as the death?'   [2] Strength.   [3] You who.
[4] Absolute.   [5] Sufficient tears to fill a handkerchief.   [6] Lay claim to.
[7] i.e. the labour pains of his spirits to separate themselves from his body.
[8] Devotion.   [9] i.e. I dare.   [10] Manifest.   [11] This brave resolution.   [12] Associate.

I durst − nay, I am bound in the revenge
Of him that's dead, since the whole world has interest
In every good man's loss − to offer it.
Dare you command me, madam?
Duch.   Not command,
But I should more than honour such a truth[1]
In man, that durst against so mighty odds
Appear Alvarez' friend and mine. The Cardinal −
Hern.   Is for the second course.[2] Columbo must
170   Be first cut up; his ghost must lead the dance.[3]
Let him die first.
Duch. But how?
Hern.   How? With a sword; and if I undertake it,
I wo' not lose so much of my own honour
To kill him basely.
Duch.   How shall I reward
This infinite service? 'Tis not modesty,
While now my husband groans beneath his tomb
And calls me to his marble bed, to promise
What this great act might well deserve: myself,
180   If you survive the victor. But if thus
Alvarez' ashes be appeas'd, it must
Deserve an honourable memory;[4]
And though Columbo, as[5] he had all power
And grasp'd[6] the Fates, has vow'd to kill the man
That shall succeed Alvarez −
Hern.   Tyranny!
Duch.   Yet if ever
I entertain a thought of love hereafter,
Hernando from the world shall challenge[7] it;
Till when, my prayers and fortune shall wait on you.
Hern.   This is too mighty recompense.
190 *Duch.*   'Tis all just.
Hern.   If I outlive Columbo I must not
Expect security at home.
Duch.   Thou canst
Not fly where all my fortunes and my love
Shall not attend to guard thee.[5]
Hern.   If I die −
Duch.   Thy memory
Shall have a shrine, the next within my heart
To my Alvarez'.
Hern.   Once again your hand.

---

[1] Fidelity.   [2] i.e. of a meal. 'We will consider him later.'   [3] The Dance of Death (to the grave).   [4] Memorial.   [5] As if.   [6] Controlled.   [7] Claim.   [8] Cf. Webster, *The Duchess of Malfi*, III, ii, 211-3.

  Your cause is so religious [1] you need not
  Strengthen it with your prayers; trust it to me.

  Enter Placentia *and* Cardinal

Plac. Madam, the Cardinal.

            [*Exit* Placentia.]

200 *Duch.* [*To* Hernando] Will you appear?
  Hern. And he had all the horror of the devil
  In's face I would not balk[2] him.

      He stares upon the Cardinal *in his exit.*

  Card. [*Aside*] What makes[3] Hernando here? I do not like
  They should consult. I'll take no note. – The king
  Fairly salutes Your Grace, by whose command
  I am to tell you, though his will and actions
  Illimited stoop not to satisfy
  The vulgar inquisition,[4] he is
  Yet willing to retain a just[5] opinion
210 With those that are plac'd near him; and although
  You look with nature's eye upon yourself,
  Which needs no perspective[6] to reach nor art
  Of any optic[7] to make greater what
  Your narrow sense applies[8] an injury,
  Ourselves still nearest to ourselves, but there's
  Another eye that looks abroad, and walks
  In search of reason and the weight of things,
  With which, if you look on him, you will find
  His pardon to Columbo cannot be
220 So much against his justice as your erring
  Faith[9] would persuade your anger.
  Duch.   Good my Lord,
  Your phrase has too much landscape,[10] and I cannot
  Distinguish[11] at this distance. You present
  The figure[12] perfect, but indeed my eyes
  May pray Your Lordship find excuse, for tears
  Have almost made them blind.
  Card.   Fair peace restore 'em!
  To bring the object nearer,[13] the king says
  He could not be severe to Don Columbo

[1] Godly. [2] Shun. [3] Does. [4] Inquiry. [5] Uniform. [6] Telescope. [7] Magnifying glass. [8] Ascribes. [9] Belief. [10] 'Your words encompass too large a vista.' [11] Make out the details. [12] Form. [13] 'To come to the point.'

Without injustice to his other merits,
230   Which call more loud for their reward and honour
Than you for your revenge; the kingdom made
Happy by those,[1] you only by the last[2]
Unfortunate.   Nor was it rational –
I speak the king's own language – he should die
For taking one man's breath, without whose[3] valour
None now had been alive without dishonour.

Duch.   In my poor understanding 'tis the crown
Of virtue to proceed in its own tract,[4]
Not deviate from honour. If you acquit
240   A man of murder 'cause he has done brave
Things in the war, you will bring down his valour
To a crime, nay, to a bawd,[5] if it secure
A rape, and but teach those that deserve well
To sin with greater licence. But dispute
Is now too late, my Lord; 'tis done, and you
By the good king, in tender[6] of my sorrows,
Sent to persuade me 'tis unreasonable
That justice should repair[7] me.

Card.   You mistake;
For if Columbo's death could make Alvarez
250   Live, the king had given him up to law,
Your bleeding sacrifice, but when his[8] life
Was[9] but another treasure thrown away
To obey a clamorous[10] statute, it was wisdom
To himself and common safety to take off
This killing edge of law, and keep Columbo
To recompense the crime by noble acts
And sorrow, that in time might draw your pity.

Duch.   This is a greater tyranny than that
Columbo exercis'd. He kill'd my lord,
260   And you not have the charity to let
Me think it worth a punishment!

Card.   To that
In my own name I answer. I condemn
And urge the bloody guilt against my nephew.
'Twas violent and cruel, a black deed,
A deed whose memory doth make me shudder,
An act that did betray a tyrannous nature,
Which he took up[11] in war, the school of vengeance;
And though the king's compassion spare him here,

[1] i.e. those merits.   [2] i.e. Columbo's latest deed.   [3] Columbo's.   [4] Track, course.   [5] i.e. to the level of a crime, nay, to that of a pander.   [6] Considera-tion.   [7] Compensate.   [8] Columbo's.   [9] i.e. would have been.   [10] Importunate.   [11] Adopted.

       Unless his heart

270   Weep itself out in penitent tears, hereafter —
   Duch.   This sounds
     As you were now a good man.
   Card.   Does Your Grace
     Think I have conscience to allow[1] the murder?
     Although when it was done I did obey
     The stream of nature, as he was my kinsman,
     To plead he might not pay his forfeit life,
     Could I do less for one so near my blood?
     Consider, madam, and be charitable.
     Let not this wild injustice make me lose[2]

280   The character I bear and reverend habit.
     To make you full acquainted with my innocence
     I challenge[3] here my soul and Heaven to witness:
     If I had any thought or knowledge with[4]
     My nephew's plot or person, when he came,
     Under the smooth pretense of friend, to violate
     Your hospitable laws, and do that act
     Whose frequent mention draws this tear, a whirlwind
     Snatch me to endless flames!
   Duch.   I must believe,
     And ask Your grace's pardon. I confess

290   I ha' not lov'd you since Alvarez' death,
     Though we were reconcil'd.
   Card.   I do not blame
     Your jealousy[5] nor any zeal you had
     To prosecute revenge against me, madam,
     As I then stood suspected, nor can yet
     Implore your mercy to Columbo. All
     I have to say is to retain[6] my first
     Opinion and credit with Your Grace,
     Which you may think I urge, not out of fear
     Or ends[7] upon you — since, I thank the king,

300   I stand firm on the base of royal favour —
     But for your own sake, and to show I have
     Compassion of your sufferings.
   Duch.   You have clear'd
     A doubt, my Lord, and by this fair remonstrance
     Given my sorrow so much truce to think
     That we may meet again and yet be friends.
     But be not angry if I still remember
     By whom Alvarez died, and weep and wake
     Another Justice with my prayers.

---

[1] Sanction.   [2] i.e. lose in your eyes.   [3] Call to account.   [4] Concerning.
[5] Suspicion.   [6] i.e. is intended to retain.   [7] Purpose.

Card.   All thoughts
     That may advance a better peace dwell with you.

                                                                    Exit.

310 *Duch.*   How would this cozening statesman bribe my faith[1]
             With flatteries to think him innocent?
             No; if his nephew die, this Cardinal must not
             Be long liv'd. All the prayers of a wrong'd widow
             Make firm Hernando's sword, and my own hand
             Shall have some glory in the next revenge.
             I will pretend my brain with grief distracted;[2]
             It may gain easy credit,[3] and beside
             The taking off examination[4]
             For great Columbo's death, it makes what act
320   I do, in that believ'd want of my reason,
             Appear no crime, but my defense. Look down,
             Soul of my lord, from thy eternal shade,
             And unto all thy blest companions boast
             Thy duchess busy to revenge thy ghost.

                                                                    Exit.

                    [ACT IV SCENE 3]

                    [*An isolated spot near the city*]
                    Enter Columbo, Hernando, Alphonso, Colonel[5]

Col.   Hernando, now I love thee, and do half
     Repent the affront my passion threw upon thee.
Hern.   You wo' not be too prodigal o' your penitence!
Col.   This makes good[6] thy nobility of birth.
     Thou may'st be worth my anger and my sword
     If thou dost execute as daringly
     As thou provok'st a quarrel. I did think
     Thy soul a starveling or asleep.
Hern.   You'll find it
     Active enough to keep your spirit waking,

[1]i.e. my loyalty to D'Alvarez.   [2]*Hamlet* (I, v, 171-2) is the best known of
many Elizabethan and Jacobean plays to utilize this device.   [3]Trust.
[4]The removal of inquiry.   [5]They probably enter from opposite sides of
the stage as two pairs, Columbo and Alphonso, Hernando and the Colonel.
[6]Confirms.

10   Which to exasperate, for yet I think
         It is not high[1] enough to meet my rage –
         D'ee smile?
Col.   This noise is worth it.[2] Gentlemen,
         I'm sorry this great soldier has engag'd
         Your travel;[3] all his business is to talk.
Hern.   A little of your lordship's patience.
         You shall have other sport, and swords that will
         Be as nimble 'bout your heart as you can wish.
         'Tis pity more than our two single lives[4]
         Should be at stake.
Colonel.   Make that no scruple, sir.
20 *Hern.*   To him, then, that survives, if fate allow
         That difference, I speak, that he may tell
         The world I came not hither on slight anger,
         But to revenge my honour, stain'd and trampl'd on
         By this proud man, when general, he commanded
         My absence from the field.
Col.   I do remember,
         And I'll give your soul now a discharge.[5]
Hern.   I come
         To meet it, if your courage be so fortunate.[6]
         But there is more than my own injury
         You must account for, sir, if my sword prosper,
30   Whose point and every edge is made more keen
         With[7] young Alvarez' blood, in which I had
         A noble interest. Does not that sin benumb
         Thy arteries, and turn the guilty flowings
         To trembling jelly in thy veins? Canst hear
         Me name that murder, and thy spirits not
         Struck into air, as thou wert shot by some
         Engine from Heaven?
Col.   You are the duchess' champion.
         Thou hast given me a quarrel now.
         [*To the others*]   I grieve
         It is determined all must fight, and I
         Shall lose much honour in his fall.[8]
40 *Hern.*   That duchess –
         Whom but to mention with thy breath is sacrilege –
         An orphan[9] of thy making, and condemn'd

---

[1] Violent. [2] 'Your protest is worth a smile.' [3] Travail, trouble. [4] In seventeenth-century England seconds of a duel sometimes fought at the same time as the principals, to demonstrate that they were worthy of their friends. [5] i.e. a release from your body. [6] i.e. to be victorious. [7] i.e. with the need to avenge. [8] Perhaps by condescending to duel with someone of lower social rank. [9] One bereft of parents or guardian, i.e. husband.

By thee to eternal solitude, I come
To vindicate, and while I am killing thee,
By virtue of her prayers sent up for justice,
At the same time in Heaven I am pardon'd for't.
Col.   I cannot hear the bravo.[1]
Hern.   Two words more,
And[2] take your chance. Before you all I must
Pronounce that noble lady without knowledge
50   Or thought of what I undertake for her.[3]
Poor soul, she's now at her devotions,
Busy with Heaven, and wearing out the earth
With her stiff knees, and bribing her good angel
With treasures of her eyes, to tell her lord
How much she longs to see him. My attempt
Needs no commission[4] from her; were I
A stranger in Navarre, the inborn right
Of every gentleman to[5] Alvarez' loss
Is reason to engage their swords and lives
60   Against the common enemy of virtue.
Col.   Now have you finish'd? I have an instrument
Shall cure this noise and fly up to thy tongue
To murder all thy words.
Hern.   One little knot
Of phlegm that clogs my stomach, and I have done.
You have an uncle call'd a Cardinal;
Would he were lurking now about thy heart,
That the same wounds might reach you both, and send
Your reeling souls together.[6] Now have at you!
Alph.   [*To* Hernando's *second, the* Colonel]
We must not, sir, be idle.

They fight, Columbo's *second*[7] *slain*

Hern.   What think you now of praying?
70 *Col.*   Time enough.

He kills Hernando's *second*

[*To* Colonel] Commend me to my friend.[8] The scales are even.
I would be merciful and give you time
Now to consider of the other world;
You'll find your soul benighted presently.

[1] Boast.   [2] And then.   [3] This statement is not true (see IV, ii, 162-99,
312-5), but Hernando here makes an effort to absolve the duchess of com-
plicity.   [4] Command.   [5] i.e. to compensate for.   [6] To death.   [7] Alphonso.
[8] The dead Alphonso.

Hern.   I'll find my way i' th' dark.

> *They fight and close.* Columbo *gets both the swords, and* Hernando *takes up the second's weapon*

Col.   A stumble's dangerous.
   Now ask for thy life. Ha!
Hern.   I despise to wear it
   A gift from any but the first bestower.
Col.   I scorn a base advantage.

> Columbo *throws away one of the swords. They fight.* Hernando *wounds* Columbo

                         Ha!
Hern.   I am now
   Out of your debt.
Col.   Th'ast done't, and I forgive thee.
80   Give me thy hand. When shall we meet again?
Hern.   Never, I hope.
Col.   I feel life ebb apace, yet I'll look upwards
   And show my face to Heaven.

                                             [*Dies*]

Hern.   The matter's done.
   I must not stay to bury him.

                                             Exit.

[ACT V SCENE 1]

[*A garden in the* Cardinal's *palace*]
Enter two Lords

1 Lord.   Columbo's death doth much afflict the king.
2 Lord.   I thought the Cardinal would have lost his wits
   At first for's nephew; it drowns all the talk
   Of the other[1] that were slain.
1 Lord.   We are friends.[2]
   I do suspect Hernando had some interest,
   And knew how their wounds came.

[1] i.e. others.   [2] i.e. we may speak freely.

2 Lord.   His flight confirms it,
For whom the Cardinal has spread his nets.
1 Lord.   He is not so weak to trust himself at home
To his enemies' gripe.
2 Lord.   All strikes me not so much
10   As that the duchess, most oppressed lady,
Should be distracted, and[1] before Columbo
Was slain.
1 Lord.   But that the Cardinal should be made
Her guardian is to me above that wonder.
2 Lord.   So it pleas'd the king, and she, with that small stock
Of reason left her, is so kind and smooth
Upon[2] him.
1 Lord.   She's turn'd a child again. A madness
That would ha' made her brain and blood boil high,
In which distemper she might ha' wrought something, –
2 Lord.   Had been to purpose.
20 *1 Lord.*   The Cardinal is cunning, and howe'er
His brow does smile, he does suspect Hernando
Took fire from her, and waits a time to punish it.
2 Lord.   But what a subject of disgrace and mirth
Hath poor Celinda made herself by pride
In her belief Columbo was her servant.[3]
Her head hath stoop'd much since he died, and she
Almost ridiculous at court.

Enter Cardinal, Antonelli, *servant*

1 Lord.   [*To* 2 Lord]   The Cardinal
Is come into the garden now.
Card.   Walk off.

                                          [*Exeunt* Lords.]

[*Aside*] It troubles me the duchess by her loss
30   Of brain is now beneath my great revenge.
She is not capable to feel my anger,
Which, like to unregarded thunder spent
In woods and lightning aim'd at senseless trees,
Must idly fall and hurt her not, not to
That sense[4] her guilt deserves. A fatal stroke,
Without the knowledge for what crime, to fright her
When she takes leave, and make her tug with death
Until her soul sweat, is a pigeon's torment.
And she is sent a babe to the other world,

[1] i.e. and that.   [2] Concerning.   [3] Lover.   [4] Realization.

40   Columbo's death will not be satisfied,
        And I but wound her with a two-edg'd feather.
        I must do more; I have all opportunity,
        She by the king now made my charge, but she's
        So much a turtle[1] I shall lose by killing her,
        Perhaps do her a pleasure and preferment.
        That must not be.

        Enter Celinda *with a parchment*

        Antonelli.   [*Aside*] Is not this she that would be thought to have been
             have been
             Columbo's mistress? -- Madam, His Grace is private
             And would not be disturb'd. You may displease him.
50 *Cel.*   What will your worship wager that he shall
             Be pleas'd again before we part?
        Antonelli.   I'll lay this diamond, madam, 'gainst a kiss,
             And trust yourself to keep the stakes.
        Cel.   'Tis done.
        Antonelli.   [*Aside*] I have long had an appetite to this lady,
             But the lords keep her up so high[2] -- This toy[3]
             May bring her on.
        Card.   [*To* Celinda] This interruption tastes not of good manners.
        Cel.   But where necessity, my Lord, compels,
             The boldness may meet pardon, and when you
60   Have found my purpose I may less appear
             Unmannerly.
        Card.   To th' business.
        Cel.   It did please
             Your nephew, sir, before his death to credit me
             With so much honourable favour I
             Am come to tender to his near'st of blood,
             Yourself, what does remain a debt to him.
             Not to delay Your Grace with circumstance,[4]
             That deed,[5] if you accept, makes you my heir
             Of no contemptible estate.

                                                    He reads

        [*Aside*]   This way
             Is only left to tie up scurril tongues
70   And saucy men, that since Columbo's death
             Venture to libel on my pride and folly.
             His[6] greatness and this gift, which I enjoy

        ---

        [1] i.e. turtle-dove; notably affectionate, gentle.   [2] Proud.   [3] Trinket, gift.
        [4] Details.   [5] Legal document.   [6] The Cardinal's.

          Still for my life, beyond which term a kingdom's
          Nothing, will curb the giddy spleens of men
          That live on impudent rhyme[1] and railing at
          Each wandering fame they catch.
Card.   Madam, this bounty
          Will bind my gratitude and care to serve you.
Cel.   I am Your Grace's servant.
Card.   Antonelli!

                                                              Whisper

          And when this noble lady visits me,
80   Let her not wait.
Cel.   [*To* Antonelli] What think you, my officious sir? His Grace
          Is pleas'd, you may conjecture. I may keep
          Your gem; the kiss was never yours.
Antonelli.   Sweet madam, —
Cel.   Talk if you dare; you know I must not wait.
          And so farewell for this time.

                                                              [*Exit.*]

Card.   [*Aside*] 'Tis in my brain already, and it forms
          Apace. Good, excellent revenge and pleasant!
          She's[2] now within my talons. 'Tis too cheap
          A satisfaction for Columbo's death
90   Only to kill her by soft charm or force.
          I'll rifle first her darling chastity;
          'Twill be after[3] time enough to poison her,
          And she to th' world be thought her own destroyer.
          As I will frame the circumstance, this night
          All may be finish'd. For the colonel,
          Her agent in my nephew's death, whom I
          Disturb'd at counsel with her, I may reach him
          Hereafter, and be master of his fate.
          We starve our conscience when we thrive in state.

---

[1] Popular ballads.   [2] The duchess is.   [3] Afterward.

[ACT V SCENE 2]

[*The* duchess's *house*]
Enter Antonio *and* Placentia

Ant.   Placentia, we two are only left
        Of my lady's servants. Let us be true
        To her and one another, and be sure,
        When we are at our prayers, to curse the Cardinal.
Plac.   I pity my sweet lady.
Ant.   I pity her too, but am a little angry.
        She might have found another time to lose
        Her wits.
Plac.   That I were a man!
10 *Ant.*   What would'st thou do, Placentia?
Plac.   I would revenge my lady.
Ant.   'Tis better being a woman; thou may'st do
        Things that may prosper better, and the fruit
        Be thy own another day.
Plac.   Your wit still loves
        To play the wanton.[1]
Ant.   'Tis a sad time, Placentia;
        Some pleasure would do well. The truth is, I
        Am weary of my life, and I would have
        One fit of mirth before I leave the world.
Plac.   Do not you blush to talk thus wildly?
20 *Ant.*   'Tis good manners
        To be a little mad after[2] my lady.
        But I ha' done. Who is with her now?
Plac.   Madam Valeria.
Ant.   Not Celinda? There's a lady for my humour.[3]
        A pretty book of flesh and blood, and well
        Bound up, in a fair letter[4] too. Would I
        Had her, with all the errata.
Plac.   She has not
        An honourable fame.
Ant.   Her fame? That's nothing.
        A little stain. Her wealth will fetch again
30   The colour, and bring honour into her cheeks
        As fresh.[5] If she were mine, and I had her
        Exchequer,[6] I know the way to make her honest,
        Honest to th' touch, the test, and the last trial.[7]

---

[1] Antonio's remarks have sexual overtones.   [2] After the manner of.
[3] Inclination. [4] Type. [5] i.e. as fresh as earlier. [6] Possessions.
[7] The processes of testing precious metals for purity.

Plac.   How, prithee?
Ant.   Why, first I would marry her; that's a verb material.[1]
         Then I would print her with an *Index*
         Expurgatorius,[2] a table[3] drawn
         Of her court heresies, and when she's read
         Cum Privilegio[4] who dares to call her whore?
Plac.   I'll leave you if you talk thus.
40 *Ant.*   I ha' done.
         Placentia, thou may'st be better company
         After another progress.[5] And now tell me,
         Did'st ever hear of such a patient madness
         As my lady is possess'd with? She has rav'd
         But twice. And she would fright the Cardinal,
         Or at a supper if she did but poison him,
         It were a frenzy I could bear withal.
         She calls him her dear governor —

         Enter Hernando *disguised, having a letter*

Plac.   Who is this?
Hern.   [*Aside*] Her secretary! — Sir,
50   Here is a letter, if it may have so
         Much happiness to kiss Her Grace's hand.[6]
Ant.   From whom?
Hern.   That's not in your commission, sir,
         To ask or mine to satisfy. She will want
         No understanding when she reads.
Ant.   Alas,
         Under your favour, sir, you are mistaken.
         Her Grace did never more want understanding.
Hern.   How?
Ant.   Have you not heard? Her skull is broken, sir,
         And many pieces taken out. She's mad.
60 *Hern.*   The sad fame[7] of her distraction
         Has too much truth, it seems.
Plac.   If please you, sir,
         To expect awhile, I will present the letter.
Hern.   Pray do.

---

[1]Concrete.   [2]The *Index Librorum Expurgatorius,* devised in 1607, a short-
lived list of works which might be read by Roman Catholics after passages
had been expurgated or amended. Antonio means that he would 'publish'
her after her court misbehaviours had been suppressed.   [3]List.   [4]i.e. when
she is read after receiving 'the exclusive permission to publish' (*cum
privilegio imprimendum solum*) ....   [5]A royal tour or visit, reputed to
encourage immoral activities among hangers-on.   [6]Variations of this
phrase occur repeatedly in both Webster and Shirley.   [7]Rumour.

Exit Placentia.

  How long has she been thus distemper'd, sir?
Ant. Before the Cardinal came to govern here,[1]
  Who for that reason by the king was made
  Her guardian. We are now at his devotion.[2]
Hern. A lamb given up to a tiger! May diseases
  Soon eat him through his heart!
Ant.   Your pardon, sir,
70 I love that voice; I know it too a little.
  Are not you −? Be not angry, noble sir;
  I can with ease be ignorant again
  And think you are another man, but if
  You be that valiant gentleman they call −
Hern. Whom? What?
Ant. That kill'd − I would not name him if I thought
  You were not pleas'd to be that very gentleman.
Hern. Am I betray'd?
Ant.   The devil sha' not
  Betray you here. Kill me, and I will take
80 My death[3] you are the noble colonel.
  We are all bound to you for the general's death,
  Valiant Hernando. When my lady knows
  You are here, I hope 'twill fetch her wits again.
  But do not talk too loud; we are not all
  Honest i' th' house. Some are the Cardinal's creatures.
Hern. Thou wert faithful to thy lady. I am glad
  'Tis night. But tell me how the churchman uses
  The duchess.

  Enter Antonelli [*and stands apart*]

Ant. He carries angels in his tongue and face, but I
90 Suspect his heart. This is one of his spawns. −
  Signior Antonelli.
Antonelli. Honest Antonio.
Ant. And how, and how − a friend of mine.[4] Where is
  The Cardinal's Grace?[5]
Hern. [*Aside*] That will be never answer'd.
Antonelli. He means to sup here with the duchess.
Ant.   Will he?
Antonelli. We'll have the charming[6] bottles at my chamber.

[1] In the house of the duchess. [2] Command. [3] Stake my life. [4] i.e.
Hernando. [5] Antonio nervously stumbles as he speaks. His use of 'Grace'
puns on the Cardinal's 'favour with God'. [6] Enchanting. He refers to
bottles of liquor.

Bring that gentleman; we'll be mighty merry.
Hern.   [*Aside*] I may disturb your jollity.
Antonelli.   Farewell, sweet.

                                                              [*Exit.*]

Ant.   Dear Antonelli. − A round[1] pox confound you!
100   This is court rhetoric at the back stairs.[2]

        Enter Placentia

Plac.   Do you know this gentleman?
Ant.   Not I.
Plac.   My lady presently dismiss'd Valeria
        And bade me bring him to her bed chamber.
Ant.   The gentleman has an honest face.
Plac.   Her words
        Fell from her with some evenness[3] and joy.
        [*To* Hernando] Her Grace desires your presence.
Hern.   I'll attend her.

                                    Exit [*with* Placentia].

Ant.   I would this soldier had the Cardinal
        Upon a promontory. With what a spring
        The churchman would leap down! It were a spectacle
110   Most rare to see him topple from the precipice,
        And souse in the salt water with a noise
        To stun the fishes; and if he fell into
        A net, what wonder would the simple sea-gulls[4]
        Have, to draw up the o'ergrown lobster,
        So ready boil'd?[5] He shall have my good wishes!
        This colonel's coming may be lucky; I
        Will be sure none shall interrupt 'em.

        Enter Celinda

Cel.   Is Her Grace at opportunity?[6]
Ant.   No, sweet madam;
        She is alseep, her gentlewoman says.
120 *Cel.*   My business is but visit;[7] I'll expect.
Ant.   That must not be, although I like your company.
Cel.   You are grown rich, Master Secretary.
Ant.   I, madam? Alas!

---

[1] Severe.   [2] i.e. from the servants' quarters.   [3] Calmness.   [4] i.e. fishermen.
[5] A further allusion to the Cardinal's red robes.   [6] At leisure.   [7] i.e. brief.

Cel.   I hear you are upon another purchase.[1]
Ant.   I upon a purchase?
Cel.   If you want any sum –
Ant.   If I could purchase your sweet favour, madam, –
Cel.   You shall command me and my fortune,[2] sir.
Ant.   [*Aside*] How's this?
Cel.   I have observ'd you, sir, a staid
130   And prudent gentleman, and I shall want –
Ant.   Not me?
Cel.   [*Aside*] A father for some infant.[3] He has credit
    I' th' world. I am not the first cast lady
    Has married a secretary.
Ant.   Shall I wait upon you?
Cel.   Whither?
Ant.   Any whither.
Cel.   I may chance lead you then –
Ant.   I shall be honour'd to obey. My blood
140   Is up, and in this humour I'm for anything.
Cel.   Well, sir, I'll try your manhood.
Ant.   'Tis my happiness;
    You cannot please me better.
Cel.   [*Aside*]   This was struck
    I' th'opportunity.[4]
Ant.   I am made for ever.

                                    [*Exeunt.*]

[ACT V SCENE 3]

[*Another room. The duchess's house*]
Enter Hernando *and* Duchess

Hern.   Dear madam, do not weep.
Duch.   Y'are very welcome.
    I ha' done. I wo' not shed a tear more
    Till I meet Alvarez; then I'll weep for joy.
    He was a fine young gentleman and sung sweetly;
    And you had heard him but the night before
    We were married, you would ha' sworn he had been

---

[1] Acquisition by buying, as opposed to inheritance. [2] Wealth, destiny.
[3] The implication is that she is pregnant by Columbo. [4] At an opportune time.

A swan and sung his own sad epitaph.[1]
But we'll talk o' the Cardinal.

Hern.   Would his death
Might ransom your fair sense, he should not live
10   To triumph in the loss.[2] Beshrew my manhood,
But I begin to melt.

Duch.   I pray, sir, tell me –
For I can understand, although they say
I have lost my wits. But they are safe enough,
And I shall have 'em when the Cardinal dies,
Who had a letter from his nephew too
Since he was slain.

Hern.   From whence?

Duch.   I know not where he is, but in some bower
Within a garden he is making chaplets,
And means to send me one, but I'll not take it;
20   I have flowers enough, I thank him, while I live.[3]

Hern.   But do you love your governor?[4]

Duch.   Yes, but I'll never marry him; I am promis'd
Already.

Hern.   To whom, madam?

Duch.   Do not you
Blush when you ask me that? Must not you be
My husband? I know why, but that's a secret.
Indeed, if you believe me, I do love
No man alive so well as you. The Cardinal
Shall never know't; he'll kill us both, and yet
He says he loves me dearly, and has promis'd
30   To make me well again; but I'm afraid
One time or other he will give me poison.

Hern.   Prevent him, madam, and take nothing from him.

Duch.   Why, do you think 'twill hurt me?

Hern.   It will kill you.

Duch.   I shall but die, and meet my dear lov'd lord,
Whom, when I have kiss'd, I'll come[5] again, and work
A bracelet of my hair for you to carry him
When you are going to Heaven. The poesy[6] shall
Be my own name in little tears that I
Will weep next winter, which,[7] congeal'd i' th' frost,
40   Will show like seed-pearl. You'll deliver it?
I know he'll love and wear it for my sake.

---

[1] All swans were believed to be mute, but to be capable of singing just
previous to death. [2] i.e. your present loss of reason. [3] Cf. Webster,
The White Devil, V, iv, 70-3, and *Hamlet*, IV, v, 173-84. [4] i.e. guardian
(the Cardinal; see V, i, 12-3). [5] Appear. [6] Posy, a motto or short poem,
usually inscribed inside a ring. [7] i.e. which tears.

Hern.   [*Aside*] She is quite lost.
Duch.   I pray give me, sir, your pardon.
    I know I talk not wisely, but if you had
    The burden of my sorrow, you would miss
    Sometimes your better reason. Now I'm well.
    What will you do when the Cardinal comes?
    He must not see you for the world.
Hern.   He sha' not.
    I'll take my leave before he come.
Duch.   Nay, stay.
    I shall have no friend left me when you go.
50 He will but sup; he sha' not stay to lie wi' me.[1]
    I have the picture of my lord abed;
    Three are too much this weather.

    Enter Placentia

Plac.   Madam, the Cardinal.
Hern.   He shall sup with the devil.
Duch.   I dare not stay;[2]
    The red cock[3] will be angry. I'll come again.

                              Exeunt [Duchess *and* Placentia].

Hern.   This sorrow is no fable. Now I find
    My curiosity is sadly satisfied.
    Ha! If the duchess in her straggl'd[4] wits
    Let fall words to betray me to the Cardinal,
    The panther will not leap more fierce to meet
60 His prey, when a long want of food hath parch'd
    His starved maw, than he to print[5] his rage
    And tear my heart-strings. Everything is fatal;[6]
    And yet she talk'd sometimes with chain of sense,
    And said she lov'd me. Ha, they come not yet.
    I have a sword about me, and I left
    My own security to visit death.
    Yet I may pause a little and consider
    Which way does lead me to't most honourably.
    Does not the chamber that I walk in tremble?[7]
70 What will become of her and me and all
    The world in one small hour? I do not think
    Ever to see the day again. The wings

---

[1] See V, i, 88-91, where the Cardinal plans her seduction or rape. The
duchess's indecorous comments are reminiscent of Ophelia's.   [2] i.e. remain
here, keeping the Cardinal waiting in an anteroom.   [3] i.e. the Cardinal.
[4] Wandering.   [5] Express.   [6] Fated.   [7] i.e. with the premonition of death.

Of night spread o'er me like a sable hearse-cloth.
The stars are all close[1] mourners too; but I
Must not alone to the cold, silent grave;
I must not. If thou canst, Alvarez, open
That ebon curtain, and behold the man,
When the world's justice fails, shall right thy ashes
And feed their thirst with blood. Thy duchess is
80   Almost a ghost already, and doth wear
Her body like a useless upper garment,
The trim and fashion of it lost. Ha!

Enter Placentia

Plac.   You need not doubt me, sir. My lady prays
You would not think it long. She in my ear
Commanded me to tell you that when last
She drank she had happy wishes to your health.
Hern.   And did the Cardinal pledge it?
Plac.   He was not
Invited to't, nor must he know you are here.
Hern.   What do they talk of, prithee?
90 *Plac.*   His Grace is very pleasant

                                                                A lute is heard

And kind to her, but her returns[2] are after
The sad condition of her sense, sometimes
Unjointed.
Hern.   They have music.
Plac.   A lute only,
His Grace prepar'd; they say the best[3] of Italy
That waits upon my Lord.
Hern.   He thinks the duchess
Is stung with a tarantula.[4]
Plac.   Your pardon;
My duty is expected.

                                                                Exit.

Hern.   Gentle lady.
A voice too?

---

[1] Strict, deep.   [2] Replies.   [3] i.e. the best musician.   [4] Its bite was reputed
to cause melancholy, leading to death. The depression could be relieved
only by lively music, to which the patient must dance vigorously; hence
the later dance, tarantella.

Song within[1]

Strephon.	Come, my Daphne, come away,
100	We do waste the crystal day.
	'Tis Strephon calls.
Daphne.	What says my love?
Strephon.	Come follow to the myrtle grove,
	Where Venus shall prepare
	New chaplets for thy hair.
Daphne.	Were I shut up within a tree[2]
	I'd rend my bark to follow thee.
Strephon.	My shepherdess, make haste,
	The minutes slide too fast.
Daphne.	In those cooler shades will I,
110	Blind as Cupid, kiss thine eye.
Strephon.	In thy bosom then I'll stay.
	In such warm snow who would not lose his way?
Chorus.	We'll laugh and leave the world behind,
	And gods themselves that see
	Shall envy thee and me,
	But never find
	Such joys when they embrace a deity.

[*Hern.*] If at this distance I distinguish, 'tis not
    Church music; and the air's wanton,[3] and no anthem
120 Sung to't, but some strange ode of love and kisses.
    What should this mean? Ha, he is coming hither.
    I am betray'd! He marches in[4] her hand.
    I'll trust a little more, mute as the arras,
    My sword and I here.

He [*draws his sword and, standing behind the arras,*] *observes
Enter* Cardinal, Duchess, Antonelli, *and attendants*

Card.   Wait you in the first chamber,[5] and let none
    Presume to interrupt us.

                  Exeunt [Antonelli *and*] *servants.*

[*Aside*]   She is pleasant.

[1] Shirley's song, which he published in *Poems &c.* (1646), with three minor variants, was set to music by the distinguished composer, William Lawes (1602-45); see John Playford, *The Musical Companion* (1673), or V. Jackson, *English Melodies from the Thirteenth to the Eighteenth Centuries* (1910).   [2] In classical lore Daphne was pursued by Apollo, and to escape from him she pleaded to be transformed into a laurel tree. [3] Gay. [4] While holding. [5] Anteroom.

Now for some art to poison all her innocence.

Duch. [*Aside*] I do not like the Cardinal's humour. He
Little suspects what guest is in my chamber.

Card. Now, madam, you are safe.[1]

[*Embraces her*]

130 *Duch.*   How means Your Lordship?

Card. Safe in my arms, sweet duchess.

Duch.   Do not hurt me.

Card. Not for the treasures of the world. You are
My pretty charge.[2] Had I as many lives
As I have careful thoughts to do you service
I should think all a happy forfeit to
Delight Your Grace one minute. 'Tis a Heaven
To see you smile.

Duch.   What kindness call you this?

Card. It cannot want a name while you preserve
So plentiful a sweetness. It is love.

140 *Duch.* Of me? How shall I know't, my Lord?

Card.   By this and this; swift messengers to whisper
Our hearts to one another.

Kisses [*her*]

Duch. Pray, do you come a-wooing?

Card.   Yes, sweet madam.
You cannot be so cruel to deny me.

Duch. What, my Lord?

Card.   Another kiss.

Duch.   Can you
Dispense with this, my Lord? [*Aside*] Alas, I fear
Hernando is asleep or vanish'd from me.

Card. [*Aside*] I have mock'd[3] my blood into a flame, and what
My angry soul had form'd for my revenge

150 Is now the object of my amorous sense.
I have took a strong enchantment from her lips
And fear I shall forgive Columbo's death
If she consent to my embrace. – Come, madam.

Duch. Whither, my Lord?

Card.   But to your bed or couch,
Where, if you will be kind and but allow
Yourself a knowledge,[4] love, whose shape and raptures
Wise poets have but glorified in dreams,

---

[1] A *double entendre;* secure, harmless.   [2] Ward.   [3] Tantalized.   [4] Sexual
intimacy.

Shall make your chamber his eternal palace,
And with such active and essential[1] streams
160   Of new delights glide o'er your bosom, you
Shall wonder to what unknown world you are
By some blest change translated. Why d'ee pause
And look so wild? Will you deny your governor?

Duch.   How came you by that cloven foot?
Card.   Your fancy[2]
Would turn a traitor to your happiness.
I am your friend; you must be kind.
Duch.   Unhand me,
Or I'll cry out a rape!
Card.   You wo' not, sure?
Duch.   [*Aside*] I have been cozen'd with Hernando's shadow.
Here's none but Heaven to hear me. – Help, a rape!
170 *Card.*   Are you so good at understanding?[3] Then
I must use other argument.

He forces her. [Hernando *comes forward*]

Hern.   Go to, Cardinal!

Strikes him. Exit Duchess.

Card.   Hernando! Murder! Treason! Help!
Hern.   An army sha' not rescue thee. Your blood
Is much inflam'd. I have brought a lancet wi' me
Shall open your hot veins and cool your fever.[4]
To vex thy parting soul, it was the same
Engine[5] that pinc'd[6] Columbo's heart.

[*Stabs him*]

Card.   Help! Murder!

Enter Antonelli *and servants*

Antonelli.   Some ring the bell; 'twill raise the court.
180 My Lord is murder'd! 'Tis Hernando!

The bell rings[7]

---

[1] Vital. [2] Whim. [3] 'Are you sane?' [4] Bloodletting was the traditional
remedy for relief of fever. A sanguine humour was hot and moist. See
also II, i, 142-5. [5] Device. [6] Pinched, hurt. [7] Cf. *Macbeth*, II, iii, 79-85,
and Middleton and Rowley, *The Changeling*, V, i, 74-6.

Hern.   I'll make you all some sport.

[*Fights with* Antonelli *and servants, and is mortally wounded*] [1]

So, now we[2] are even.
Where is the duchess? I would take my leave
Of her, and then bequeath my curse among you.

Hernando *falls*

Enter King, Duchess, Valeria, Lords, *guard*

King.   How come these bloody objects?
Hern.   With a trick of my sword found out. I hope he's paid.
1 Lord.   [*Aside*] I hope so too. – A surgeon for my Lord Cardinal!
King.   Hernando?
Duch.   Justice, oh, justice, sir, against a ravisher!
Hern.   Sir, I ha' done you service.
King.   A bloody service.
190 *Hern.*   'Tis pure scarlet.[3]

Enter Surgeon

Card.   [*Aside*] After such care to perfect my revenge,
        Thus bandied out o' th' world by a woman's plot!
Hern.   I have preserv'd the duchess from a rape.
        Good night to me and all the world for ever.

Dies

King.   So impious![4]
Duch.   'Tis most true; Alvarez' blood
        Is now reveng'd. I find my brain return
        And every straggling sense repairing home.
Card.   I have deserv'd you should turn from me, sir.
        My life hath been prodigiously wicked.
200   My blood is now the kingdom's balm. Oh, sir,
        I have abus'd your ear, your trust, your people,
        And my own sacred office. My conscience
        Feels now the sting. Oh, show your charity,
        And with your pardon, like a cool soft gale,[5]
        Fan my poor sweating soul that wanders through
        Unhabitable climes and parched deserts.
        But I am lost, if the great world forgive me,

---

[1] [*Stabs himself.*] Gifford and other editors.   [2] The Cardinal and I.   [3] An
oblique allusion to the scarlet blood, sins, and robes of the Cardinal.
[4] Presumably the attempted rape of the duchess.   [5] A light wind.

Unless I find your mercy for a crime
You know not, madam, yet, against your life.
210   I must confess more than my black intents
Upon your honour: Y'are already poison'd.
King.   By whom?
Card.   By me,
In the revenge I ow'd Columbo's loss.
With your last meat[1] was mix'd a poison that
By subtle and by sure degrees must let
In death.
King.   Look to the duchess, our physicians!
Card.   Stay. I will deserve her mercy, though I cannot
Call back the deed. In proof of my repentance,
220   If the last breath of a now dying man
May gain your charity and belief, receive
This ivory box; in it an antidote
'Bove that they boast the great magistral medicine.[2]
That powder, mix'd with wine, by a most rare
And quick access to the heart, will fortify it
Against the rage of the most nimble poison.
I am not worthy to present her with it.
Oh, take it and preserve her innocent life.
1 Lord.   Strange he should have a good thing in such readiness.
230 *Card.*   'Tis[3] that which in my jealousy and state,[4]
Trusting to false predictions of my birth,
That I should[5] die by poison, I preserv'd
For my own safety. Wonder not I made
That my companion was[6] to be my refuge.

Enter servant with a bowl of wine

1 Lord.   Here's some touch of grace.
Card.   .In greater proof of my pure thoughts, I take
This first, and with my dying breath confirm
My penitence. It may benefit her life,
But not my wounds. Oh, hasten to preserve her,
240   And though I merit not her pardon, let not
Her fair soul be divorc'd.[7]

                                    [Duchess *drinks*]

King.   This is some charity. May it prosper, madam.

[1] Food. [2] i.e. the Grand Magisterium, the perfect substance to promote transmutation of base metals, etc., the philosopher's stone. [3] This Q. [4] i.e. perturbed state of mind. [5] sh' Q. [6] i.e. which was. [7] i.e. from her body.

Val.   How does Your Grace?
Duch.   And must I owe my life to him whose death
             Was my ambition? Take this free acknowledgement,
             I had intent this night with my own hand
             To be Alvarez' justicer.
King.   You were mad,
             And thought past apprehension[1] of revenge.
Duch.   That shape[2] I did usurp, great sir, to give
250   My art more freedom and defence, but when
             Hernando came to visit me I thought
             I might defer my execution,
             Which his own rage supplied without my guilt,
             And when his[3] lust grew high, met with his blood.
1 Lord.   The Cardinal smiles.
Card.   Now my revenge has met
             With you, my nimble duchess. I have took
             A shape to give my act more freedom too,
             And now I am sure she's poison'd, with that dose
             I gave her last.
King.   Th'art not so horrid?
Duch.   Ha! some cordial![4]
260 *Card.*   Alas, no preservative
             Hath wings to overtake it. Were her heart
             Lock'd in a quarry, it would search and kill
             Before the aids can reach it. I am sure
             You sha' not now laugh at me.
King.   How came you by that poison?
Card.   I prepar'd it,
             Resolving when I had enjoy'd her, which
             The colonel prevented, by some art
             To make her take it, and by death conclude
             My last revenge. You have the fatal story.
270 *King.*   This is so great a wickedness it will
             Exceed belief.
Card.   I knew I could not live.
Surg.   Your wounds, sir, were not desperate.
Card.   Not mortal? Ha! Were they not mortal?
Surg.   If[5] I have skill in surgery.
Card.   Then I have caught myself in my own engine.
2 Lord.   It was your fate, you said, to die by poison.
Card.   That was my own prediction, to abuse
             Your faith. No human art can now resist it;
             I feel it knocking at the seat of life.
280   It must come in. I have wrack'd[6] all my own

---

[1] Understanding.   [2] Form (of revenger).   [3] The Cardinal's.   [4] Medicine.
[5] i.e. not if.   [6] Destroyed.

To try your charities. Now it would be rare
If you but waft me with a little prayer;
My wings that flag may catch the wind. But 'tis
In vain; the mist is risen, and there's none
To steer my wandering bark.

Dies

1 Lord.   He's dead.
King.   With him
   Die all deceived trust.
2 Lord.   This was a strange impiety.
King.   When men
   Of gifts and sacred function once decline
   From virtue, their ill deeds transcend example.
290 *Duch.*   The minute's come that I must take my leave too.
   Your hand, great sir, and though you be a king,
   We may exchange forgiveness. Heaven forgive,
   And all the world. I come, I come, Alvarez.

Dies

King.   Dispose their bodies for becoming funeral.
   How much are kings abus'd by those they take
   To royal grace, whom when they cherish most
   By nice[1] indulgence, they do often arm
   Against themselves;[2] from whence this maxim springs:
   None have more need of perspectives than kings.

Exeunt.

Epilogue
Within.   Master Pollard![3] Where's Master Pollard, for the epilogue?

He is thrust upon the stage, and falls

Epilogue.   I am coming to you, gentlemen. The poet
   Has help'd me thus far on my way, but I'll

---

[1] Luxurious.   [2] These lines may allude to the relationship between Charles
I and his confidant, George Villiers, Duke of Buckingham (murdered
1628), whose arrogance and misjudgment contributed to the unpopularity
and to the ultimate downfall of the king.   [3] Thomas Pollard was for
many years a comedian with the King's men; he died *c.* 1648.

Be even with him. The play is a tragedy,
The first that ever he compos'd for us,[1]
Wherein he thinks he has done prettily,

Enter Servant

And I am sensible.[2] [*To* Servant] I prithee look.
Is nothing out of joint? Has he broke nothing?
Serv.   No, sir, I hope.
10 *Epilogue.*   Yes, he has broke his epilogue all to pieces.
Canst thou put it together again?
Serv.   Not I, sir.
Epilogue.   Nor I. Prithee be gone. [*Exit* Servant.] Hum. Master Poet,

I have a teeming mind to be reveng'd.[3]
[*To audience*] You may assist and not be seen in't now
If you please, gentlemen, for I do know
He listens to the issue of his cause;[4]
But blister not your hands in his applause,
Your[5] private smile, your nod or hum, to tell
My fellows that you like the business well;
20   And when without a clap you go away,
I'll drink a small-beer health[6] to his second day,[7]
And break his heart or make him swear and rage
He'll write no more for the unhappy stage.
But that's too much. So should we lose.[8] Faith, show it,
And if you like his play, 'tis as well he knew it.

---

[1] Shirley was associated with the King's men from 1640; of the six plays he wrote for them only *The Cardinal* is a tragedy.   [2] Cognizant of it.   [3] i.e. a mind prolific with thoughts of revenge.   [4] The consequence of his action.   [5] i.e. offer your private smile....   [6] i.e. a weak toast.   [7] By agreement with the company, a portion of the receipts from the second performance was sometimes assigned to the playwright. See also Alternate Prologue, line 20 (p. 264).   [8] 'Actions such as I have suggested would be excessive, and we the actors should be the losers'.

Appendix

Alternative Prologue[1]

Does this look [like] a term?[2] I cannot tell.
Our poet thinks the whole town is not well,
Has took some physic lately, and for fear
Of catching cold dares not salute this air.
How like a wither'd and forsaken place
Hath this appear'd? No influence, no grace
From any star, as[3] Nature meant to be
At loss, and show here dwelt vacuity;
As Time, with age turn'd child, had got a fall,
10   Broken a limb, and lost his usual
Motion, which strikes a lameness in the year.
We are to have but little summer here.[4]
But now I guess the reason.[5] I hear say
London is gone to York.[6] 'Tis a great way.
Pox o' the proverb,[7] and of him, say I,
That look'd o'er Lincoln,[8] 'cause that was, must we
Be now translated north?[9] I could rail too

---

[1] First printed, in this form, in Shirley's *Poems &c.,* 1646, entitled "Prologue to his Tragedy call'd *The Cardinal;*" it appeared again, modified slightly, as the prologue to Shirley's *The Sisters,* published in *Six New Playes,* 1653. (*The Cardinal* was first published in this collection, with the original 1641 prologue which prefaces the present edition of the play.) Shirley evidently wrote the Alternative Prologue for *The Sisters,* first produced in 1642, but he subsequently transferred this prologue to the stage version of *The Cardinal,* hence the title of the piece in *Poems &c.* Before the publication of both plays in 1653 Shirley reattached the prologues to their original plays.   [2] Conclusion (i.e. to plays or playing), end.   [3] As if.
[4] Lines 5-12 were added to the poem subsequent to its apparent first appearance prefacing *The Sisters* (produced in 1642). Three additional modifications from the *Poems &c.* version (1646) are noted below. They too contribute to the effect of a deepening mood of depression as the playwright surveyed English life between 1642 and 1646. See also Richard Brome's Dedication and Prologue to *A Jovial Crew* (1641).   [5] But there's another reason. *The Sisters.*   [6] Charles I reigned from York between mid-March and early August 1642.   [7] 'Lincoln was, London is, and York shall be the fairest city of the three.'   [8] Possibly an allusion to the Lincoln imp, a stone figure of a devil on Lincoln Cathedral, which looked over, perhaps in the sense of bewitched, the city.   [9] 'Merely because part of the proverb appears to have been fulfilled ("Lincoln was") we should not be compelled to abandon London only to discharge a prediction concerning the future pre-eminence of York.'

On Gammer Shipton's[1] ghost, but 't wo' not do;
The town will still be flecking,[2] and a play,
20   Though ne'er so new, starves now[3] the second day.[4]
Upon these very hard conditions
Our poet will not purchase[5] many towns,
And if you[6] leave us too we cannot thrive.
I'll promise neither play nor poet live
Till ye come back. Think what you do; you see
What audiences[7] we have, what company
To Shakespeare comes, whose mirth did once beguile
Dull hours and, buskin'd, made even sorrow smile.
So lovely were the wounds, that men would say
30   They could endure the bleeding a whole day.
He has but few friends lately — think o' that.
He'll come no more, and others have his fate.[8]
Fletcher, the Muses' darling and choice love
Of Phoebus,[9] the delight of every grove,
Upon whose head the laurel grew, whose wit
Was the time's wonder and example; yet
'Tis within memory trees did not throng,
As once the story said, to Orpheus' song.[10]
Jonson, t' whose name wise Art did bow, and Wit
40   Is only justified by honouring it,
To hear whose touch, how would the learned quire[11]
With silence stoop; and when he[12] took his lyre,
Apollo dropp'd his lute, asham'd to see
A rival to the god of harmony.
You do forsake him too. We must deplore
This fate, for we do know it by our door.[13]
How must this author fear then, with his guilt
Of weakness, to thrive here, where late was spilt
The Muses' own blood, if being but a few
50   You not conspire, and meet more frequent too?
There are not now nine Muses, and you may
Be kind to ours; if not, he bade me say,
Though while you, careless, kill the rest and laugh,
Yet he may live to write your epitaph.

---

[1] The reputed author of *The Prophesie of Mother Shipton...* (1641); she is
claimed to have anticipated during her lifetime a century earlier a civil war
that would last three years, after which the nation would be governed by
three lords.   [2] Fluttering about.   [3] *The Sisters:* will starve.   [4] See Epilogue,
l. 21, n. 8.   [5] Win.   [6] The present audience.   [7] *The Sisters:* audience.   [8] i.e.
others have a similar fate.   [9] Apollo, the Greek god of light, also of music
and poetry.   [10] In classical legend, the music of Orpheus's lyre made trees
and rocks follow him.   [11] The Muses.   [12] Jonson.   [13] i.e. the empty
entrance door of the theatre.

GLOSSARY

Obscure and obsolete words that recur in the plays are listed here. Unfamiliar words that appear only once or twice are clarified in footnotes.

and, if
antic, grotesque
brave, handsome
cates, delicacies
challenge, claim
charge, responsibility, expense
confusion, destruction
desert, worth
doubt, fear
expect, wait
fame, reputation

honest, chaste
How! Indeed!
intelligence, information
motion, proposal
nor...nor, neither ... nor
or ... or, either ... or
own, acknowledge
presently, immediately
still, always
want, lack
What! Indeed!